Retail Management

Principles and Practices

Retail Management

Principles and Practices

Edited by
R. Sudarshan
S. Ravi Prakash
M. Subrahamanya Sarma

School of Management
University College of Arts and Science
Kakatiya University, Warangal

in association with

New Century Publications
New Delhi, India

NEW CENTURY PUBLICATIONS
4800/24, Bharat Ram Road,
Ansari Road, Daryaganj,
New Delhi-110 002

Tel.: 23247798, 65396605
Telefax: 011- 41017798
E-mail: indiatax@vsnl.com
www.newcenturypublications.com

Editorial office:
34, Gujranwala Town, Part-2,
Delhi - 110 009
Tel.: 27247805, 27464774

First Published - June 2007

ISBN: 81-7708-148-9 (*10 digit*)
978-81-7708-148-0 (*13 digit*)

Published by New Century Publications and printed at Singhal Print Media, New Delhi -110 005

PRINTED IN INDIA

ABOUT THE BOOK

Indian retail business is undergoing dramatic transformation. The retail sector employs about 8 per cent of the country's workforce and is characterised by a high degree of fragmentation with over 5 million outlets. Due to their small size, Indian retailers have very little bargaining power vis-à-vis manufacturers unlike in the case of retailers in developed countries.

The corner grocer or the *kirana* store is a key element in the retail business in India due to the housewife's unwillingness to go long distances for purchasing daily needs. In the emerging scenario, traditional formats of retailing (like hawkers, grocers and paan shops) are now co-existing with modern formats like supermarkets and non-store retailing channels such as multi-level marketing and teleshopping.

The structure of a country's retail sector has an enormous influence on marketing strategy and marketing activities of firms. The Indian retail sector has arrived at a very critical stage. Stores in modern formats have emerged in the metropolitan cities but the bulk of the retail sales still take place through traditional retail formats. The development of modern retailing is of great interest to marketing scholars, practitioners and policy makers.

The emergence of new formats of retailing has attracted the attention of government functionaries, company managers and economic analysts.

This book analyses the developments in retailing in India. It consists of 20 papers authored by scholars in the field. This work will appeal to all categories of readers, particularly students of business management, economics and commerce, company executives, government officials, and non-governmental organisations monitoring developments in the Indian economy.

ABOUT THE EDITORS

Professor R. Sudarshan is a faculty member in the Department of Commerce and Business Management, Kakatiya University, Warangal since 1978. He obtained his M.Com. (with distinction and first rank), M.Phil. and Ph.D. degrees from Kakatiya University in 1978, 1982 and 1987 respectively. Ten scholars have been awarded Ph.D. degrees and an equal number of scholars M.Phil. degrees under his supervision. He has served as Head, Department of Commerce and Business Management (1998-2000) and Dean, Faculty of Commerce and Business Management (2000-2002) of Kakatiya University.

Professor S. Ravi Prakash is a faculty member in the Department of Commerce and Business Management, Kakatiya University, Warangal since 1977. He obtained M.Com degree from Osmania University in 1977 and Ph.D. degree from University of Pune in 1982. He has guided ten scholars for M.Phil. degree and twenty- five scholars for Ph.D. degree. He successfully completed a Major Research Project sponsored by the University Grants Commission (UGC) on Corporate Governance in India. He has published twenty-five papers in various journals on Small Industry and Entrepreneurship Development.

Professor M. Subrahamanya Sarma is a Professor in the Department of Commerce and Business Management, Kakatiya University, Warangal. He was awarded Ph.D. degree in 1989 for his work on Management Information Systems in Public Enterprises. He has been guiding research scholars in the areas of Banking, Capital Market Reforms and Retailing. He has published thirty papers in reputed journals. So far he has guided six Ph.D. scholars and ten M.Phil. scholars. His area of specialisation is Accounting and Finance.

PREFACE

Retailing has been defined as a business activity involving sale of goods and services to consumers for their personal, family or household use. Although retailing has been around since times immemorial, it was in the 20th century that significant changes occurred in the retail sector, especially in the developed countries. Modern formats of retailing, such as department stores, discount stores, supermarkets, convenience stores, fast food outlets, specialty stores, warehouse retailers and hypermarkets, are now making inroads into developing countries of the world. Retailing has become more organised and chain stores (using sophisticated information technology and communication to manage their operations) are coming up at the expense of independent shops.

The emergence of new formats of retailing has attracted the attention of government functionaries, company managers, economic analysts and the public at large.

Indian retail business is undergoing dramatic transformation. The retail sector employs about 8 per cent of the country's workforce and is characterised by a high degree of fragmentation with over 5 million outlets. Due to their small size, Indian retailers have very little bargaining power vis-à-vis manufacturers unlike in the case of retailers in developed countries.

The corner grocer or the *kirana* store is a key element in the retail business in India due to the housewife's unwillingness to go long distances for purchasing daily needs. In the emerging scenario, traditional formats of retailing (like hawkers, grocers and paan shops) are now co-existing with modern formats like supermarkets and non-store retailing channels such as multi-level marketing and teleshopping.

Modern stores tend to be larger, carry more stock and have a self-service format. Modern formats also tend to have higher levels of sales per unit of space, stock turnover and gross margin but lower levels of net margin as compared to traditional formats. Modernisation in retail formats is likely to happen quicker in categories like dry groceries, electronics, men's apparel, books and music. Some reshaping and adaptation my also happen in fresh groceries, women's apparel, fast food, and personal care products.

At present the new format stores cater mostly to households belonging to the higher income families. The catchments area for these modern stores has to be fairly large as the number of such households is small in relation to the total population.

Manufacturing firms will need to develop new strategies for dealing with powerful retailers. The first change required will be one of mind-set. Negotiations with powerful retailers will have to be carried out at much higher executive levels within the firm. New structures such as national account managers and category managers would need to be deployed. Firms will have to reconsider their brand promise, brand promotion and their brand building policies to deal with store brands that will be introduced by retail chains. Firms will also have to re-engineer their logistic policies to meet the demands of powerful retailers for in-time delivery to their distribution centres/stores. New product introductions will have to be coordinated with the retail chains so that adequate shelf space is available at the time of launch. The firms will need to carefully look at their product cost structures both in terms of variable cost and fixed costs in order to maintain profitability in the face of pressure for price reductions from powerful retailers.

The Indian retail sector is largely traditional, but stores in modern format are emerging. The contribution of organised retailing in the share of retail sales in India is currently very small. Based on the experience of retail developments in countries like Thailand, Brazil and Greece, it is possible to conclude that modernisation of retailing in India is round the corner. The development of modern retail system will have several implications for managerial practices in manufacturing firms. Firms will have to proactively review their sales structures, brand activities, logistics policy and price structure to cope with pressures from powerful retailers.

The structure of a country's retail sector has an enormous influence on marketing strategy and marketing activities of firms. The Indian retail sector has arrived at a very critical stage. Stores in modern formats have emerged in the metropolitan cities but the bulk of the retail sales still take place through traditional retail formats. The development of modern retailing is of great interest to marketing scholars, practitioners and policy makers.

This book analyses the developments in retailing in India. It consists of 20 papers authored by scholars in the field. We place on record our deep appreciation and gratefulness to each of them for their worthy contributions.

June 20, 2007
Warangal

R. Sudarshan
S. Ravi Prakash
M. Subrahamanya Sarma

LIST OF CONTRIBUTORS

A. Sathish Babu	Reader, P.G. Department of Commerce and Management Studies, V.R.S. and Y.R.N. P.G. College Chirala, A.P.
A. Suryanarayana	Chairman, Board of Studies, Department of Business Management, Osmania University, Hyderabad.
B. Raj Kumar	Lecturer, Department of Business Management, Balaji Institute of Technology and Sciences, Warangal.
B. Srinivas Raj	Senior Business Manager, ICFAI, Hyderabad.
C. Ram Mohan	Assistant Professor, Department of Business Management, Vathsalya Institute of Science and Technology, Anantharam, Bhongir.
C.J.S. Prasad	Research Scholar, School of Management Studies, Jawaharlal Nehru Technological University (JNTU), Hyderabad.
D. Guna Sankar	Assistant Professor, P.G. Department of Commerce and Management Studies, V.R.S. and Y.R.N. P.G. College Chirala, A.P.
D. Harikanth	Lecturer, Department of Commerce and Business Management, University Arts and Science College, Kakatiya University, Warangal.
D. Raghunatha Reddy	Associate Professor, School of Management Studies, Jawaharlal Nehru Technological University (JNTU), Hyderabad.
Dhanya Menon	Technical Writer with Ocimum Biosolutions Ltd., Hyderabad.
G. Deepika	Assistant Professor, Vivek Vardhini School of Business Management, Jambagh, Hyderabad.
G. Rathnakar	Lecturer, Department of Business Management, Kakatiya Institute of

	Technology and Sciences, Warangal.
Jai Raj Nair	Faculty Member, M.P. Birla Institute of Management, Bangalore.
K. Krishna Reddy	Chairman, Board of Studies in Commerce and Business Management, Kakatiya University, Warangal.
K. Rama Mohana Rao	Department of Commerce and Management Studies, Andhra University, Visakhapatnam.
M. Prabhakar Reddy	Reader, Department of Commerce, Badruka College, Hyderabad.
M. Subrahamanya Sarma	Professor, Department of Commerce and Business Management, Kakatiya University, Warangal.
M. Nalini	Assistant Professor, V.V. School of Business Management, Jambagh, Hyderabad.
M.S.R. Seshagiri	Assistant Professor, Gayatri College for Degree and Post-graduate Courses, Rushikonda, Visakhapatnam.
Mohd. Mujahed Ali	Faculty Member, Department of Business Management, Mahboobia Panjetan P.G. College, Warangal.
N. Kusuma	Faculty Member, Department of Commerce and Business Management, Kakatiya University, Warangal.
P. Krishnama Chary	Professor and Head, Department of Commerce and Business Management, Kakatiya University, Warangal.
P. Pinakapani	Associate Professor, Gayatri College for Degree and Post-graduate courses, Rushikonda, Visakhapatnam.
Priya Deshpande	Assistant Professor, V.V. School of Business Management, Jambagh, Hyderabad.
R. Sudarshan	Faculty Member, Department of Commerce and Business Management, Kakatiya

	University, Warangal.
S. Ravi Prakash	Professor, Commerce and Business Management, Kakatiya University, Warangal.
Satyanarayana	Associate Professor, Department of Commerce and Business Management, Vaagdevi Post-graduate College, Warangal.
Shaik Masood	Faculty Member, Nizam Institute of Engineering and technology, Department of Business Management, Hyderabad.
Smitha Sambrani	Associate Professor, School of Business Management, Vivek Vardhini College, Jambagh, Hyderabad
Sowmya Katyayini	Assistant Professor, Vivek Vardhini School of Business Management, Jambagh, Hyderabad.
Srikanth Verma	Research Scholar, Department of Commerce and Business Management, Kakatiya University, Warangal.
Syeda Parveen	Faculty Member, Kakatiya Institute of Technology and Science, Warangal.
T. Suchitra Rani	Faculty Member, Siva Sivani Institute of Management Studies, Secunderabad.
V. Krishna Mohan	Professor, Department of Commerce and Management Studies, Andhra University, Visakhapatnam.
V.V. Vara Prasad	Associate Professor, Department of P.G. Courses, Raghu Engineering College, Dakammari, Visakhapatnam.

CONTENTS

1

Conceptual Issues in Retail Equity and Retail Loyalty

A. Suryanarayana

Brand equity is the value a brand adds to a product. Retail equity is the value a retail outlet adds to the brands or products it sells. Point of purchase happens at the retail outlet and, hence, the equity added at this point enhances the image of the outlet. In fact, retail equity draws consumer traffic in product categories like jewellery though names like Carbon and Tanishq have been attempting to build brands in this category. BPL, Titan, Carrier Aircon, Ceat, and MRF are some of the brands which have exclusive showrooms it is this exclusivity that helps brands to build equity. Titan virtually changed the experience of buying watches from the regular bazaar shops to a retail world of comfort and feel-good ambience. This is not to say that multi-branded outlets are not required. The Titan example only reflects the importance of retail equity in building brands.

Importance of Image

As in the case of brand associations, retail outlets also have to nurture and cultivate specific associations in the mind of consumers. In urban cities, the 'retail ladder' can be the hot spot for marketeers and retailers. Like 'brand ladders' in which consumers form a mental hierarchy of brands when they think of a product category, retail equity aims at creating specific associations which create a high degree of recall by placing a retail outlet on top of the 'retail ladder'. For example, when consumers think of value associated with consumables (groceries, and commodities), Food World may be on top of the consumer's mind, and it may be Music World for music and Health and Glow for health products. Retail equity also serves as a differentiator when consumers are confronted with hundreds of retail outlets. Retail equity also helps the outlet have a better buying power with large companies because of the volumes it is capable of achieving.

Developing Retail Equity

While the actual process of developing retail equity differs from one product category to another, there are a few aspects which may be useful to any outlet concerned with retailing and point of purchase.

Target Segment: The type of target segment *being considered* by a retail outlet defines the expectations that the outlet will have to fulfill in terms of service, availability, product assortment and layout. A typical buyer of a Titan watch is unlikely to be the one who wants a watch in the range of Rs 150-250. There is a huge unorganized market operating in the watch category (50-60 per cent of the total market) and a high percentage of watches (around 50-60 per cent) are sold below Rs 500. A consumer at the lower end of the market may, in fact, feel uncomfortable in an outlet selling high-end watches. A grocer will only display the products and brands in which the consumers in his neighbourhood are interested. This is the reason why these outlets select product categories and brands with great care. For example, Mother's Recipe-a brand of pickles-may not be available at most retail outlets (including shops) which sell pickles. But Priya, another pickle brand, is more likely to be available at most outlets. Awareness of brands and expectations from retail outlets from the target segment is an important criterion for developing retail image. The concept can be extended to any product category – Baskin Robbin's ice-cream outlets and the watch outlets of Tanishq are examples which substantiate the point.

Dimensions of Expectations: The next aspect is to consider the various dimensions which a specific consumer segment is interested in. There may be a few situations in which the retail outlet may cater to a broad segment. This happens when a brand appeals to a big segment. A typical example is of McDonald outlets allover the world. McDonald is known all over the world for its value, cleanliness and convenience. These expectations have been built over a period of time and, hence, it draws consumers from all income, age and lifestyle groups. Even a brand like McDonald today offers a variety which appeals to distinctive segments.

An outlet should research the target segment and identify specific dimensions which can be developed to attract consumers. Convenience for a fast food outlet, fast check-out during peak hours for a departmental store and variety for a music store are important dimensions. At a time when life is fast, time is scarce and pressures many, an emerging dimension is the need to enjoy the atmospherics and shop at leisure. Shoppers Stop has positioned itself on this dimension. It highlighted the total shopping experience in its visuals, backed by the spread, ambience, decor, product variety and consumer-friendliness. Black and white advertisements made a powerful statement on the feel-good shopping experience. Then, there were advertisements in which customers 'talked' of their experience. Having created an association with enjoyable shopping (to be the first in the 'retail ladder'), the outlet also ensured that this association/image did not get diluted. For instance, when a sales promotion is planned, it is conducted through an event. Fountain Head, the Chennai-based book store, has also positioned itself on a leisurely shopping experience-something that also acts as a differentiator for the book store.

Expectations grow and change with changes in the environment. The concept of Outlet Malls (normally situated on the outskirts of the city) is another point of purchase retailing option which is becoming popular in the West. Manufacturers manage these outlets and offer a good shopping experience apart from discounted, but not damaged, merchandise. Large layouts, open spaces, comfortable car parks, apart from low prices, attract a specific segment to these outlets.

Planning the POP Process: Retailing is about point of purchase and this is the final place at which sale happens. POP strategies have to be planned as a part of the overall strategy of the brand/retail store. In the present context of multi-promotional plans, the POP process has to be integrated into the entire promotional plan. This process can be called integrated POP plan. Apart from conventional POP like posters and brochures, a POP plan today also considers factors like store layout, parking place, atmospherics (which include mood enhancing elements like music, decor and temperature systems) and systems which enable consumers to transact business with ease and comfort.

Promoting Brands in an Era of Brand Proliferation

A supermarket in today's context sells a number of brands within a category. The display or shelf space is limited. Besides, from the consumers' point of view, certain brands may generate greater recall than other brands in the category. In the category of soaps, Liril may generate greater recall than a new brand of herbal soap in the same price range because of the impact of its advertising over the years. While a strongly established brand attempts to retain its existing consumers and also attract new ones from competitive brands, a new brand has to entice consumers try out the new offering. Added to that is the tendency of even loyal consumers to try out new brands in a category like soaps. This is the backdrop against which a typical FMCG brand attempts to use POP material in the store. A store which deals with 20 brands of soaps or toothpastes may have to promote all the brands most of the time. A special display and POP material have to be organized when the brand is on sale. But as the number of brands increase in most categories, a store may find itself under pressure to promote all of them simultaneously. And is that isn't enough, there are as many variants (across FMCG categories) to ensure that the consumer stays with the brand. Colgate may have a herbal version, gel version and a Colgate Total which offers several benefits. All these variants may need to be promoted. Even manufacturers need to be convinced that they are getting a fair share of the retailer's attention.

Retail equity establishes a retail association in the psyche of consumers and also enables the retailer to deal more competitively with manufacturers, depending on how the latter executes that equity.

Retail Service

Service at the point of purchase has been often written about and discussed in great detail. A contemporary dimension is the nature of the service consumers expect in a specific retail setting and the nature of the product category itself. Service in the retail context is the overall attention given to consumers which can enhance their (retail) experience. This retail experience can also extend to certain services beyond the point of purchase in the case of durables.

Importance of Appropriate Service: A retailer is concerned with the store image and service, a vital aspect, can affect his/her image. The direct result of the service provided can be seen in the way consumers talk about it with their friends/peer-groups. A positive word of mouth (WOM) is the best 'advocate' for the store while a negative one can spell disaster. The importance of WOM is reflected in the fact that large brands developed markets conduct research studies to quantify its impact in terms of sales gained or lost! Service also helps the store to establish for itself a specific proposition. This is important as it functions as a differentiator. A consumer will appreciate a service which ensures faster billing with separate counters for less than five items bought in a large store.

Service varies with the types of products and retail outlets. But the basic aspect of providing service is concerned with the identification of consumers who need to be serviced after entering a large retail outlet. Sales personnel should be trained to provide appropriate, not unwanted service. Unfortunately, service is mixed up with over enthusiasm, which is reflected in artificial hospitality at the retail outlet which certain consumers may not like. The attention given to a consumer should always be perceived as warm, spontaneous and appropriate. It should never be associated with unnecessary intrusion.

FMCG products, commodities and groceries are categories which require little 'on-store' service. Normally, consumers are discerning enough to sift through the information on brands, prices and sale offers (if this kind of basic information is made available). The 'off-store' service becomes important. Apart from free home delivery (on certain conditions) offered by super markets, the reassurance provided on the quality of products is extremely important-especially in the case of groceries and commodities and vegetables which are not branded. Consumers visit these large retailers in the hope of finding value on such products (a combination of price and quality). Dissatisfaction on this count can force them to return to their neighbourhood grocer or look for other options. Food World marked the success of super markets in India. The perception that super markets are shopping places for the middle class is of recent origin and is based on the variety and quality associated with their goods. Consumers should never be let down on this proposition.

Complaints about the lack of quality, freshness, improper packaging and under weight should be immediately attended to and consumers should not get the feeling that the store is doing them a favour by replacing the product. If required, changes in the procurement process or supply chain may have to be made before the store loses its reputation on its core promise. That unbranded products are (relatively) more important from the viewpoint of the store cannot be overemphasized. The store is important for the consumers because it stocks what they really need to buy as against branded FMCG products which they pick up more because of the 'pull' effect created by manufacturers.

Speciality Products

High-end products (expensive jewellery, furniture or designer wear) are those which draw consumers because of their lifestyle and symbolic appeals. While brands may also playa role in attracting consumers, a retail store needs to offer a different kind of service. Allen Solly's exclusive showroom is a good example to illustrate this point. The consumer goes through an 'experiential' service, especially if the product is of personal significance. The product display at Allen Solly's exclusive shop was such that the consumer could go around and feel the fabric before trying it on. Digital kiosks can also be used to give an idea to the consumer about how well the product will match him/her. (These kiosks enable the consumer to try out different designs/variations of the brand enabling him/her to decide on the one which is most suitable).

In the case of readymade wear, what is usually wanting is 'fit' with which the consumer is concerned even after selecting the design. The retail store personnel can help, but in an unobtrusive manner. This aspect of service is also associated with the availability of SKUs and inventory management which takes into consideration consumer needs.

'Experiential service' which consumers experience at the point of purchase can also be extended to categories like perfumes and cosmetics. Lakme introduced a plan at the point of purchase for its Orchids range of cosmetics in which a consumer could try the product before deciding on its purchase. It should be noted that in such categories, a free trial is possible only in the premium price range.

Feel of the Product: 'Experiential service' can also be extremely effective if applied to audio and video durables. BPL has exclusive galleries in some cities that display its products. Carrier Aircon and Onida are other brands which maintain such exclusive showrooms displaying a range of products/variants. If the retail store can help the consumer simulate the experience of listening to an audio system in a 'house-like' setting or the coolness of an air-conditioner in a room similar to the consumer's, it not only helps the consumer but also the store. Such a trend can have a significant impact in detailing with the benefits of a brand. A part of the promotional budget can be allocated for such point-of-purchase experience.

Service for Durables: Leading brands like Videocon, BPL, LG or Samsung deal with a number of product categories (audio, TV, refrigerator, microwaves etc). Word of mouth has an even greater impact with regard to durables. A consumer of a black and white TV may be a prospective consumer of a refrigerator or an audio system. Millions of households may use at least one. BPL or Videocon product and the service at the retail outlet can be a potent tool for creating a base of loyal consumers. There are two aspects to be considered with regard to service for durables: service provided by multibrand outlets (like Vivek and Co) and service provided by an exclusive outlet. A leading brand is likely to be present in about 3000 to 4000 outlets in the country and not all are exclusive. Such a differentiation can also help the brand improve its infrastructure and locational considerations apart from enhancing customer satisfaction.

Credibility Factor: A multibrand outlet is one where the consumer can compare features/prices and also get a feedback from the store personnel on specific brands. Such a retail store should be very careful in dealing with the consumer when he/she asks for information on specific brands. It is not uncommon to find sales personnel in the store attempting to promote a specific brand or brands against certain others. This traditional approach of, pushing' some brands may no longer work in an environment where the consumer is more aware and has sources of information other the store personnel. For instance, when the consumer receives a negative feedback about a brand of washing machine which has a positive WOM among his friends, he begins to suspect the credibility of the store. While the retailer's influence on the consumer is still quite high in India (though the trend is declining in metros), the opportunity provided by the situation should be used to build credibility in the transaction.

Analyzing the need of the consumer is fundamental to building the credibility of the store. The clutter of brands, benefits and features may confuse the consumer. Confounding the confusion is the comparative advertising which compares brands on their features, quality, and prices and so on. A consumer attempting to upgrade to a colour TV is very different from the one who is entering the store to replace a colour TV. Pressurizing and selling a feature-ridden colour TV to the former can create post-purchase dissonance. The consumer is likely to feel 'cheated' about being sold a TV which he did not want or one that is too complicated for his needs. Mercedez has an 'S' series of cars with around 125 controls. But a consumer for this car is very different from the one who looks for an 'entry model'.

While price points are significantly apart, they are generally much clustered in TV s. Sales personnel may tend to force a price point higher than the one the consumer wants to buy. The 'need-offer' match, which takes place in the initial phase of ' customer-point of purchase' interaction is vital, especially for highly competitive products (low and middle price range). This is because the major chunk of the market exists in these ranges and the existence of most retail stores depends on these markets. The kind of the service which should be provided by a large exclusive outlet has been indicated earlier in the article (with a focus on 'experiential service'). Product-service interface at the point of purchase enhances the relationship between the retailers and consumers just as structured 'instore' and 'off-store' service enhances the customer-retailer interface.

Retail Loyalty

Loyalty being an important strategy for marketeers, it is worth analyzing how retailers retain consumers and ensure they come back after establishing retail equity. With fragmented patterns of retail locations and a high degree of area wise concentration in urban cities, sustaining consumer loyalty is a major challenge. Research, both in Indian and western contexts across categories, shows that loyal consumers significantly enhance profitability. Loyalty, here, is essentially a consumer's commitment towards a retail outlet. This aspect highlights the fact that for some reason, a consumer selects a store for repeat buying in spite of the several alternatives available to him/her.

Depending on the nature and size of the retail store, there may be different approaches to enhance the base of loyal consumers. A few aspects may provide a conceptual platform for retailers involved with the point-of purchase.

Importance of SKU Management

In products like soaps, toothpastes, blades, talcum powders, shampoos and other packaged goods (FMCG), a high degree of branding is taking place. It is not uncommon, to find consumers asking for a specific brand in urban markets. But brands like A-I, Lifebuoy and Pond's are strong even in rural markets. The critical aspect to be noted at the point of purchase (even in a super market) is the maintenance of the typical stock-keeping units (SKU) with regard to each product category and brand. Based on previous purchase data, one can find out what these SKUs are. An SKU is just a unit of the brand. For example, there are sachets, 500 gm and 1 kg packages of Surf Excel. Each is an SKU. The normal point-of-purchase strategies, which may be often associated with loyalty, are service and price. SKUs may play an important role in deciding how a consumer perceives a store. A consumer, who is unable to get an SKU of his/her choice at a store after frequenting the store a few times, may not want to return to that store again. Availability of appropriate SKUs (according to the location, product category or brand) is important for gaining store traffic-a prerequisite for store loyalty. Does the same size of Ariel or Close Up or Red Label sell uniformly in all areas in the city? How many times does a retailer run out of stock with regard to a specific SKU? Such probing also helps a retailer to manage his/her inventory more profitably.

Price-based Loyalty

Price is one of the several factors which lead to repeat purchase. Any shopper is aware of a couple of retailers in his/her neighbourhood, who may be able to offer packaged goods at a price less than the marked retail price (MRP). This is one of the reasons why consumers stick to their neighbourhood shops in spite of the super markets in their vicinity. Such retailers bank heavily on business volumes. But the catch is that 'price loyalty' may be a short-term strategy. This is not to say that retailers must not take recourse to discount sales or a reduced MRP. But they must have other plan to back up the 'price based' strategy. The emergence of a big retailer who offers better prices because of large volume can be a definite threat to small retailer who uses the 'price-based' strategy. This is the reason why some kirana stores offer home delivery during working hours even for small purchases.

Service and Profitability

While service is certainly an important factor in retaining consumers, its quality and the infrastructure at the point of purchase should be appropriate for consumers, apart from being profitable for the retailer. Quick and free home delivery may be an attractive service for consumers. But, as the retailer builds up a consumer over a period of time, this service will mean more personnel and, hence, more overheads. This is one of the reasons why large retailers specify a minimum purchase and distance limit for free home delivery. Financial bottomlines are extremely important when retailers plan for an infrastructure-be it personnel, additional space or technology. Even ambience can be a service which enhances the shopping experience. The cost of the retailer's AC, the store traffic, repeats purchases and the margin on brands have to be taken into account. The store can have a significant part of low margin-high volume products or high margin-low volume products (like CDs, foreign publications or furniture). Service provided by the store should not be allowed to offset profitability, especially when it is attempting to build loyalty. It is virtually impossible to wean away a loyal consumer from a service that he/she gets used to.

Triggering Retail Loyalty

It is not possible to have a customized strategy for each brand/retail store without specific situation-based inputs, the following guidelines may be considered to come to grips with promoting brands in a retail store:

- The identification of the target segment helps in the selection of brands/product-categories. Having done that, the store need not stock slow-moving brands or variants. This also minimizes POP efforts. For example, 'Connexions' is a retail store which carries books, CDs, gifts and toys by taking into account the needs of consumers in a specific locality.

- The store can identify fast-moving brands and plan promotional activities at the point of purchase. This will ensure that an optimal promotional plan is worked out and to-be-promoted brands get enough visibility without any major clashes (between the brands).
- Brands on sale can be placed in a specific location in the store. This helps the consumer plan his/her purchase of these brands and also compare and contrast with the variants which are not on sale. Going around the store, a consumer may find on sale a brand of squash and a brand of tea at different locations. If many brands from many categories are on sale, the consumer may miss seeing certain brands or run out of money by the time he comes to the other 'sale' locations in the store. Comparison of variants is also likely to take place better if on-sale variants are kept separately.
- POP posters have to be displayed at different locations depending on whether a brand is on sale or not. Categorizing on-sale brands also helps the retailer to spread the POP material in the store. This helps attract the attention of customers much better as it breaks the 'adaptation' process by which the latter get used to the POP plethora and end up not looking at any such material at all.
- POP brochures are best placed within the vicinity of the respective product category. Placing brochures at the entrance of the store (or distributing them) fails to identify consumers who may be interested in that product category. If awareness is to be created on a new category/brand, it will have to be done in synchronization with media planning.
- It makes sense for a brand to advertise its sale in local media vehicles which are also popular in the area where the store is located. This generates awareness and selective use of POP material within the store can serve as recall stimuli. POP planning is an elaborate and structured process, which can

improve the image of the retailer in the long run.

Retail loyalty may help retailers deal better with manufacturers, especially when brand differentiation becomes small. Managing the experiences and expectations of the target segment is a prerequisite for retail equity, which can, eventually, lead to retail loyalty.

2

Torrential Forces in Indian Modern Retailing

S. Ravi Prakash and G. Rathnakar

The paper is well thought-out into three sections. In the first section academic journal articles about Indian retailing are reviewed in order to identify established findings about Indian retailing. The second section consists of a review of the literature relating to the development of modern retailing in a few newly industrialized countries with a view to examine if the patterns of retail development in these countries could occur in India. The third section analyses the process of modernization in the Indian retail sector, makes a prognosis about the likely pattern of future development of retailing in India and derives implications for practice and policy

Prelude

Retailing has been defined as business activities involved in selling goods and services to consumers for their personal, family or household use. Although retailing has been around for millennia, the 20th century witnessed a lot of change in the retail sector, especially in the developed countries. Modern formats such as department stores, discount stores, supermarkets, convenience stores, fast food outlets, specialty stores, warehouse retailers and hypermarkets have emerged. Retailing has become more organized and chain stores have been growing at the expense of independent shops. The chains are utilizing sophisticated information technology and communication to manage their operations and have grown rapidly not only within their home countries like US, UK, France, Germany and Holland but to other developed countries. Walmart Stores, the US retailer, was recognized as the largest firm in terms of sales in 2002 in Fortune magazine's list of 500 largest global firms. Modern retail formats have also spread beyond developed countries.

Modernisation in Indian Retailing

The emergence of new formats and the evolution of modern retail in India have attracted attention in recent years. The business press in India has carried several articles and news items in the last three years about the modern formats (Shukla 2001; Anand & Rajshekhar, 2001; Bhattacharjee, 2001). The consulting firm KSA Technopak has organized retail meetings or summits in major metros which have witnessed participation from major domestic and international retailers, and also from manufacturers. In the Marketing Channel Management -a Customer Centric Approach has discussed that the census studies of retail outlets that the market research firm ORG MARG conducted in the 1990's. This census provided data and estimates on a number of parameters relating to Indian retail such as number and type of outlets and growth of outlets over time separately for urban and rural areas. Due to these reports and activities, there is good deal of information available about what is happening in Indian retail. However Indian retailing has received sparse attention by way of academic research with the exception of a few articles in academic journals and some case studies.

An Overview of Indian Retail Sector

Indian retailing is undergoing a process of evolution and is poised to undergo dramatic transformation. The retail sector employs over 8 per cent of the national workforce but is characterized by a high degree of fragmentation with over 5 million outlets, The retail universe more than doubled between 1978 and 1996 and the number of outlets per 1000 people at an All India level, increased from 3.7 in 1978 to 5.6 in 1996. For the urban sector alone, the shop density increased from 4 per 1000 people in 1978 to 7.6 per 1000 people in 1996 (Venugopal, 2001). Because of their small size, Indian retailers have very little bargaining power with manufacturers and perform only a few of the flows in marketing channels unlike in the case of retailers in developed countries, (Sarma , 2000).

The corner grocer or the ' kirana' store is a key element in the retail in India due to the housewife's unwillingness to go long distances for purchasing daily needs. An empirical study was carried out by Sinhaetal (2002) to identify factors that influenced consumers' choice of a store. Although convenience and merchandise were the two most important reasons for choosing a store, the choice criteria varied across product categories. Convenience was indicated by consumers as the most important reason in the choice of groceries and fruit outlets, chemists and lifestyle items while merchandise was indicated as the most important in durables, books and apparel. The traditional formats like hawkers, grocers and paan shops co exist with modern formats like supermarkets, and non store retailing channels such as multi level marketing and teleshopping. Example of modern formats include department stores like Akbarallys ,supermarkets like Food World, franchise stores like Van Heusen and Lee, discount stores like Subhiksha, shop-in-shops, factory outlets and service retailers (Nathan , 2001).

Modern stores tend to be larger, carry more stock keeping units have a self service format and an experiential ambience. Modern formats also tend to have higher levels of sales per unit of space, stock turnover and gross margin but lower levels of net margin as compared to traditional formats (Radhakrishnan, 2003). Modernisation in retail formats is likely to happen quicker in categories like Dry groceries, electronics, Mens' apparel, Books, Music. Some reshaping and adaptation my also happen in Fresh groceries, Women's apparel, fast food, and personal care products (Fernandes et al, 2000).

In recent years, there has been a slow spread of retail chains in some formats like supermarkets, department stores, malls and discount stores. Factors facilitating the spread of chains are the availability of quality products at lower prices, improved shopping standards, convenient shopping and display, and blending of shopping with entertainment, and the entry of industrial houses like Goenkas, Rahejas, Piramals and Tatas into retailing (Ramaswamy and Namakumari, 2002).

However formats are not easily scalable across the country. Several companies have found that it is not easy to expand beyond some regions and cities as evident from the examples of Margin Free Market and Foodworld, which are active only in a few states or cities. Affordable real estate prices and availability of sufficient number of economically well off households in the catchment area are critical requirements that will determine new store viability and thus the possibility of further expansion (Anand and Rajashekhar, 2001). According to Rao (2001), foreign direct investment in the retail sector in India, although not yet permitted by government, is desirable, as it would improve productivity and increase competitiveness. New stores will introduce efficiency. Customers also gain as prices in the new stores tend to be lower. The consequences of modernization in India may be somewhat different due to lower purchasing power and the new stores may cater to only to branded products aimed at upper income segments. However it will be wise for old style stores to join together into wholesale and retail groups to improve bargaining power as experience in developed markets such as UK has shown that the modernization in retail has led to the decline of independent mom and pop stores.

The need for a fresh perspective while developing theories to explain the new developments has been stressed by Bennett et al (1998). The Indian retail environment is witnessing several changes on the demand side due to increased per capita income, changing lifestyle and increased product availability. Experience of retailing in US shows that existing theories of retail development based on changing consumer needs, are inadequate to explain new developments. In developed markets, there has been a power shift with power moving from manufacturers towards retailers. The strategies used by retailers to wrest power include the development of retailers own brands, and the introduction of slotting allowances which necessitate payments by manufacturers to retailers for providing shelf space for new products. Retailers have also used technology effectively to obtain usable information about consumer buying patterns. The increased power of retailers has led to the introduction of new tactics by manufacturers such as everyday low pricing, partnerships with retailers and increased use of direct marketing methods. Because of these issues, a supply side perspective needs to be fused with the demand side in developing theories for explaining modernization in retail.

Evolution of Modern Retail in India

The foregoing review has provided some information that enables the construction of a framework for analyzing the retail development in India. The driving forces towards development can be broadly classified into six categories and which is followed by a discussion on each of the torrential forces.

Economic Development: The development of the Indian economy is a necessary condition for the development of the Indian retail sector. The example of Thailand shows that the impetus to modernization of retail was provided by the economic boom in Thailand (Feenyetal, 1996). Development increases the disposable income in the hands of consumers and leads to an increase in the proportion of spending on discretionary non- food items. Economic development also enfranchises new households as potential customers for modern retail and leads to increased ownership of personal transportation among consumers, which in turn can increase their willingness to travel longer distances to shop in new format stores. The growth of the economy can also provide gainful employment to those who would otherwise enter retailing in areas like hawking, roadside vending and other similar low cost entries into the retail sector.

Rapid economic development may also positively influence the views of international retailing companies about the business prospects and investment attractiveness in a country. A high degree of inflation in the economy is however, not conducive to modernization of the retail sector. In Brazil, the real progress in retail was noticed only after the stabilization of the economy and control of inflation (Alexander and Silva, 2002). Development also has an influence on the regions and cities where modern formats are initially set up. In the Greek, Thai and Brazilian cases, modern formats initially appeared in the important cities. This has been noticed in India as well as the modern formats first appeared in the metros like Delhi, Mumbai and Chennai and the mini metros like Bangalore and Hyderabad due to the comparatively higher level of disposable incomes available in these cities.

Improvements in Civic Situation: The civic situation includes factors like safety and security in the city and the various municipal regulations governing the opening, location and operation of stores, and the nature of public transport available. A safe and secure environment will encourage the setting up of 24 hour convenience stores and the operation of shopping plazas and encourage shopping expeditions for the whole family. The presence of adequate parking facilities or excellent public transportation will encourage consumers to be more mobile in their choice of store. City or state regulations on opening or closing hours, rent control laws, availability of adequate electrical power and regulations relating to licensing will affect both the time required to set up a new store as well as the cost of store operation and its viability. Many of the civic factors mentioned above would be dependent on the economic development and administrative policies in the area. The impact of the civic situation may influence the choice of the cities, states, zones in which the modernization investments will be made.

Changes in Consumer Needs, Attitudes and Behaviour: The growth of modern retail is linked to consumer needs, attitudes and behaviour. Marketing channels including retailing emerge because they receive impetus from both the supply side, and the demand side. On the demand side, the marketing channel facilitates provides service outputs that consumers value. These service outputs may include but are not limited to bulk-breaking, spatial convenience, waiting and delivery time and assortment (Coughlan et al, 2001, pg 30). In Indian retailing, convenience and merchandise appear to be the most important factors influencing store choice, although ambience and service are also becoming important in some contexts (Sinha et al, 2002). Modernisation will have to address convenience issues while presenting strong alternatives to the weaknesses of traditional formats in selection of merchandise available for sale. Modern formats need not be expensive and can offer lower prices to consumers (Rao, 2001).

Lower prices in turn will increase the attractiveness of modern formats and rapid growth in the preference for purchasing from new format stores. Store ambience includes issues such as lighting, cleanliness, store layout and space for movement. Modern stores can offer a far better ambience compared to traditional stores. On the service front, traditional stores especially kirana stores offer credit and home delivery. These needs will have to be addressed by new format. Experience from Brazil shows that the combination of entertainment and shopping provided by some shopping centers, is attractive to consumers. This may become important in India as well because of the limited entertainment options currently available in cities. While consumer needs, attitudes and behaviour will influence the development in retail; it is likely that investments in retailing and the creation of new stores offering value will in turn influence consumers. This appears to have happened in Greece, Thailand and Brazil.

Changes in Government Policies: The Indian government has clarified on a number of occasions that foreign direct investment will not be permitted in India. Major international retailer organizations will be watching for signals of policy change especially because China has permitted foreign investment in retail. In opening up the retail sector, the government may consider various approaches such as insisting on joint ventures, limiting the foreign stake, or specifying the cities areas where investment is permitted. Thailand's example shows that in case of joint ventures, the local partner can play a significant role in the success of the joint venture. The Brazilian experience shows that local retailing groups can successfully compete against international chains if they adopt innovations and restructure operations in accordance with market needs. Some policy protection can be given to consumer cooperatives which have been providing value to their members and customers. This protection can be in the form of allowing these organizations to access capital from the local market and operate in a more professional manner. The government can also play a positive role in simplifying or eliminating the plethora of regulations governing retailing. Specific laws relating to franchising will also be desirable for foreign and Indian brand owners to adopt the franchise route in a bigger way.

Increased Investment in Retailing: The prospects for significant modernization and development in retailing will depend on the nature of investment in this sector. The investment will be of two types- foreign and domestic. The quantum and nature of investment will depend on the factors outlined earlier namely economic development; civic situation; consumer needs, attitudes and behaviour; and government policies. Although FDI is not yet permitted in retailing, a number of global retailers are testing the waters by signing technical agreements and franchises with Indian firms. Fast food chains like McDonalds and Pizza Hut are already operating in the metros. A Marks and Spencer store is already operational in Mumbai. Several global retailers are awaiting a change in policy. However, the development of the Indian retail sector is dependent not just on foreign investment but on Indian investment as well. Since the 1980's industrial groups such as Reliance and Raymonds have been active in encouraging development of well appointed exclusive showrooms for their textile brands. In the 1990's industrial houses like Rahejas, Piramals, and Tatas have entered retailing. Several Indian and foreign brands have used franchising to establish exclusive outlets for their brands.

At present the new format stores cater mostly to households belonging to the higher income families. The catchments area for these modern stores has to be fairly large as the number of such households is small in relation to the total population. This limits the number of stores and constrains the growth of chains. The modern stores have also been plagued by low conversion in relation to the number of footfalls. This means that although a large number of people visit the store, the number of buyers and the average bill amount is small. Due to low sales, the bargaining power of the retailers with suppliers and manufacturers is low and this restricts their average gross margin. On the other hand the expenses involved in setting up and maintaining a modern format store tend to be much higher than traditional store due to the additional expenses on larger size, better locations and superior ambience. Therefore if the returns on investment in the new formats have to be attractive, modern retailers have to develop a strong supply chain that provides them significant gross margins while delivering merchandise at attractive prices to customers. In order to do this, modern retailers will need to eliminate middlemen and buy directly from suppliers and make use of technology to control inventory. These developments will impact the survival and existence of middlemen such as wholesalers and agents who will have to find new business models to survive. Manufacturing firms will also face pressure from strong buyers on price, delivery and service terms.

Increase in Power of Organised Retail: Bargaining power of organized retail translates directly into higher gross margins for the retailers. At present there are a large number of independent retailers with little bargaining power vis-à-vis manufacturers, distributors and wholesalers. Manufacturers have been promoting their brands and generating consumer demand for branded products. This makes it necessary for all varieties of stores especially in urban areas to stock branded products. Manufacturers take advantage of the consumer pull to limit margins to the retailers. Retailers manage their profitability by operating on a very low cost basis. This is possible because of low rental expenses due to historical reasons and low labour costs due to employment of family members in the store. The modern stores have somewhat higher gross margins, but their net margins are not very significant for providing the cash flow required to fuel rapid growth in outlets.

Retailers can increase their power in several ways. They can invest efforts in developing their own store brands. The supermarket chain Food world has begun doing this in a limited way with food grains and pulses. Secondly they can invest in supply chain, buy directly from the sources and eliminate middlemen. Thirdly they can attempt to obtain volumes in buying by aggregating the requirements of various stores, and bargaining for better prices by placing large orders. Although this strategy suits chain stores, independent grocers may also get together by forming a cooperative or buying club in order to benefit from scale economies in purchasing. Retailers can also obtain several benefits from using information technology. They can monitor their stocks and sales using IT and thus manage their working capital more efficiently. They can also analyze data about customers and their buying habits and be in a position to develop marketing strategies and promotional offers to increase customer purchasing at the outlet.

Manufacturing firms will need to develop new strategies for dealing with powerful retailers. The first change required will be one of mind-set. Negotiations with powerful retailers will have to be carried out at much higher executive levels within the firm. New structures such as National account managers, Category managers etc. would need to be deployed. Firms will have to reconsider their brand promise, brand promotion and their brand building policies to deal with store brands that will be introduced by retail chains. Firms will also have to re engineer their logistics policies to meet the demands of powerful retailers for just in time delivery to their distribution centers or stores. New product introductions will have to be coordinated with the retail chains so that adequate shelf space is available at launch. The firms will need to carefully look at their product cost structures both in terms of variable cost and allocated fixed costs in order to maintain profitability in the face of pressures for price reductions from powerful retailers.

Conclusion

The Indian retail sector is largely traditional, but stores in modern format are emerging. The contribution of organized retailing in the share of retail sales in India is currently very small. Based on an analysis of retail developments in countries such as Thailand, Brazil and Greece, and some experience in India, it is possible to conclude that modernization of retailing in India would be influenced by some important factors. These factors include economic development; improvements in civic situation; changes in consumer needs, attitudes and behavior; changes in government policies; increased investment in retailing and rise in the power of organized retail. The development of modern retail will have several implications for managerial practice in manufacturing firms. Firms will need to proactively review and their sales structures, brand activities, logistics policy and price structure to cope with pressures from powerful retailers.

References

Aggarwal, A. Current issues in Indian retailing, European Retail Digest , Issue 25 70-71

Alexander, N. and Silva, M..D. (2002). Emerging markets and the internationalization of retailing: The Brazilian experience", International Journal of Retail Distribution and Management, 30, (6) 300-314

Anand, M. and Rajshekhar, M. The retail puzzle, Business World, 29 October, 2001.38-42

Bennett, R.C., Livstack, D.S., and Singh, D. Merging theories to explain Recent retail evolution", Vision, 2 (1) 27-32

Bennison, D. and Boutsouki, C. 1995. Greek retailing in transition", International Journal of Retail Distribution and Management, 23 (1) 24-31

Berman, B. and Evans, J.R. 2001. Retail Management, (8th ed) , Upper Saddle River, N.J., Prentice Hall

Bhattacharjee, P. (2001). Retail's new Godzilla" Business World, 28 May, 44-46

Coughlan, A.T., Anderson, E., Stern, L.W. and El-Ansary, A.I. 2001. Marketing Channels, (6th Ed). New Delhi: Prentice Hall of India Pvt. Ltd.

Radhakrishnan, K. (2003). Organised retail: Forging ahead, Praxis, 4 (1) 47-51

Ramaswamy, V.S. and Namakumari, S. Marketing Management. Delhi: Macmillan India Ltd.

Venugopal, P. (2001). Marketing Channel Management: A Customer Centric Approach. New Delhi: Response Books

3

Role of Information Technology in Indian Retailing

D. Harikanth and B. Raj Kumar

In any industry there are two methods available to an organisation for making business productivity. The first method focuses on improving the organisation's impact on the market place while the second focuses on improving the internal operations, thereby, lowering costs or improving services.

In retail, there exists a significant opportunity to use technology to deliver revolutionary new processes and in effect, redefine the industry or to change the approach towards business. Investments in technology are expensive and technology needs vary, depending on the size of the business and the forward and backward linkages that the retailer is able to seize.

The technological footprint that a retailer creates is a strong indicator of his ability to leverage people and managerial talent. The information technology strategy adopted has to be based on the business strategy so as to enable synchronisation with the key success factors of the business.

Retailers like Wal-Mart, Zara, Amazon.com and Metro continue to effectively use new and emerging technologies to stay continually relevant to the ever-changing consumer.

In India, organisations like GCMMF, Asian Paints, HLL and McDonald's have effectively harnessed the power of emerging technologies to control costs, enhance supply chain efficiencies and achieve differentiation in the marketplace in terms of product and service. The main aim of the study is to examine the role played by the technology and the factors effecting its usage.

Importance of Information Technology in Retailing

The importance of information technology in retail stems from the importance of data. Data is nothing but information which aids decision-making. The right data, in the right form to the right set of people at the right time, is one of the greatest tools in the hands of the retailer. Information is always with reference to a particular time frame.

For example, a customer at a department store. After selecting some goods, he proceeds towards the billing counter. Here, the billing clerk scans each product at the POS (Point of Sale) terminal, the total number of items and the bill amount is added up. While doing so, he has also checked with the customer if he is a member of the store's loyalty programme. The customer confirms that he is a member gives him the store card for entry, makes the payment by way of a credit card and exits the store with his purchases. While to the customer it is just a routine purchase, the information that the store has gathered from this transaction helps the retailer in many ways. They are

- Efficient Stocking of Merchandise: The items purchased provided information on merchandise sold in the stores; this is the base of sales analysis and decisions on replenishment, re-ordering and merchandise planning. If the information is passed on to the manufacturer, it can help reduce production time.
- Collection of Data: The use of technology aids data collection. Data can be collected about consumers, their purchase the frequency of buying and the typical basket size. This information helps the retailer distinguish the customers who shop at his store frequently and also reward them. The data on purchases made also passed on to the credit card organisation for payment to the merchant establishment and also for billing the customer.
- Efficiency in Operations: The use of information technology serves as a basis for integrating the functioning of various departments. When a retailer decides to use the power of technology to aid his business, the investment in terms of

money is usually high. However, the benefits of the use of information technology are many. As the processes get automated, the time involved in a particular task is reduced.

- Helps Communication: Communication within the organisation can be faster with the use of software like Lotus Notes. Retail stores can also communicate with each other and with the warehouses. This can be done 24 hours a day and seven days a week. Electronic Data Interchange (EDI) can also be used for communication with suppliers and vendors. The information needs of the retailer largely depend on the size and the spread of the organization.

With an increase in the number of stores and/or an increase in the number of products sold in the store, gathering of information becomes crucial. Technology plays a vital role in gathering this information and making it available to the right set of persons.

Unique Needs of Technology in Retailing

The retail business has been an early adapter of Information Technology (IT). This is one business where the need to capture accurate information and make it available not only within the store, but to the warehouses, distributors and manufacturers as soon as it has been acquired, has been an important requirement. The need for making information available in real time emerges out of the need to manage the short shelf life of goods and the need to manage the costs of inventory.

The spread of the Internet has opened up a number of opportunities for using IT innovatively, to extend the reach of the retailer into the homes of his customers. While the Internet was expected to revolutionise the retailing business and take it into the virtual world, it has been found to be appropriate only for some categories of goods.

IT has been applied to some of the unique requirements of the retail business, such as the need for product identification, the need for quick billing and settlement of bills electronically and specialised logistics applications. The use of information technology in retail includes a wide swathe of technologies covering software, hardware and wire line and wireless communication. Typically, a mature user of IT in retail uses a number of technologies such as: POS terminals, software's for managing inventory and to interact with financial services organisations to complete transactions, in addition to standard applications. The industry uses advanced constructs such as data warehousing/mining for trend analysis and customer management and highly specialised solutions for Supply Chain Management.

A single customer transaction has implications on wide range of areas. For example, a customer who has made a purchase at retail store for goods worth Rs. 1,000. Typically, to record this transaction, a barcode scanner will be used to scan the item/s being purchased.

The customer may choose to pay cash or may pay by way of a credit card. In case the customer chooses to pay by cash, a simple transaction is required which will record the sale. However, in case of a card transaction, the data also needs to be furnished to the bank to ensure that the retailer receives the payments. The customer may also be a member of a loyalty programme offered by the store, hence, that is also information which has to be checked and recorded.

Sales would need to look at the consolidated effect of each transaction to understand the achievement of targets and take decisions as may be necessary. Merchandising will look at the data in the form of movement of merchandise which has to be replaced and therefore, reordered, as the case may be. Finance will have to look into the movement of merchandise and the sales in terms of the inflow of cash into the company and payments that have to be made to the suppliers. Marketing may look at the transaction to understand and evaluate new campaigns, sales promotions/spot offers which may be offered.

Applications of Technology

A typical retail store offers at least a few hundred units of products to the consumer. In order to keep track of what has been sold and to be able to re-order products, the retailer needs to know the quantities, the types, colours, sizes and other characteristics of the products sold. It is not humanly possible to remember all these variations over a period of time. Even if attempted, it is a time consuming exercise and could be error ridden. Thus, a need was fell for developing a machine readable system which could help identify the product across various retail locations and provide all information associated with it quickly.

The Universal Product Code (UPC) or Barcode as it is popularly known, was developed from this need. While the first barcode patent was issued in 1952, the retail industry adopted it much later, since to implement a barcode system, hardware to produce the codes and software to interpret the information contained in them was required. Once this was developed, the grocery retailers were the first to adopt the barcode.

Bar coding is one of the IT tools used for automatic data capture. As opposed to manual data entry, which is tedious and prone to inaccuracies and errors, bar coding enables data capture with 100 per cent accuracy and in micro-seconds. Barcodes can be used to represent information related to product attributes, other supplementary information like batch number, manufacturing and expiry dates, consigner/consignee, etc.

Electronic Data Interchange (EDI)

Electronic Data Interchange (EDI) is defined as the exchange of business information, through standard interfaces, by using computers. It can also be interpreted as transmission of business data between organisations in a computerised format that does not require the re-keying of information. Since EDI is defined as the exchange of electronic documents between organisations, the EDI acronym has also been sometimes interpreted as the Electronic Document Interchange.

EDI is at the core of the overall concept of Electronic Commerce (EC). The advantages of the use of EDI are listed below:

- EDI saves time, as the transmission of data can be immediate. If there is an EDI exchange between a retailer and the supplier, the supplier at his end, can spot trends in purchase and accordingly realign production.

- A manual error, which may arise while keying in data, is also avoided.
- It reduces costs involved in paper handling, filing, storage and mailing and,
- It serves as a tool for strengthening the relationship between the retailer and the supplier.

Database Management, Data Warehousing, Data Mining

A simple purchase at any retail store can enable the store to gather a vast amount of information about its customers and products. The use of systems to organise, retrieve, search and manage that data is termed as *database management.* Data can be with respect to products, customers, vendors and suppliers or a combination of them put together.

The elements of database management are data warehousing and data mining. Let us take the example of a customer who buys a pair of cotton chino trousers from a large department store chain in Mumbai. The customer is also a member of the loyalty programme run by this chain and visits the store frequently.

By swiping the customer loyalty card at the time of purchase, an entire information system starts functioning. The store's computer sends the information to the company's central computer, which usually hosts the *data warehouse.* From this data warehouse, the organisation is able to retrieve-data that will give important information about the purchase made, the total number of purchases made, the colour, size and demographic data of the customer.

The concept of data mining is not new, as for many years, statisticians, used to mine data manually. Technology has enabled the automation of data mining process and has integrated in with a data warehouse, which enables the availability of data in a manner relevant for various business. Data mining can help extract information from a database that the user did not know existed. The information unearthed by data mining can also help the customer relationship management process (CRM).

Radio Frequency Identification (RFID)

Radio frequency identification or RFID is fast transforming the way business is being conducted and monitored across the supply chain. It can be described as a wireless bar code which provides wireless communication between objects and readers. RFID uses tags or transponders that collect data and manage it in a portable, changeable database.

While there are a great deal of similarities between the barcode and the RFID tag, the chief differentiator is the level of technology used. Bar coding scans a printed label with either optical laser or imaging technology, while RFID scans or interrogates a semiconductor tag using radio frequency (wireless) technology.

Bar Code

The Universal Product Code or the bar code is basically a product identifier, made up of a series of bars and spaces, which represent alphanumeric information. In 1972, manufacturers and distributors of 12 European countries formed a council to explore the development of a standard numbering system for Europe, similar to and compatible with the UPC.

The European Article Numbering (EAN) was born as a result. It is a superset of the UPC and is followed in India. EAN International has 09 member organisations across the world, representing 101 countries. Any organisation which requires automated stock control or identification systems can benefit from the adoption of the EAN code. It is useful for organisations which perform one or more of the following activities.

- Produce products that arc ultimately sold at the retail outlets;
- Distribute or store goods on a large scale;
- Export their products; and
- Repackage goods for further selling.

Most items manufactured for sale through retail outlets bear a number and a barcode symbol. The whole number is made up of two sets of digits and a check digit. The first set is the country prefix, followed by the item reference number and the last digit is the check digit.

Future IT Trends and Benefits for Retailers

The hardware and software tools that have now become almost essential for retailing can be into three broad categories.

1. Systems that Affect the Customer Directly

Bar Coding and Scanners: Point of sale systems use scanners and bar coding to identify an item, use pre-stored data to calculate the cost and generate the total bill for a client. Tunnel Scanning is a new concept where the consumer pushes the full shopping cart through an electronic gate to the point of sale. In a matter of seconds, the items in the cart are hit with laser beams and scanned. All that the consumer has to do is to pay for the goods.

Payment: Payment through credit cards has become quite widespread and this enables a fast and easy payment process. Electronic cheque conversion, a recent development in this area, processes a cheque electronically by transmitting transaction information to the retailer and consumer's bank. Rather than manually process a cheque, the retailer voids it and hands it back to the consumer along with a receipt, having digitally captured and stored and image of the cheque, which makes the process very fast.

Internet: Internet is also rapidly evolving as a customer interface, removing the need of a consumer physically visiting the store.

2. Retail Operation Control Systems

Retail Exchanges: Various retail exchanges have been set up in the US and in Europe. One of them is the World Wide Retail Exchange, which enables retailers to interact with vendors and with other retailers for B2B transactions. Such exchanges help in reducing transaction costs. They need to be set up in India, too.

ERP Systems: Various ERP vendors have developed retail-specific systems which help in integrating all the functions from warehousing to distribution, front and back office store systems and merchandising. An integrated supply chain helps the retailer in maintaining his stocks, getting his supplies on time, preventing stock-outs and thus reducing his costs, while servicing the customer better.

3. Retail ERP Packages: In the future there would be a need to evaluate if retail ERP packages like JDA, SAP, and Retek are suitable for Indian retailers. These products have an integrated solution for demand forecasting, merchandising, replenishments, supply chain, etc. Most of these packages have built-in CRM, OLAP tools, collaborative planning and supply chain systems that are tightly integrated with the merchandising and forecasting functionality.

Though the flip side is that these packages are costly, the return on investment takes longer and expertise to implement the systems is gradually being developed in India. Hence, it would be a good idea to evaluate these packages, determine the cost-benefit analysis, and wherever possible, source the software from one vendor organisation that would provide all the functional requirements of the retailer from information

Role of Information Technology in Indian Retailing

The e-commerce market in India witnessed a great deal of activity a few years ago, with just about everybody getting into the act. However, things seem to be abuzz again, and the total Internet business is estimated to be worth over Rs. 2,200 crore. About Rs. 500 crore comes from advertising, ecommerce (not including billings) and other revenues. Add in access charges at a minimum of Rs. 200 per month, and multiply it with the 7 million-odd subscriber base. This gives us a figure of Rs. 1,700 crore + being spent just to get on to the Internet.

The advantage of a young nation to many, means a nation that is going to be Internet savvy, and hence, holds tremendous potential. India also has the lowest broadband prices worldwide (S4-S5 monthly) and is seeing one of the world's fastest growing mobile revolutions. It is believed that India had 38.5 million internet users (54 per cent growth last year) in June 2005, according to IAMAI (Internet and Mobile Association of India). Table 3.1 indicates the leading websites in India.

Table 3.1: Leading Websites in India.

Websites	Size of Business (Rs. crore)
India Times	175
India Bulls	126
Rediff	144
Naukri	75-85
Shaadi	20-30
Sify	20-25
Makemytrip	20
Hungama	17
Contests2win	15-20

Source: Internet Industry Comes of Age, *Business World,* February 2006

It is interesting to note that the travel business in India is worth Rs. 750 crore and has shown a growth of 100% over the last year. Broking also has shown the same growth over the last year and is growth respectively and are said to worth Rs.180 crore and 162 crore respectively.

With the size of organised retailing growing, the bar-coding technology has become completely indispensable, especially at the POS applications due to its inherent benefits and cost effectiveness. Bar-coding coupled with Mobile computing and WLAN technologies is also gaining ground at the back door applications like inventory and warehousing operations.

Major international players in the bar-coding technology like Symbol, Zebra, Intermec have targeted India as a much focused market. These companies have been offering special pricing for the Indian market to promote the technology and to make the products affordable for even medium scale operations and thus opening up the large volumes. Reduction in import duties has further helped in increasing the popularity of these technologies.

This technology will be further boosted if the Government decides to open Retail for FDI, since MNCs are already using these technologies abroad very extensively across the complete supply chain.

The Indian experience in implementing Retail ERPs has been difficult due to the lack of trained ERP package implementers in India. Hence, the cost of implementation has gone up, as package experts have to be brought in from abroad. But this is true for all ERP implementation in India, whether in the retail sector or in the manufacturing sector.

In the past, manufacturing industries also faced difficulties in implementing ERP packages specifically meant for the industry, but over time, with expertise in the packages and in their implementation building up within India, the success rates of such implementations have increased.

Hence, over the next two to three years, Retail ERP expertise will grow and will be able to support the needs of Indian retailers, who in that timeframe would have progressed up the learning curve on the benefits of information technology.

However, one has to learn where to draw the line and cannot go on with adapting new technologies which some times may not be cost effective solutions. At the same time, growth is rapidly evolving and change is the only thing that is constant. If we in Indian retail business don't adapt ourselves with the changing times we will be left way behind in another day and age.

Factors Affecting the Use of Technology

Every retailer may want to harness the power of technology and use it to its optimum advantage factors affect its use. The chief among them are:

- **Scale and Scope of Operations:** As stated earlier, the size or the scale of operations is the key factor influencing the decision on the type of systems required. In case of a small retailer, the significance is much lower as compared to that for a large chain retailer, who operates at a national or international level.

- **Financial Resources Available to the Organisation:** Many a times, the financial resources available to the firm for investment in technology are a crucial differentiating factor. The retailers in mature markets may invest significantly higher amounts in technology than their Indian counterparts. In India, investment in technology varies significantly with the type and size of operations and the estimated payback period.
- **Nature of the Business:** The industry that the retailer operates in is an important factor affecting the requirement and the use of technology. For example, a retailer who is a part of the fashion industry, needs to track consumer demands and changes in buying patterns at a much faster pace than a retailer operating in the consumer durables industry. While both need technology, the changes in demand are significantly higher in the fashion industry. By analysing sales data, changes in the buying patterns can be tracked. Changes can be made at the production level if this information is passed on to the supplier. On the other hand, an increase in demand for certain products can also be tracked and production can be realigned much earlier to avoid a stock-out situation.
- **Human Resources Available:** The retailer needs people to build and implement technology solutions-people who understand the complexities of the business that the retailer operates in and at the same time, the type of technology that will suit the business. They not only need to implement the system, but also to train people within the organisation on its use and applications. It is for this reason that Information Technology is many a time, termed as the backbone of retail.

The above decisions revels that the retailing business growing at a faster rate and benefiting the economy in many ways at the same time it posses certain challenges to adopt technological benefits in retailing sectors in India.

References

Internet Industry Comes of Age, Business World, February 2006.
Old Markets, New Battles, Business World, February 2006.

Swapna Pradhan, Retailing Management, Tata McGraw-Hill Publishing Company Ltd, New Delhi.

4

Consumerism and Retailing in India

C.J.S. Prasad and D. Raghunatha Reddy

Introduction

Most of the business organizations are customer-centric and customer-driven as it is known that customer is the king and demi-god of retail business activities. Retailing is all about understanding the articulated and unarticulated needs and wants of customers. Today's customer is empowered with many alternatives and choices, supported by competitive environment. Consumers enjoy an enormous freedom to choose the products and services; they are sovereign and have only the power of not buying it. However, the consumer often feels that while he has the power of veto, he is not fully equipped to exercise that power in his best interests. This situation may be the effect of lack of information, too much indigestible information or even misinformation from one or several competing producers. This problem facing the consumer has led to 'consumerism'. Consumer niches have begun propelling the market and the concept of 'value for money' is picking up. As consumers move from the 'feel-good' to the 'feel-great' zone, those turning to the retail industry know the bounty that awaits them. Philip Kotler defines Consumerism as "a social movement seeking to augment the rights and powers of the buyers in relation to sellers." [1]

Boyd and Allen state that "although often abused as a term, consumerism may be best defined as the dedication of those activities of both public and private organizations which are designed to protect individuals from practices that impinge upon their rights as consumers. [2] So, consumerism is aptly interpreted as a collective endeavor of the consumers to protect their interests, is a manifestation of the failure of the business, including that of public sector, and the government to guarantee and ensure the legitimate rights of the consumers. Consumers should accept consumerism as a means of asserting and enjoying their rights. Consumerism is a social force to (i) make the business more honest, efficient, responsive and responsible, and (ii) pressurize the government to adopt the necessary measures to protect consumer interests by guaranteeing their legitimate rights. As Philip Kotler observes, "consumerism is a clarion call for a revised marketing concept. [3] Consumerism also refers to the official standards and measures that protect people, so that we can trust what we buy. Consumerism is a term used to describe the effects of equating personal happiness with purchasing material possessions and consumption. It is often associated with criticisms of consumption starting with Karl Marx and Torstein Veblen. Consumerism is also used to describe the social effects of demand side economic policies associated with Keynesian economics. [4]

Consumerism describes the shift in Indian culture from a producer-oriented society in the nineteenth century to a "consumerist" society in the twentieth century. Changes in domestic demographics and advances in industrialization, manufacturing, transportation, and communication all contributed to the change. Consumerism also contributed greatly to the liberal thrust of the Progressive Era and spawned a long-running trend of consumer advocacy and consumer protection legislation. Retailing is a customer oriented service sector which is solely on the benign grace of the enigmatic customer. The liberalization and globalization policies and practices have completely changed the consumption patterns of urban population. The information and communication technology have unleashed revolution in the mindsets and activities of consumers. Hence it is imperative to understand the concept of consumerism and the variables influencing the paradigm shift in consumerism that led to the origin and growth of retailing in India. This paper keenly monitored the implications of growing consumerism in the existence and survival of retailing in India. This paper puts great focus upon selected retail sector areas like food and grocery, apparel and entertainment that how consumerism wield power in its formation and development. This paper observes in detail the chief contribution of retail sector to the Indian economic growth.

Section 1

Overview of Consumerism in India

An important socio-political and economic environment confronting the business is the growth of consumerism and the legislative measures to protect the consumers. Consumer movement has its conspicuous beginning and development in the United States. While consumerism is not a new phenomenon, it has only become widespread over the 20th century and particularly in recent decades, under the influence of neo-liberal capitalism and globalization. The consumer movement in India is as old as trade and commerce. In Kautilya's Arthashastra, there are references to the concept of consumer protection against exploitation by the trade and industry, short weighment and measures, adulteration and punishment for these offences. However, there was no organised and systematic movement actually safeguarding the interests of the consumers. Prior to independence, the main law under which the consumer interests were considered were the Indian Penal Code, Agricultural Production, Grading and Marketing Act, 1937, Drugs and Cosmetics Act, 1940. Even though different parts of India exhibited different levels of awareness, in general, the level of awareness was pretty low. Indian economy is evolving as a service exporting economy of the world. At home, it has evolved as a domestic consumption economy.

Though consumerism is not well developed in India, yet it is growing slowly. Consumerism has spread far and deep. It is an intrinsic part of India's evolution today as it should be of any emerging market which attempts to embrace global standards, both for its consumers and for its products. Consumerism and consumer spending levels are increasingly contributed to the economy in the post-liberalized period in India. India has been growing at 6 per cent per annum on an average which has increased to 7-8 per cent growth that has additionally facilitated by a change in the lifestyles of people during the last few years.

Overall Indian consumer goods market is about US$ 450 billion. It is expected to double to about US$ 800 billion in about 5 years, if the country maintains its 8 per cent growth trajectory. Of this amount only 4 per cent is in the organized sector, remaining bulk of consumer sales are handled by the unorganized sector. Surprisingly there is only 8 per cent of the total population base, which is involved in the retail trade. They run 5 million plus retail stores, of which 90 per cent are small stores of less than 500 square feet. Hence these stores carry a very limited variety and still smaller inventory. That is a drawback both for the retailer as well as the consumer. Monopoly and price level is maintained with brand agencies limiting supply. The latter offers only a few agencies in a given geographic area and forces the consumer to pay their price.

Lack of competition also helps to maintain prices high. Inspite these draw backs, India is ready for consumer goods revolution. The country's burgeoning wealthy middle class which constitute major source to the ever growing consumerism, is estimated at over 300 million, which equals that of the entire population of the US (source: Business Standard on 27/01/07). This will increase to 628 million middle-class Indians by 2015 as per experts forecast, which in turn create a massive demand for consumer goods. Most of the India (i.e. 660 million) lives in villages. This is two third of the population largely untouched by the consumer revolution sweeping the cities. Slowly and steadily the village India is getting accustomed to Consumerism.

The village folks are getting educated, moving to cities and returning home with new ideas and new values. They are changing the landscape in favor of consumerism. The younger people, i.e. 100 million (source: Business Line on 25/02/07) will have a higher propensity to spend compared to the not so young people who have a tendency to save. The consumerism in India is utterly influenced by consumers intrinsic and extrinsic factors. It is revealed that although people are willing to spend money, their expectations of return from every spent are much more than what they were earlier. Consumers today are seeking better deals and better bargains, and are looking to get more than they bargained for, not just from a product but also from the entire experience. This substantiated the growing trend of consumerism. Reinforcement of consumerism and retailing is vigorously going on in urban areas. There is a reciprocal relationship between consumerism and retailing. Retail evolution and consumer changes are often slow to occur. Labeling these changes as “revolutions” has been a highly misleading metaphor for decades.

The structural shifts in consumption pattern have contributed to the growing importance of retailing and strengthening of the retail shops. In recent days, due to the improvement of technology, change life styles and improvement in standard of living, increasing urbanization and time sensitivity are mostly influencing the consumerism. Hence, the number of options open to them is enlarged from time to time. This diversification reinforces the strategic economic position of the shop keeper also leading to mutual impact of retailing and consumerism. Consumerism is a big business with opportunities galore in India. Obviously, every multinational company now wants to sell in India. Some companies have failed and others succeeded. The ones that failed did so because they were not sensitive to the cultural factors that affect consumer behavior in India. "Consumerism" is likely to dominate the Indian market in the next Millennium, thanks to the economic reforms ushered in and the several agreements signed under the World Trade Organization.

The transition will be from a predominantly "sellers market" to a "buyers market" where the choice exercised by the consumer will be influenced by the level of consumer awareness achieved. By "consumerism" we mean the process of realising the rights of the consumer as envisaged in the Consumer Protection Act (1986) and ensuring right standards for the goods and services for which one makes a payment. This objective can be achieved in a reasonable time frame only when all concerned act together and play their role. The players are the consumers represented by different voluntary non-government consumer organisations, the government, the regulatory authorities for goods and services in a competitive economy, the consumer courts, organisations representing trade, industry and service providers, the law-makers and those in charge of implementation of the laws and rules. The India of today, like any developed and sensitive economy, must recognise the intrinsic worth of consumerism and the role it plays in not just freeing markets but in the ultimate empowerment of the consumer. And if for nothing else but this empowerment, it is time to declare India a country of consumers who, finally have acquired the right to choose and therefore the right to reject.

Overview of Retailing in India

The changing face of consumption patterns and consumerism styles has necessitated the need of organized retailing in India. Retail marketing is not a new phenomenon, but gained momentum in India for the last couple of years for various reasons. In fact, consumerism is one of the chief attributes for the growth and development of retail trade in India. Organized retailing is the future of Indian Consumerism. Malls across India's urban landscape are the new face of changing consumerism across India and more importantly the new reality of Retailing as an industry. Retailing consists of a conclusive set of activities or steps used to sell a product or a service to consumers for their personal or family use. Retail sector in India is highly fragmented with organized retail contributing to only 3 per cent of total retail sales. The retail sector in India is quite different from that prevailing in developed countries like U.S, U.K and France in many ways such as Indian cities are congested, a large part of the population is still concentrated in rural areas, Indian houses are smaller and Indian consumer is not still used to buying in bulk on weekends. The paper gives the close picture of over view of retailing in India.

The retail industry in India is largely unorganized and predominantly consists of small, independent, owner-managed shops. The sun rise retailing sector is India's largest industry after

Info Tech, in terms of contribution to GDP and constitutes 13 per cent of the GDP (gross domestic product). This is the second largest employer after agriculture of generating employment for some 2.5 million people in various retail operations and over 10 million additional workforces in retail support activities including contract, production & processing, supply chain & logistics, retail real estate development & management etc. The contribution of the Indian retail sector to the total employment has been 7 per cent as compared to 6 per cent, 11.7 per cent and 11 per cent in case of china, USA and UK respectively 1 (Source Mr. Kamal Nath, Commerce & Industry Minister releasing the IMAGES India Retail Report 2007 on 09 Jan 2007).

Of the estimated 12 million retail outlets in the country, only about 4 per cent of them are larger than 500 sq. ft. in size. This is in comparison to 0.9 million outlets only in USA, catering to more than 13 times of the total retail market size as compared to India. India has one of the highest density of retail outlets per capita in the world with a widely spread retail network but with the lowest per capita retail space (@ 2 sq. ft per person. Only 3 per cent of the Indian retail sector is organised while this has been 20 per cent, 80 per cent and 70 per cent in case of China, United States of America (USA) and United Kingdom (UK) respective (Source: India retail report 2007 released on 09 Jan 2007).

It is observed that although the retail outlet density in India is one of the highest in the world (the country has 15 million outlets); Indian retailing continues to be one of the least evolved industries. Unlike in China and Brazil, where organized retailing has registered explosive growth in the last decade, in India organized retailing accounts for a mere 3 per cent of all goods sold in the country. In China organized retailing accounts for a 20 per cent share, whereas in Brazil it is 40 per cent. The Indian retail is poised for a transformation owing to a plethora of changes within and outside its marketplace, like a paradigm shift in increase in the disposal income of the middle-class households, exponential growth in per capital income, rapid changes in technology and lifestyles, imitation of western culture, double income families, emphasis on lower prices, conveniences and the time value.

India has its own dynamics, which cushion global shocks as in no other country. India had kept the retail sector largely closed to outsiders to safeguard the livelihood of nearly 15 million small storeowners consists of 97 per cent of the total retail business and only allows 51 per cent foreign investment in single-brand retail with prior government permission. Dynamic and robust retailing buoyed by favorable political and economic outlook with government legislation permitting higher foreign direct investment from January 2006, retailing is expected to be dynamic and sales are expected to follow an upward trajectory with a healthy 8 per cent constant value CAGR (compound average growth rate) of the present total retail business is estimated as US$ 320 billion of US$ 6.6 trillion of world retail trade, which is forecast to grow to US$ 637 billion by 2015. (Source: KSA Techno Pack).

The organized sector accounted for Rs. 55,000 crore (US$ 12.4 billion) business at current prices in the calendar year 2006 increasing its share to 4.6 per cent of the total Indian Retail Value that stood at Rs. 12,00,000 crore (US$ 270 billion). Moving forward, organized retailing is projected to grow at the rate of about 37 per cent in 2007 and 42 per cent in 2008. The organized retail sector was expected to generate 10 to 15 million jobs over the next 5 years, and that the value of the organized retail sector in India by 2010 would be around Rs. 2,00,000 crore or US$ 45 billion (Source: India Retail Report, 2007).

The modern retail formats are showing robust growth as several retail chains have established a base in metropolitan cities, especially in south India, and are spreading to tier II and tier III cities at a rapid pace in the form of departmental stores, discount stores, specialty stores and hypermarkets. Western-style malls have begun appearing in metros and second-rung cities alike, introducing the Indian consumer to an unparalleled shopping experience. Indian retailing industry is thus in the second gear and is moving slowly but steadily towards sophistication as in other developed and developing countries. Going by the current growth trend and considering the fact that existing prominent players in organised retail have stepped up their expansion drive with domestic industrial giant Reliance entered with a huge investment of Rs. 25000 crore and other Indian corporate houses too evincing keenness on investing heavily in this sector as also the inking of the joint-venture between the world's largest retailer Wal-Mart and Bharti – the organised retail in India has indeed gained top speed and is now on the verge of take-off.

Section 2

This section elucidates the various underpinnings of external and internal factors contributing to the growing consumerism that led to the growth and development of retail sector in India.

Social Factors

The social class factors are prominent in changing consumer spending patterns. Different social classes exhibit characteristically different behavior pattern in consumerism. Social class as a relatively permanent and homogeneous group/ strata in society which differ from one another in their status, wealth, education, possessions, values, beliefs, and attitudes, etc. Social stratification and social class categorization has led different lifestyles and different way of living among consumers. Out of these, upper class has access to prosperity, prestige, and power which tempts them to consume designer clothing, luxury goods, leisure related items, etc. for conspicuous consumption purposes. India's middle-income group (popularly called middle-class) is about 25 per cent of the total population base. Of this segment about 4 per cent are extremely rich and about 10 per cent have just graduated into the middle class and are feeling their way through the material world. In addition about 1 per cent of the poor in the country are graduating into this middle-income group every year for the last ten years. This trend not only will continue but also will get accelerated.

The wealthy middle class is estimated at over300million and

go up to 400 million middle-income earning segments that believe in good things of life style and indulge in conspicuous consumption in India by 2025, would have about US$ 2.8 Trillion a year to spend is a Good news for the consumer goods industry of the world and welcome to consumerism in India. Working class is mostly interested in fun oriented, parochial and focus on possessions and their purchase tendencies are newest appliances, novelty items, sports and other entertainment events. The gradual shift in income levels has changed the social class and consumer buying behavior. Each social group follows a certain culture (i.e. norms, mores, and value system) which then determines shopping and consumption pattern for that group in general. The basic hypothesis behind attempting to link social class with distinctive consumption pattern seems to be that the needs and wants of members of a particular class are product of social conditioning by the environment. The competition in the hierarchy of social class stratification to excel and emulate each other class tends to increase the consumer spending which is very palpable.

Cultural Factors

The broadest environmental factor affecting consumerism is culture, which is a very intriguing and complex factor as reflected by the values and norms society emphasizes. Both material cultures involve man-made things and non-material culture includes such factors as dress, language, ideals, beliefs, values, music, habits, etiquettes etc. are almost in metamorphosis stage. Changing cultural values are stoutly influencing consumer's purchases and consumption patterns. Culture not only influences consumer behavior, it reflects it. Consumer acculturation occurred by observation, word of mouth communication, and through communication from internet and mass media has shown major influence on consumerism especially in middle class income group.

Cross-cultural influences trigger a rapid change in consumer preferences, beliefs and eating habits that results the formation of fast food outlets, Chinese restaurants, and Domino's pizza, burgers, ketchup, popcorn and coffee cafes. Cultural meaning of products and services is often expressed in sign and symbolic form increases the consumption of products because it has become a means of communicating social status, self-expression, sharing experiences and hedonic. Dress culture and code has taken complete turnaround that led to apparel retailing conforming to the western style. Cultural vicissitudes has too influenced the consumption rituals like brushing teeth, using deodorants and shampoos, dyeing hair and personal makeup, etc. Cross-cultural and sub cultural influences are the manifestation of global influences and technology diffusion changed the entire existing profile of consumerism. In a nutshell, imitation, impersonation, adaptation and transmission of western culture have brought a dramatic shift in consumerism.

Demographic Factors

The demographic changes are the utmost influential factors in consumer spending and augmenting the consumerism patterns. The size of the population is an important determinant of demand for many products and services. In India, out of the total population of 1027 million as on 1st March, 2001, about 742 million live in rural areas and 285 million in urban areas. The net addition of population in rural areas during 1991-2001 has been to the tune of 113 million while in urban areas it is 68 million. The percentage decadal growth of population in rural and urban areas during the decade is 17.9 and 31.2 per cent respectively. The burgeoning population growth has significant influence on retail market. The percentage of urban population to the total population of the country stands at 27.8 in 2001 census, as against 25 per cent in 1991 Census because of migration from rural to urban areas and the urbanization of rural areas. 70 per cent of the country's 1027 million population is concentrated in rural areas consisting of 6 lakh villages thereby creating a demand for products such as toothpaste, instant coffee, deodorants, etc. likely to increase by 60 per cent by 2012. (Source: ASSOCHAM Report, New Delhi)

These figures will speak about the need for more consumer

goods. The average household income in urban areas has grown at a 5 per cent CAGR (Compounded Annual Growth Rate) over the last decade. The total number of house holds as per their income levels have shown in table 8.This means more purchasing power and, in turn, more scope for improvement in consumption. The important demographic pattern in India is the age composition, where the median age of an average Indian is about 27 years i.e., 100 million. The largest young population in the world – over 890 million people below 45 years of age is in India. And 550 million-plus people will be under the age of 20 by year 2015 in India. This creates whopping 600 million-plus effective consumers by year 2010 (Source: Business Line on 25/02/07).

Working-age population between 15 and 64 years will increase by a staggering 71 million in India to reach 762 million by 2010 (Source: The UN report, 2005) which is a huge source of appetite for consumption of goods and services. Life expectation at birth for male will increase from 61.9 years in 2001 to 63 years in 2015 and from 63.7 years for females in 2001 to 65 years in 2015 (Source: NCAER Report, 2001) which will some what contribute to the consumption patterns. Rapid changes have taken place in family size (5.4 people) and family life cycle played cardinal role in consumerism.

The disintegration of joint family system has led to the formation of nuclear families with or with out children. The changing composition of work force and growing number of women employees in public and private organizations i.e. the participation of women in the labour force and in professional and technical workforce in India is 34 per cent and 21 per cent respectively (Source: NCAER Report, 2005) contribute a lot in the emergence of retail outlets because lack of abundant time for doing all house hold chores. While the latest National Sample Survey shows an increase in female work participation, it has also shown an increase in the gender gap in wages for all categories of workers, urban or rural, regular or casual The conspicuous shift in income levels and surging DIG's (Double income group) with or without children has given an enormous disposable income to purchase consumer goods.

The number of people who earn over US$ 5,000 plus per annum is growing at an intense pace and this is primarily attributed to the rapid rise in young earners (those in their mid twenties). The 70 million-plus people earn over Rs. 8,00,000 (US$ 18,000) a year – number to rise to 140 million by year 2011. The 2001 census figures show an increase in literacy levels (i.e. 65.5 per cent), the female literacy percentages were up to 26.2 per cent and the male literacy rates were 39.3 per cent shows the trend toward increasing levels of awareness of consumerism and women participation in consumer spending. The results of 61st round of the National Sample Survey have shown that the annual growth in employment has accelerated from 1.6 per cent levels of 1993-2000 to 2.5 per cent during 1999-2005. This augurs well for the Indian economy and creating multiplier effect for the consumerism.

Economic Factors

Consumer behavior and spending are widely influenced by the economic characteristics and economic policy dimensions. The economic factors include the structure and nature of economy, the stage of development of economy, economic resources, the level of income, the distribution of income and assets, global economic linkages, and lastly economic policies. India's G.D.P is invariably going high for the last couple of years and stood at 9.2 per cent for the year 2006-2007, the Indian economy is among the fastest growing in the world. It has the world's fourth largest GDP of US$ 4.042 trillion as measured by purchasing power parity(PPP). India's percapital income(PPP) of US$ 3,700 is however ranked 117 th in the world. When measured in terms of USD exchange rate, India's GDP is US$ 785.47 billion, which makes it the twelfth largest economy wealth distribution in India, adeveloping country, is fairly uneven, with the top 10 per cent of income groups earning 33 per cent of the income. However, iIncome levels are tremendously increased by average salary hike at 14.4 per cent in the year 2006, which is the highest salary hike within the Asia pacific region.

India has a labour force of 509.3 million, 60 per cent of which is employed in agriculture and related industries. The agricultural sector accounts for 28 per cent of GDP; the service and industrial sectors make up 54 per cent and 18 per cent respectively. The second best performing sector is consumer goods sector with 8.2 per cent annual growth. It contributed 42 per cent to industrial production in the year 2005-2006 compared to 24 per cent in the year 1999-2000. This is a reflection of rapid rise in consumer demand driven by jump in the per capital income at 6.4 per cent compared to 1.5 per cent during the first 30 years of after independence (Source: Rakesh Mohan, RBI Bulletin, December, 2006, p. 1481). The standard of living in India is modest and is constantly improving. The single most common indicator used to quantify standard of living is the per capita purchasing power parity (PPP) adjusted gross domestic product (GDP). In 2005, the per capita PPP adjusted GDP for India was US$ 3,460. These figures can be compared to US$ 6,660 for China a neighbouring country.India is fast on way to become a large and globally important consumer economy.

The Indian, touched to be anywhere between 200 and Indian middle class 300 million, is fast becoming used to theWestern life style. If current trends continue, Indian per capita purchasing power parity will grow to be approximately one third that of the developed world by the middle of the 21st century. The recent economic developments have helped upper and middle class Indians. The National sample survey organisation (NSSO) estimated that 22.15 per cent of the population was living below the poverty line in 2004–2005, down from 51.3 per cent in 1977–1978. 75 per cent of the poor are in rural areas (27.1 per cent of the total rural population) with most of them comprising daily wages,self-employed households and landless labourers. 34.7 per cent of India's poorest population still live on less than US$ 1 a day and 79.9 per cent live on US$ 2 per day. Lower interest rates, savings,borrowing patterns, hassel-free personal loans, easily available cheap credit,debit, ATM , internet phone bnking and a sharp reduction in the retail lending rates will, in turn, help in reviving the latent consumer demand and consistently facilitated the increae in consumerism.

Technological Factors

Technology includes the tools – both machines (hard technology) and ways of thinking (soft technology) contribute in a terrific way to the growth and development of consumerism in India. The information communication technology has really shrunk the whole world into a small village with its wide spread wings of advanced technological tools and techniques like E-mail, internet, web enabled services, etc. The prevailing advanced 'IT' technology has truly enabled the consumers to keep abreast of the current trends occurring in consumerism in and around the country as well as the world. The technology advancements have equipped the consumer with more knowledge and information for the purpose of better decision making in consumer goods purchase. The Indian consumer has also recognized that the media will not only provide him with an insight into what's available in the markets, it will also help him determine what to buy. This is why it is not unusual for an Indian brand of consumer durables to be amongst the most-respected brands. Consumer preferences and choices are extremely influenced by mass media and integrated communication technological factors.

Section 3

This section exclusively deals with the contribution of consumerism in select retail sectors like food and grocery, apparel and entertainment. Change is rather perennial and inevitable. The conspicuous changes observed in socio-cultural, economic and demographic environment, as the purchasing power of the middle-class had grown substantially; propelled the growth of consumerism in India. Retail growth solely relies on evolving consumer needs, wants and preferences. The spending pattern and latent shift in consumerism have fuelled the need of retailing in food and grocery, apparel and entertainment sector. The consumption pattern of the Indian households is undergoing a radical change. Organized Retail - This is one sector that would be a killer application in the future, as they start from almost nil, and would soon have over US$ 50 billion investment in the next couple of years. The total retail sector is valued at US$ 320 billion (Rs. 14, 40,000 crore) of which organized retail accounts a miniscule 6 per cent (Rs. 86,400 crore). The organized retail has 35 per cent growth in multiples of 7-8 per cent forecast for the sector has a whole (Source: AT Kearney and CII Report published in Business Standard on 30/01/07). The organized retail in India would be at a staggering US$ 11 billion by 2011 from the current US$ 6 billion. The chief contribution of consumerism in select sectors areas is as follows.

Food and Grocery Retail Sector

Though India is one of the largest producers of food products, very little attention has been given to organized processing and marketing of the agricultural output. Household groceries and apparel are the key drivers in India's organized retail industry. Food retail in particular is the sunrise sector. The changing trends in food and eating habits of consumers have contributed immensely to the growth or food retailing in India. The south of India has been witnessing frenetic activity in food retail especially the organized grocery segment. Stores built on the format of Food world and Nilgiris in the south have started to expand their boundaries of grocery markets that have so far been extremely localized. The west and north of India are also expected to provide good growth opportunities for retail. The supermarkets and hypermarkets/discount stores and fresh produce store formats complementing each other is going to be the way of the future.

In a developing country like India, a large chunk of consumer expenditure is on basic necessities, especially food related items. Hence food, beverages and tobacco account for 60 per cent of the consumer spending and sales constitute 70 per cent of total retail sales (Mulky and Nargundakar). AT Kearney claimed that most of the growth in India would be in the food and apparel sectors. It shouldn't come as a surprise that Indian consumers spend 53 per cent of their money on food and grocery and this category is the 'way to go' for retailers to attract consumers initially.

Thus, it seems that the food retail industry is indeed the hottest in India and truly has the potential to go miles. According to KPMG study entitled 'Grocery Retailing in Asia pacific.' the organized Indian food/grocery-retailing sector is forecast to grow at a compound annual rate of 33 per cent between 2004-2007 even as the Economic Times Intelligence Group (ETIG) has predicted a CAGR of 13 per cent, from 2001-2007,for the entire Indian retail industry. But the growth of organized retailing in India has changed the business landscape and buyer behavior. According to IMAGES India Retail Report 2007, of the Rs. 12,00,000 crore retail market, food & grocery retail is by far the single largest block estimated to be worth a whopping Rs. 7,43,900 crore, but more than 99 per cent of this market is dominated by the neighborhood kirana stores. The food and beverage retail market in India is estimated at US$ 4.6 billon (Rs. 21,000 crore) and makes up for 2 per cent of the country's total retail market, out of which organized food and beverage retail market accounting for 5 per cent of the total food and beverage market is valued at US$ 230 million (Rs.1,050 crore) and constitutes 3 per cent of the total organized retail market in India.

The organized food and beverage retail sector is represented by mid-priced fast food restaurant chains (both Indian and International) modern format retail chains, such as (Barista, Café Coffee Day and Qwiky's) and fine dining restaurant chains, which account for only about 8-10 per cent of the organized food and beverage segment, with the presence of limited players such as TGIF, Ruby Tuesday, Geoffrey's and so on. The coffee retailing segment is estimated at US$ 45 million (Rs. 200 crore) and growing at the rate of 25 per cent per year. (Source: Technopak Report published in Business Standard on 30/01/07).

Apparel Retail Sector

The Indian apparel sector is one of the most profoundly influenced by the consumerism in India. The astonishing shift in socio-cultural, demographic, economic and technological factors observed in Section 2 has fueled the growth and development of apparel retailing in India. The Indian fashion and retail sector is at a crossroads today; facing as it does, both opportunities and challenges. Following a boom in communication across India due to satellite television, internet and other forms of media, the Indian customer is now becoming aware of fashion trends across the world, as they happen, and demanding the same in India. The wardrobe of young girls and boys is changing with more prominence to Western wear and Indo-western wear. A market with 600 million people of less than 25 years of age, more than a lakh people with annual incomes greater than Rs 50 lakh, more than 7 lakh people with annual incomes greater than Rs 15 lakh and growing exponentially, is an indicator of increasing consumer spending even across categories which were earlier price-driven. India ranks as one of the world's top ten apparel exporters. 1265 million ready-made garments, valued at US$ 4.54 billion, were exported in 2001 and contributed to 3 per cent of the world's apparel market (Source: Images-Technopak Annual Apparel Report).

The organized apparel segment is of US$ 1.8 billion and is expected to grow at a steady 9.5 per cent per annum over the next three years. Multi-brand outlets are becoming the popular destination for customers and will outrank manufacturer retailers in size. Large retailers such as Shoppers' Stop, the RPG group, Pantaloon Retail and Trent have stabilized their retail models, and are rolling out more stores to grow in size Kids retailing is growing by leaps and bounds in India and those in the industry say it is likely to see 30-35 per cent growth per annum. When it comes to clothing, men are as conscious as women. It would come as a surprise that men's wear constitute one-sixth of India's domestic market for clothing, textiles, and fashion accessories that stands at Rs. 1,13,500 Crore. Starkingly, accessories have also grabbed an 11 per cent share in the growing apparel market. The Indian consumer's particularly wealthy middle class is unmindful and unapologetic in purchasing branded apparel goods. Riding on back of buoyant consumer sentiment and demand, the Indian apparel market has galloped to over Rs 1, 00,000 crore. Indian consumers across income strata are buying apparel, evident from the number of new brands being launched across categories and by marketers as diverse as big organised retailers to small entrepreneurs in mofussil towns.

Entertainment Retail Sector

The entertainment retail sector consists of electronic, music and media, which is riding high on growing income and education levels, fast growing urbanization, technological improvements and consumerism has brought in huge investment in the media and entertainment retail sector. This sector is expected to cross turnover of Rs. 1,00,000 crore by 2011 from the present Rs. 43,700 crore there by registering 18 per cent compounded annual growth (Source: FICCI-Pwc Report published in Business Standard on 19/03/07). The reading habits of people are seeing a lot of drastic change and there is more thirst for gaining knowledge. That creates a need for book retail outlets such as Landmark, Oxford, Crossword, RPG, Pantaloon etc. have gone national and more book stores have mushroomed across the country with an average retail space 1500 sq. ft. to 10,000 sq. ft. The total print media industry is expected to register 13 per cent growth to reach Rs 23,200 crore from the current size of 12,800 crore by 2011 (Source: FICCI-Pwc Report published in Business Standard on 19/03/07).

The conspicuous change observed in mobile retail market, is estimated at Rs. 70,000 crore and growing at the rate of 15-20 per cent. This is the one segment expected to cross 220 million mobile users by the year end and 500 million by 2010 as about 6 million subscribers will be added every month (Source: Economic Times on 18/03/07). Though the internet media has a small base, it is expected to show the highest compounded annual growth rate of 43 per cent to reach Rs 950 crore in 2011 from Rs 160 crore at present. (Source: FICCI-PwC report).

Section 4

Summery and Conclusions

It is observed that retailing in general and organised retailing in particular is acting as a promoter of consumerism. In the light of the above observations, it is important to conclude that this paper adds to our understanding of consumerism attitudes towards the different characteristics of the retail stores. Because of changing consumer moods, increasing purchasing power and more frequent visits of teenagers are the catalysts for growing consumerism in India. "Today consumerism plays a vital role in the society. In one-way or another, everyone falls in line with consumerism. Consumers face a lot of difficulties in the market. The interest of consumers must be kept in mind by the entire society". There was imbalance in the world, that only one-sixth of the world population enjoyed all the facilities. Consumerism had gained importance due to the Industrial revolution and rise of Capitalism.

After a thorough analysis of consumerism and retailing in India, we believe that there are some of unresolved and enigmatic issues to be addressed in order to protect the consumer rights and safe guard their interests to creative conducive environment for both the consumer and retailer. As it is pretty well known that most of the India lives in villages and village consumers are not so advanced and knowledgeable. So, it is imperative to adopt measures to protect and create awareness about consumerism because organised retailing is almost saturated in tier 1 cities. It is rather paradoxical that the customer is advertised as the "king" by the seller and service provider; but in actual practice treated as a slave or servant. Goods are purchased by him along with the label "Items once sold by us will never be received back under any circumstances whatsoever." This unethical, illegal and unilateral declaration has to be viewed in the light of the practice in developed countries where the seller declares, "In case you are not fully satisfied with our product, you can bring the same to us within a month for either replacement or return of your money." This is to be viewed seriously.

An average Indian consumer is noted for his patience and tolerance. Perhaps because of these two traditional traits and due to the influence of the mythological epics, he considers the receipt of defective goods and services as an act of fate or unfavorable planetary position in his horoscope. Such weakness should not become a weapon in the hands of retailers. However, things are changing - slowly but steadily - and the momentum has increased considerably since the establishment of consumer courts and due to the efforts of a number of consumer organizations like the Consumer Guidance Society of India (CGSI), Mumbai, and the Consumer Education and Research Centre (CERC), Ahmedabad, which are doing commendable work. Some of these organizations are very active in conducting product testing and exposing substandard quality and adulteration. There is a great need to encourage such organizations to create consumer awareness and facilitate in redressing the consumer grievances.

It is felt that Consumerism should make the government more responsive to consumer interests, prompt it to take necessary, statutory measures, and to make the required institutional arrangements to safeguard the consumer rights. There is an urgent need to encourage the development of market conditions which provide consumers with greater choice at lower prices and high quality. Consumerism in India to be well organised developed. Whatever the number of laws available to safeguard the interests of consumers, ensure that they are to be implemented and enforced to achieve the objectives. There are a number of areas where the procedure has to be made simple and consumer-friendly. The one more issue of protection of consumers from the private sector dealing with goods and services. It is not to be construed that the entire business sector is keen on exploiting the consumers. There are established business firms which really care for consumer satisfaction, their own reputation and goodwill. Voluntary bodies like the Fair Business Practices Forum are functioning effectively and are quick in removing the grievances of the consumers. These can go a long way in reducing the number of cases in the consumer courts. The consumer has to be aware of his rights and play a key role.

The success of "consumerism" is a strong function of consumer awareness and the assistance the movement gets from the government. The next millennium will witness a high degree of consumer awareness and the concepts of "comparative costs", "consumer preference/ resistance/ abstinence" and "consumer choice" will become vital aspects of the economy. Retailing in India is growing leaps and bounds. There is a high positive correlation exists between consumerism and retailing in India. In fact, it is not an exaggeration to say that entire Retailing is surviving at the mercy of consumerism. All retailing activities must focus upon the consumer interests and growing importance of consumerism to foster a healthy consumer environment. Consumerism and Retailing are the Siamese twins. Consumerism acts like an umbilical cord between consumer and retailer.

Notes

1. Philip Kotler, "What Consumerism Means for Marketers", Harvard Business Review, May-June 1972, p. 49
2. Harper, W. Boyd jr., and David, B. Alien. jr., "Caveat Emptor, Caveat Venditor, Caveat Omnis", in Marketing Management and the Indian Economy, New Delhi: Vikas Publishing House Pvt. Ltd., 1982. p.310
3. Philip Kotler, Ibid.,p. 54
4. en.wikipedia.org/wiki/consumerism

References

Biswas Ranjan (2006), "India's Changing Consumers", Retail news, Spring,2-6.

Chetan Bajaj, R. Tuli, N.V. Srivastava, " Retail Management", Oxford University press,2005, p.201-250.

Fracis Cherunilam, "Business Environment", H.P House, 2002, p.164-185.

Harper, W. Boyd jr., and David, B. Alien. jr., "Caveat Emptor, Caveat Venditor, Caveat Omnis", in Marketing Management and the Indian

Economy , New Delhi: Vikas Publishing House Pvt. Ltd., 1982., p. 310.

Henry Assel, "Consumer Behaviour and Marketing Action", Asian Books Private Limited, 2001, p.380-450.

Levy, Michael and Weitz, Barton (2002), Retailing Management, Tata McGraw Hill, 5e.

Philip Kotler, "What Consumerism Means for Marketers", Harvard Business Review, May-June 1972,p.49

Pradhan, Swapna (2007), Retailing Management, 2/E, Tata McGraw-Hill, New Delhi, pp30-34.

Srivastava, Kandai, "Consumer Behavior in Indian Context", Galgotia Publishing Company, 2003, p.113-157.

5

Retail Banking: Strategies and Perspectives

M. Subrahamanya Sarma and N. Kusuma

The health and wealth of the economy are reflected in the structure growth and performance of Banking Industry. Developments in information technology and entry of private/foreign banks have forced the public sector banks to investigate mechanisms to face the present competitive environment more efficiently. Retail Banking is a marketing strategy to penetrate in to the market. Increasing connectivity, automation, business process re-engineering, strategic cost management and market research are being included in the corporate strategic plans of the public sector banks to gain competitive advantage in retail banking. The purpose of the present paper is to examine the recent perspectives in retail banking and to suggest strategies for market penetration in the present complex dynamic market environment.

What is Retail Banking?

Retail Banking encompasses retail deposit schemes, retail loans/credit cards, debit cards, insurance products, mutual funds, depository services including demat facilities and a host of other services in the form of one stop financial supermarket or even at the customer door step, by offering the best services through latest delivery channels. Targeted marketing, designing improved products and solutions, I.T. enabled customer service, franchising, cross selling, up-selling and Customer Relationship Management (CRM) and direct to customer are the key elements of retail banking. Today public sector banks are faced with competition from globally reputed companies offering world class products. The objective of Commercial Banks is not just to build a profitable and healthy portfolio, but to create and retain loyal customer base by attending their total requirements.

Salient Features: Retail banking can be described in terms of the following characteristics.

1. Retail Banking is more customer centric and direct to customer.
2. Retail Banking adopts new smart delivery channels like Net-Banking, Credit Cards, Debit Cards, ATM, Mobile Banking etc.
3. Retail Banking focuses on personal banking rather than corporate /business finance.
4. Retail Banking follows a policy of segmenting the market on the basis of the purpose of the loan/deposit. Product differentiation and the price differentiation are made based on the purpose of the loan. E.g., Educational Loan, Housing Loan, Car Loan etc.
5. Retail Banking concentrates on enhancing the quantity number of customers and number of loans rather than value.
6. Retail Banking implies the provision of different banking products under a one roof including value added services/products.
7. Retail banking involves adequate attention to each customer i.e. a different ambience and atmosphere at the Branch to attend each customer personally, some times routed through a call center with due care and concern.
8. Another prominent feature of retail banking is retail lending/retail credit with help of franchised agents. They posses the required skills for credit assessment, documentation counseling and follow up including customization of loan products.

Growth Drivers of Retail Banking

The present boom in retail banking is attributed to the following growth drivers:

1. The LPG Fever;
2. The I.T. Boom;

3. Economy Growth with Greater Market Potential.
4. Thinner Margins and Growing NPAs;
5. Change in Family System;
6. Security and Convenience off take Cost and Income;
7. Failure of NBFCs and frequent crash of Stock Markets;
8. Supportive Role by Government and RBI; and
9. A timely alternative with low default rate.

The LPG Fever: Globalization has opened the flood gates for a lot of new players in the market. Indian banking system also witnessed sweeping ramifications resulting from the economic reform process of Liberalization, Privatization and Globalization (LPG). Increased capital mobility, Increased Standard of Living, Improved Employment Opportunities, Increased Income Levels, Growth in Financial Sector, Industrial Sector, I.T. Sector have enhanced Purchasing Power, Per Capita Consumption and Credit Appetite in the Economy.

The IT Boom: The recent advances in Information Technology have enhanced the opportunities. Increased connectivity. Electronic Money Transfer, Electronic Clearing, Automation of Bank Products and Solutions have led to the unprecedented growth in Retail Banking. The cost of handling a transaction/maintaining a customer account has become much cheaper. Speed, Accuracy, Transparency, Security have created a favorable atmosphere for the growth this sector.

Economy Growth with Greater Market Potential: The size of the retail banking market is enormous and the prospects of the industry are bright. The size of retail banking market in India of the order of Rs. 50,000 crore. While there has been impressive growth in retail credit during the last few years, the fact is that market is still on its nascent stage in India. Even today the level of market penetration in India is just 2 percent of GDP whereas it is about 20 percent of GDP in respect of South East Asia and 50 percent in the case of US. The annual growth rate of economy is also quite optimistic with 6-7 percent. Retail Assets portfolio of bank as grown at (CAGR) of 25 per cent. A recent study undertaking CRISIL has revealed that even a growth rate of 40%

in retail credit is sustainable.

Thinner Margins and Growing NPAs: Sharp decline in interest rates and the slim interest spread forced the banks to investigate new profitable products and solutions. A significance proportion of NPAs being from the corporate business, commercial banks have to think for an alternative business opportunity for deployment of loans. Retail banking with potential return became a boon for consolidation and stabilization. Now the balance sheet of any commercial bank include wide range of loan products such as housing loans, mortgage loans, consumption loans for the purchase of durables, personal loans for specified activities like Auto Loans, Educational Loans etc. Retail banking has many advantages like stable deposits, low cost of funds, larger customer base etc., on the resources side. On the assets side the advantages are better yields and higher profitability, larger volume of credit, credit absorption, well diversified risk and lower NPAs.

Change in Family System: Shift in the pattern of GDP from agriculture and manufacturing sectors to service sectors with increased per capita income led to increased middle income segment and their income levels. The attitude and family culture had also significantly changed resulting increased number of dwelling units with growing concept of nuclear families created vast demand for housing loans and personal loans from this segment.

Security and Convenience take off Cost and Income: There is a perceptible shift in the customer preferences from cost and income to security, convenience and flexibility. This attitude shift has transformed the banking culture from mere depositing and borrowing to more flexible and friendly products like credit cards, debit cards. Any time any where banking has virtually increased the value of banking. As a result, in spite of increase in transaction costs, decrease in interest rates on savings deposits, stipulation of AQMB, saving deposits continued to record an impressive annual growth rate of 31 to 35 percent.

Failure of NBFCs and Frequent Crash of Stock Markets: Large scale scams and failure of Non Banking Finance Company has positive contributed for the growth in bank deposits. Depressed stock market and sudden crash situations have induced the investors to shift their investment portfolios to bank deposits.

Supportive Role of the Government and RBI: Housing Loans are included in priority sector for financing. As a result Banks have concentrated on housing loans to attain their targets of priority sector lending. Reduction in risk weightage, capital adequacy ratio requirement have doubled the credit disbursement capacity of banks.

Tax exemption on Housing Loans removal of Urban Land (Ceiling and Regulation) Act. Have further induced the borrowers to avail house loans. Similarly the aggressive marketing effort put by the commercial banks for selling house loans, personal loans, car loans, followed by incentives and initiatives have also resulted the boom in retail segment.

Timely Alternative with Low Default Rate: The incidence of bad advances is lesser in the case of retail credit compared to corporate credit. This is particularly true in respect of housing finance where the average default rate on an annualized basis is less than 1%. Housing Finance to considered to be safer with mortgage and collateral security and lesser incidence of delinquency. The quantum and tenure of house loan assure long term business. Further the emotional sentiments, people attach to their residential dwellings enhance the security and prospects of recovery. Corporate, commercial and business sectors are restoring to alternative sources of obtaining cheaper finance both from the domestic and overseas markets. This has left the commercial banks with excess liquidity.

Strategies for Sustainable Growth

Retail Banking includes a very large and comprehensive range of financial products. Banks now found themselves in a perfect market environment with increasing emphasis on winning competition, customer retention, industry leadership and market penetration. Hence all the public sector banks should adopt an appropriate marketing strategy for attaining sustainable competitive advantage. Some of the important strategies often adopted by the Banks for winning the competition in Retail Banking are discussed here.

1. Product Innovation;
2. Pricing of the Products;
3. Customer Relationship Management;
4. Branding the Retail Products;
5. Customer Segmentation and Targeted Marketing;
6. Technology sets a True Competitive Edge;
7. Strategic Alliance; and
8. Human Resources – The Real Assets of Banking Sector.

Product Innovation: Product Innovation should be a continuous process. Market Research should bring new solutions to the customer problems. Banks need to innovate products suiting the needs and requirements of different types of customers. Revising the features of the existing products to continue to keep them on demand should be also given due importance. Improvements in the existing products are possible by adding some new features are removing some existing clauses or by offering complementary value added services along with main product. Product differentiation is the need of the hour to attract/retain customers.

Pricing of the Products: Banking industry is also witnessing a price war, with each bank competing for a larger market share. In pricing of products, its importance on strengthening the bottom line of banks has to be borne in mind i.e. enhancing the shareholders return. In the scenario of shrinking spreads, banks will have to walk on the edge in meeting the depositors demand for increasing interest and borrowers claim for a lower rate of interest on advances by cutting the cost of operations drastically. Banks should also encourage multi-product relationships, use of ATM and Debit Cards to reduce transaction costs.

Private Banks, ICICI, HDFC have adopted penetration pricing for house loans. The reduction in interest rates below PLR level and offering options to fixed or floating rate of interest have made the house loans attractive.

Customer Relationship Management (CRM): To survive and prosper in today's market environment customer should be the focal point of all marketing strategies. Understanding the customer total requirements retaining the customers and maintaining large pool of loyal customers for life time relationship is the essence of CRM. In addition to cross selling and upselling you should not forget that a delighted customer is your brand ambassador. The concept should become part of organisation culture. Customer centric approach in product development, pricing, delivery channel and documentation will go a long way in retail marketing. The retail product marketing strategy of banks should have around the basic principle of improving the bottom line of the bank by increasing the number of desirable customers and profit per customer.

Branding the Retails Products: Branding helps to distinguish the Bank products from the competitors or stand out from the Crowd. For e.g. Abhay Gold of Andhra Bank. Branding is a means to communicate unique strength of the product to the customers. Customers today are looking for convenience. Branding will be of immense help in the era of severe competition. Financial Products offered by most bank is are not significantly different from that of others, hence financial products for many years have proved particularly difficult to create a brand identity. But with increased competition financial products are no more exception to branding. Winning brands have three things in common a product insight, customer insight and value insight.

Customer Segmentation and Targeted Marketing: For the purpose of targeted marketing, customers should be classified on the basis of demographics, value and attitudes. Design a product that targets a market segment provide opportunity for one to one customer interaction. After segmenting the customers to various segments appropriate strategies should be tailored to enhance the share of profitable segments. Product development efforts can also be focussed to that segment. Product, should be identified with market segment. That delivery channel and promotion strategy should be selected that is more appropriate to that segment.

Technology sets a True Competitive Edge: Retail Banking calls for huge investment in technology. Have an I.T. strategy that helps to reduce costs of delivery, and be scalable for future growth. Be a pioneer by launching mobile banking, online/net-banking, branch net-working, debit cards, credit cards (National/International).,

Retail marketing is highly technological intensive in nature because of the large volumes of business. Retail banking needs instant service, on line response, faster processing and maintenance and integration of complex data base. Data warehousing and data mining would come to play crucial role in the marketing strategy of cross selling which is an integral part of e-CRM. Data mining enables banks to understand and predict client behavior and develop appropriate customer strategy. Public sector banks have to go long way for maintaining, updating and integrating vast customer data base. Such data base helps in market research and new product development.

Strategic Alliance: Strategic Alliance is a mutually beneficial long-term formal relationship for supplying, sharing and exchanging business capacities, strengths between two parties. Alliances in retail banking are often described in two ways:

- Alliances with Non-Banking Finance Companies, Insurance Companies, Investment or Equity Research Organisations.
- Alliances with service providers and out-sourcing.

Strategic alliances with other non-banking investment insurance companies help in reducing the customer defections. Banks which offer a wide range of banking, insurance, D.Mat products can retain the customers. The loyalty of bank customer can be increased manifold by offering diversified products. The use of internet and web technologies is an integral part of the business process of retail banking. Banks are entering into strategic alliance with service providers. Some of the critical functional solutions offered by the service providers are ATM, Credit Card management, Cash Management, New Account Generation, Central Office Accounts. They also provide customized service for end to end solutions, system integration, back office automation, call centre etc.

Human Resources: The Real Assets of Banking Sector: Skilled human resources is one of the most important pre requisites for handling large diverse retail credit product mix. Technology and product innovations are vital in retail banking but at the same time human capital of the banks is more vital. Empowering the staff with requisite skills and leadership qualities, transparency in human resource policies can go a long way in building a professional work culture and conducive organisation climate for managing the change in public sector banks. Public sector bank have to go a long way for transforming its work force into truly professional, productive accountable and customer friendly above all.

The study thus far highlighted on the recent perspectives in rural banking vis-à-vis strategies for market penetration. In fact retail banking is not an entirely new phenomenon. It is always there in the main stream banking. Now the only difference is increased emphasis on customer relationship, use of technology, multiple products under one roof. Housing loans and credit cards have given new life to the banking sector especially during the period when the interest rates have fallen drastically. Continuous innovation introduction of new products and business process re-engineering keep the present pace of retail boom ever glowing. But it is unfortunate to notice that even the most popular private sector/foreign banks, ICICI, HSBC and Citbank are often found misleading the customers with hidden charges, false statements and ambiguous clauses. ICICI life time free credit card is subject to severe criticism. MRTPC has clearly indicated that ICICI has violated the RBI guidelines and constituted an enquiry on the different types of credit cards issued by the bank. Public sector banks continue to surpass private and multinational banks in terms of popularity accessibility and safety with Average Minimum

Quarterly Balance (AMQB) in savings bank account.

References

Almedia, R.A. 2003. Retail Banking : A focus IBA Bulletin, Nov.2003.

Chansarkar, A.R. 2004. Business Strategies for Banks in the Changing Environment. State Bank of India Monthly Review, Vol.XXXXIII (1) : 6-20.

Kumar, Anand, 2002. Paradigm shift in retail. Bank Economists Conference 2002, The Economic Times 27, December, p.III.

Malhotra, Viren, 2004 – Is Retail Lending Getting out of Control ? The Economic Times, 7 December: 7.

P.S. Sodhi, Chief Manager, Punjab & Sind Bank, Retail Banking in the New Flavour, IBA Bulletin, Dec. 2004.

Sengupta, B. 2002 Emerging Issues, Bank Economists Conference 2002, The Economic Times, 27 December, p.II.

Sobti, Romesh, 2004. Is Retail Lending Getting out of Control ? The Economic Times, 7 December, 8, p.1.

6

Problems and Prospects of Retailing in India

M. Prabhakar Reddy

Gone are the days when people use to buy the groceries from the local shopkeepers or kiranawalas. Now the big retail shops are in fashion. Everyday in the news we can see any M.N.C or even an Indian company joining this band wagon. This clearly states that the retail in India will be the next big thing. Therefore first there is need to understand what is retailing.

What is Retailing?

Retailing refers to the process of selling goods and services in small quantities to final consumers. Retailers source products from different wholesalers/manufacturers and sell them to final consumers.

There are more than 12,00,000 small, medium and big retail outlets in India. Kirana shops, general stores, bangle stores, medical shops, supermarkets, etc. are examples of retail stores. Retailer is the last link in the value chains of products. From retailers, consumers can buy an assortment of products in small quantities. The value chain-of a typical FMCG product starts from sourcing raw material and goes through stages such as in-bound logistics, operations, out-bound logistics, selling and servicing.

The last two processes in the chain, namely, selling and servicing are performed by the retailer. What characterizes a retailer is not where he sources his products from, but to whom he supplies them.

Depending on the nature of the product, the link that a retailer provides could be between manufacturer and consumer or wholesaler and consumer.

Evolution of Retailing

In pre-industrial era, the same person or family performs the functions of manufacturing and selling. Individual skilled workers produced goods and sold them to buyers. Skilled workers produced goods in small quantities and sold them to consumers on a one-to-one basis.

Each product had a community of artisans and craftsmen who were experts in making it. These artisans produced products catering to the neighborhood demand. They sold them directly to the final consumers. There were no middlemen.

Nevertheless, there were traders who purchased from several such individual craftsmen and transported the goods to far away places. These traders traveled over long distances with stocks of different items and traded them in barter system or gold.

But this is more like a company sourcing from several small suppliers and selling to customers than a middleman buying from manufacturers and selling to a large number of final consumers. It is more B-to-B than B to C.

From this period of handicrafts era, business moved to an era of mass production, which was made possible by the sweeping revolution called industrialization. Industrialization changed the way people lived and traded forever. It made large-scale production possible. It brought along and perpetuated factory system.

Mass production resulted in 3 main disparities. It separated production from selling. Production was restricted to one particular place called factory but goods were sold to buyers residing in different places. Goods had to be sold to different people at different places at different times.

Another disparity was that of quantity. The quantity of goods produced by a single manufacturer was much more than the quantity that a single buyer could buy. The third disparity was related to time. There came about a long gap between the time of production and time of consumption.

These disparities led to a situation where transportation, bulk breaking, warehousing, and product assortment became important activities in business. Those who performed these intermediate activities are called intermediaries.

Intermediaries emerged to be of two different types. Wholesalers, who purchased in large quantities from manufacturers, and retailers who purchased in smaller quantities from wholesalers.

Apart from the traditional services of bulk breaking and product assortment, modern retailing provides new age benefits such as deep discounts, pleasant ambience and pleasure shopping. Retailing is changing from a one-shop-business operated by an individual to a multi-crore-business operated by a company. From being a predominantly unorganized sector, retailing is metamorphing into largely organized sector.

Indian Scenario

For centuries, retail stores in India were operated by individuals as small family businesses. Many small stores were managed within the house. Most of the owners employed members from their own families. Even when outsiders were employed, the number rarely exceeded 3.

Customers bought goods from one of the stores nearby their residences. Such retail store catered to the needs of the people living nearby.

Each store had its quota of customers living in the territory. Business depended to a considerable extent on the personal relations that retailers have with their customers. Customer relations played a very important role in business.

After years of small store retailing, one notable change happened in retailing sector. A new type of retail stores sprouted everywhere. They were known as supermarkets.

Supermarkets were bigger and neater than traditional Kirana shops. For the first time, consumers could walk around picking up what they wanted instead of giving a list of products to the shopkeeper and wait. Also, supermarkets offered better packaging and cleaner groceries.

But apart from being bigger and neater, they didn't differ from a normal Kirana shop in any significant way. They offered products at the same price as small shops did. They offered the same product assortment. The ambience was slightly better but not radically different. Like small retail outlets, individual families also owned supermarkets.

It is only very recently that Indian retailing started becoming an organized business run by companies and professionals.

- Even though India has well over 5 million retail outlets of all sizes and styles (or non-styles), the country sorely lacks anything that can resemble a retailing industry in the modern sense of the term. This presents international retailing specialists with a great opportunity.
- It was only in the year 2000 that the global management consultancy AT Kearney put a figure to it: Rs. 400,000 crore (1 crore = 10 million) which will increase to Rs. 800,000 crore by the year 2005 – an annual increase of 20 per cent.
- Retailing in India is thoroughly unorganized. There is no supply chain management perspective. According to a survey by AT Kearney, an overwhelming proportion of the Rs. 400,000 crore retail market is UNORGANISED. In fact, only a Rs. 20,000 crore segment of the market is organized.
- As much as 96 per cent of the 5 million-plus outlets are smaller than 500 square feet in area. This means that India per capita retailing space is about 2 square feet (compared to 16 square feet in the United States). India's per capita retailing space is thus the lowest in the world (Source: KSA Technopak (I) Pvt. Ltd., the India operation of the US-based Kurt Salmon Associates).
- Just over 8 per cent of India's population is engaged in retailing (compared to 20 per cent in the United States). There is no data on this sector's contribution to the GDP.
- From a size of only Rs. 20, 000 crore, the ORGANISED retail industry will grow to Rs. 160,000 crore by 2005. The TOTAL retail market, however, as indicated above will grow 20 per cent annually from Rs. 400,000 crore in 2000 to Rs. 800,000 crore by 2005 (Source: Survey by AT Kearney).

- Given the size, and the geographical, cultural and socio-economic diversity of India, there is no role model for Indian suppliers and retailers to adapt or expand in the Indian context.
- The first challenge facing the organised retail industry in India is: competition from the unorganised sector. Traditional retailing has established in India for some centuries. It is a low cost structure, mostly owner-operated, has negligible real estate and labour costs and little or no taxes to pay. Consumer familiarity that runs from generation to generation is one big advantage for the traditional retailing sector.
- In contrast, players in the organised sector have big expenses to meet, and yet have to keep prices low enough to be able to compete with the traditional sector. High costs for the organised sector arises from: higher labour costs, social security to employees, high quality real estate, much bigger premises, comfort facilities such as air-conditioning, back-up power supply, taxes etc. Organised retailing also has to cope with the middle class psychology that the bigger and brighter sales outlet is, the more expensive it will be.
- The above should not be seen as a gloomy foreboding from global retail operators. International retail majors such as Benetton, Dairy Farm and Levis have already entered the market. Lifestyles in India are changing and the concept of "value for money" is picking up.
- India's first true shopping mall – complete with food courts, recreation facilities and large car parking space – was inaugurated as lately as in 1999 in Mumbai. (This mall is called "Crossroads").
- Local companies and local-foreign joint ventures are expected to more advantageously position than the purely foreign ones in the fledgling organised India's retailing industry.
- These drawbacks present opportunity to international and/or professionally managed Indian corporations to pioneer a modern retailing industry in India and benefit from it.
- The prospects are very encouraging. The first steps towards

sophisticated retailing are being taken, and "Crossroads" is the best example of this awakening. More such malls have been planned in the other big cities of India.

- An FDI Confidence Index survey done by AT Kearney, retail industry is one of the most attractive sectors for FDI (foreign direct investment) in India and foreign retail chains would make an impact circa 2003.

According to this year's Global Retail Development Index India is positioned as the leading destination for retail investment. This followed from the saturation in western retail markets and we find big western retailers like Wal-mart and Tesco entering into Indian market. India's retail industry accounts for 10 percent of its GDP and 8 percent of the employment to reach US$ 17 billion by 2010. There are about 300 new malls, 1,500 Supermarkets and 325 departmental store being built in the cities very soon.

A shopping revolution is ushering in India where, a large population between 20-34 age groups in the urban regions is boosting demand by 11.1 percent in 2004-05 to an Rs 23,308 purchasing power. This has resulted in huge international retail investment and a more liberal FDI. This market research report "The Indian Retail Sector – An Outlook (2005-2010)" analyzes the greatly divided Indian retail market and the trends in its business. Issues such as foreign investment restrictions, modern merchandizing in India, logistics and payment terms for distribution, role of channel members and growth trends in different regions are discussed. The market research report further analyzes the sustainability of the Indian retail sector and on the basis of 25 domestic and international companies the report has given a suitable business model.

Major Retailer Types in India

- **Vegetable vendors/hawkers, etc**: Very small sellers selling in small quantities.
- **Traditional Kirana Shop (Mom and pop stores)** which sell groceries and general items. Mostly run by family members.

The smallest of these are run in huts in rural areas. One or two family members manage a typical store. All transactions are over the Counter.

- **Stationery/Medical Shop, etc:** selling staples, impulse and emergency goods excluding groceries. Specialize in one category such as stationery, automobile spare parts, etc.
- **Supermarkets.** First change in retail sectors centuries. These are bigger and neater than traditional stores. Customers can walk around and pick up goods.
- **Chain of Supermarkets operated by a company**. This is a recent development. Businessmen founded companies to run chain of supermarkets. To leverage brand familiarity, businessmen founded companies and ran chain of supermarkets within or across cities.
- **Lifestyle Department Stores** offering a wide product range in a sprawling, spacious, appealing ambience where shoppers can shop at leisure. By and large they cater to high-end consumers.
- **Hypermarkets**: Huge outlets with discount selling across product categories. Cater to both upper and middle class.
- **Malls:** Bigger than department stores. Rent out space to sellers. Provide restaurants, entertainment, multiplexes, etc. within the mall. Product range is as wide as or wider than in hypermarkets.
- **Direct Marketers.** Manufacturers directly sell to final consumers in direct marketing. They act as both manufacturer and retailer. They dispense product information and promote products through magazines, catalogues, Internet, television or phones. They take orders through internet, phone or post and deliver goods at the doorstep of the buyer.

Traditional Kirana shops are small stores of grocery and convenience items managed mostly by the members of a family without any hired help.

Supermarkets are bigger than General stores where buyers can walk around pick products on their own. Hypermarkets are bigger than Supermarkets with higher volumes and lower prices. Malls are larger than hypermarkets offering a very wide product range in a pleasant ambience making shopping a pleasure.

Organised and Unorganised Retailing

Unorganized retailing refers to a situation where there are a large number of individual, small retailers operating in the market each with limited number of customers, product range, services, efficiency and expertise.

Organized retailing refers to companies managing huge retail outlets, individual or chain of stores, within a city or across cities, using carefully selected and trained personnel on a large scale with high volumes. Their volumes and profits are high, management is professional, competition is tough are both risked and return is high. They are managed by organizations instead of individuals.

New Trends in Retailing the World Over

1. New Retail Forms and Combinations: Mom and Pop store gave way to Supermarkets and Supermarkets soon lost out department stores. Newer forms included Hyper malls and Life style malls. Every few years a new form of retailing with new utilities is coming up dealing a blow to existing forms. Some of the new forms combine features from two or more different types of existing types.

2. Growth of Intertype Competition: There was a time when target market and buying situations were different for different types of retailing. Each firm had to compete only with other firms of the same type. But as more and more forms emerged offering different combinations of values and benefits, the dividing lines became blurred. Firms now have to compete not only with fellow retailers in the same category but also with other types of retailers. Each retailer has to compete every other type of retailer within a large surrounding area for customers.

3. Growth of Giant Retailers: Gone are the days when 'small was beautiful'. Economies of scale took over retailing and the dictum now is that 'the bigger the better'. Retail outlets are getting bigger and bigger. With tight control over supply Chains, more bargaining power and high volumes these giant retailers leave no chance of fight back for smaller operators.

4. Growing Investment in Technology: Except for glow signboards and billing calculators, there was no technology in retail stores till some decades ago. As number of SKUs reached mind-boggling numbers and volumes soared sky high, there was need for more efficient management systems. Firms adapted technology to manage their businesses better. Investment was huge in using technology in inventory management, supply chain management, warehouse management, transportation, physical arrangement of stock, etc. It is no more a business with jobs performed by unskilled or semi-skilled workers. Retailing became multi-million dollar business with heavy investment in promotion and technology.

5. Global Presence of Major Retailers: American retailers are seen entering Canada and taking over the entire Canadian retailing market. Several other retailing organizations operating in developed countries are crossing borders and forming retailing business organizations in foreign countries. Retailing business has now become global.

6. Selling an Experience: In their quest to differentiate and offer extra value, firms changed the very meaning of shopping. Shopping is no more a simple job of buying goods'. Shopping now is a pleasant experience that people enjoy. Shopping involves

7. Competition between Store-based and Non-store-based Retailing: Brick and mortal retail stores find them in a situation today where they have compete with non-store-based retailing. They have to compete with virtual companies operating from the internet and phone. For example a book seller in Patna now has compete not only with other book sellers in Patna, but also with many virtual book stores on the net because consumers can buy the same book through internet without having to visit any shop.

Changing Socio Cultural Conditions

The rise of big retail outlets in India is caused and

consolidated by certain socio cultural conditions.

1. Rising Incomes: Rising incomes in IT and IT enabled services has a multiplier effect in the economy. This coupled with general overall increase in income levels, spurred expenditure on convenience goods by people. Ready to spend money, this segment needed to be attracted and satisfied in new ways. Investors invested in new, giant shopping outlets with modern, pleasing ambience complete with entertainment and other attractions.

2. Faster Pace of Life: Buyers preferred to shop at one place at their own pace for all their monthly supplies rather than visit two or three different places. Giant malls offered them almost everything under one roof.

3. Working Women: Women have more opportunities today than ever especially in IT and ITES. This meant less time to spare and more money to spend. Shopping at new age malls both these developments by providing everything at one place and combining it with pleasure thus selling an experience rather than just goods.

4. Small Families: Small families with wife, husband and children meant more demand for readymade goods and ready shopping.

5. Cross-cultural Influences: Cultures of developing countries have a profound influence on Indian psyche through media and the experiences of Indians living there. Whatever changes happen they are happening in India too.

A large young working population with median age of 24 years, nuclear families in urban areas, along with increasing working-women population and emerging opportunities in the services sector is going to be key growth driver of the organised retail sector in the country.

The highly fragmented structure of the Indian retail sector is also helping the growth of the sector. There is a great potential for the organized retail industry to prosper in India, as the market for the final consumption in India is very large.

Many researches show that the total private consumption

market in India is about Rs 15 trillion out of which about Rs 8.5 trillion is towards retail consumption. While food and grocery represents about 6.5 trillion of this consumption clothing comes second with consumption of about Rs 600 bn.

A combination of increased consumer demand, improved sourcing options and larger availability of real estate are creating the foundation for a significant growth in the organized retail sector.

Even though India has well over 12 million retail outlets of all sizes and styles, the country still sorely lacks anything that can resemble a retailing industry in the modern sense of the term. This presents international retailing specialists with a great opportunity. Most of the modern retail outlets include facilities like amusement and Water Park besides food courts, multiplex cinema and banking facilities.

The Indian retail market is the world's second largest with estimated revenue of Rs 9,000 crore. India had over 12 million retail enterprises in 2003, about 78 per cent of which are small family businesses utilizing only household labour.

Even among retail enterprises that employ hired workers most of them use only less than three workers. In a developing country like India, a large chunk of consumer expenditure is on basic necessities, especially food related items, accounting as much as for 73% in 2004. Some 40 million Indians have the same purchasing power as Americans and 7% (74 million) of Indian population is engaged in retailing.

In the last 5 years, some important changes have taken place in Indian retailing sector. Organizational players made a foray into Indian, retailing. Retail outlets have become bigger. Shopping has become a pleasure experience. Lifestyle shopping malls emerged as a major segment of retailing. These changes are discussed below.

Growing Share of Organised Players

Till a few years ago Indian retailing was made up of thousands of small and medium individual retailers. It was an out and out unorganized sector. This composition is changing. Today 4 per cent of the Indian retailing is organized and 97 per cent of it is unorganized.

The share of organized sectors is slowly but steadily increasing. More companies are entering the business opening huge malls in urban and sub-urban areas.

Big, established business groups are forming companies for the purpose of entering retail business and setting up huge shopping malls running into thousands of square feet of retail space offering a wide product range including durables in a enjoyable, modern, pleasing ambience.

Since the time the Narasimha Rao government kicked off economic reforms in 1991 and interest rates deregulation became a reality, the retail sector is seen as toddler waiting to grow big.

It has taken some time but finally it seems that the evolution of organised retailing in India is picking up momentum. During the last 10 years, many retail start-ups promised a lot. A few folded up even before they really got started, a few others struggled and then burnt out before they could develop a sustainable business model and others arc still evolving.

Shoppers' Stop, Lifestyle, Westside, Giant and Tanishq are few examples of an Indian success story in the retail business. They are now the torchbearers of a modern Indian retail sector. The second layer includes players like FoodWorld, Nilgiris, Big Bazaar Pantaloon and The Home Store.

Prospects of Retailing in India

New after understanding the retailing and its various aspects, let's elaborate the prospects of retailing in India. Let's deal with it one by one.

The first point that brightness the prospect is the highest percentage of youngsters in the Indian population. Because of it the companies be it Reliance, Tata, Birla, Big Bazar of India or Walmart, Carrefour, Metro and other global giant wants to enter into retailing in India.

Because they know that the spending power of the Indian

youth is high.

And most of them prefer to buy things from the retail stores like Reliance fresh Food world, Subhiksha, Big Bazaar etc. rather than from the local kiranawala, because of convenience, higher standard of hygiene and the attractive ambience.

If we look at the retailing scene in clothes and footwear. We will find the presence of a large no. of unorganized players. They generally display a limited range of inexpensive and popular item. Whereas in contrast modern clothing and footwear stars are spacious with sample products displayed in windows

With growth in incomes Indians have been spending more on health, beauty products, entertainment and food. Therefore, Big retailers are aiming to provide all these amenities under one roof through the mall culture. There people can go and shop with having fun and leisure.

This thing presently account for a tiny share but in the future the business is bound to grow as new and new malls will open.

Moreover, the laws are also getting more and more business friendly. Main rules regarding F.D.I in retail and real estates are getting lesser and lesser which means entry of large no. of players mainly foreign in the Indian market that will lead to a double-digit growth in this sector.

One more factor that helps in retail growth is the fact that means of entertainment are less in India. So, people generally feel these retail stores or malls as a place to end up spending amount on food and entertainment. So that means there is immerse potential in it. Therefore every one will keep this thing in mind and try to open up more avenues like this where people can enjoy and spend some quality time.

Problems of Retailing in India

Lack of Personal Touch: The ambience of these mega stores is no doubt world class but even they fail to establish a personal touch. It is because in local kiranashops the owner and worker is same therefore he can easily remember all the customers of the locality in which he is operating and can built a rapport with them.

Where as in retail stores the buyers have to walk and select the item. And the ownership is different from the workers. So, the employees just do what they are taught to do and they don't try to build bond with the customers.

Non-availability of Credit: If we observe then we will find that, as the local kiranawala knows people in the locality he can supply goods to them and get cash later as he has that rapport. Whereas retail stores cant do so they can just provide privilege card or other such schemes.

Therefore the customers will go for local ones as they are providing much flexibility to the consumers.

Ease of Purchase: There is a lot of ease in buying goods from local shops than in retail stores. For eg. If you have to buy toothpaste then you have to just tell the shopkeeper and he will give the best. But in retail stores you have to go to the counter for billing which itself is a very time consuming process. Moreover, it becomes very uneasy to go to a retail store to buy a small item.

One more problem for the retail sector is the government policies. Though we know that the government is opening up the retail sector in India but, even then there is a fear that the government may make any rule that can disrupt the retail growth in case it feels that it is against the welfare of the people. So there stays a constant fear of rule change among the companies.

There is another threat from MNCs as they are entering into Indian retail markets because of the Government policy with regard to Foreign Direct Investment.

So, we can say that there is a 50:50 chances of Retail Industry, in India. As, the traditional Indian household is not open to that type of culture but yes; even then the companies can work hard in changing that mindset.

References

Chatterjee Purvita "Advent of Merchandizing", Business Line, Dec 5, 2002.

Jeffrey W Bennet, "Challenges of a Changing Retailing Industry", published in International Trends in retailing", Vol. 16, No. 2, Dec. 1999.

M. Rajashekhar "Shoppers Stop - Adding NOW Colours", published in the Business World, Dec 18, 2000.

Mohan Devendra"Mr. Big (Bazaar)!" Business India, September, 2002.

Neil Z Stern "Tomorrow's Hot Retail Ideas", published in Retail Watch 1999.

Radha Krishnan "Organized/Retailing" - Business Line, January 2003.

Radhika Neela, "Changing Trends in Retailing and FMCG Industry in India", published in Marketing Journal – ICFAI, February 2005.

S. Ramesh Kumar "What Makes E-tailing Tick?" Associate Professor, IIM-B, published in Business Line, Aug 3, 2000.

S. Shajahan & Shankee Bharat "Retail Industry - Challenges & Opportunities" published in Marketing Maslermind in May 2004.

Uta Werner. John Me Dermott and Grea Rotz. "Retailers at the Cross Roads. How to Develop Profitable New Growth Strategies" published in Journal of Business Strategy, Vol 25, and No.2 2004.

7

Customer Retention in the Retail Industry

T. Suchitra Rani and Dhanya Menon

Introduction

Retailing, also popularly known as 'detailing', is becoming the blue-eyed sector of the new emerging LPG economy, employing nearly 21 million people and generating revenues of approximately Rs. 9,30,000 crore. Organised retailing accounts only for three percent of the entire retailing activities in the country.

To attract customers, organised retail stores need to generate value and differentiate their outlets from other unorganised retail stores. As rightly said, 'Retail is Detail', so organised retail players need to target their markets and manage the customer experience in best possible ways. This study analyzes the various factors that determine the customer experience in retail outlets. Also, the study identifies strategies to retain and attract more customers by creating a memorable shopping experience. Thus, implications are drawn for retail stores, as a result of the analysis and interpretation done.

Every one of us does render some service or other. If we cultivate the habit of doing this service deliberately, our desire for service will steadily grow stronger, and will make, not only our own happiness, but that of the world at large.

Retail, according to Concise Oxford English Dictionary is "the sale of goods to the public for use or consumption rather than for resale."

Retailing according to Wikipedia, the free Encyclopedia, refers to "the sale of goods/merchandise for personal or household consumption either from a fixed location such as a department store or Kiosk, or from a fixed location and related subordinated services."

In commerce, a retailer buys goods and products in large quantities from manufacturers or importers, either directly or through a wholesaler, and then sells individual items or small quantities to the general public or end-user customers, usually in a shop, also called a store. Retailers are at the end of the supply chain. Marketers see retailing as part of their over all distribution strategy.

In today's competitive world, retailing is not just about selling at the shop. It entails a host of other activities such as conducting market surveys, providing choice to consumers, managing consumer experience, maintaining competitive price levels and retaining consumers.

Considered to be one of the most happening industries after IT, retailing industry has many big players competing with each other to gain an edge over the other. Owing to a steady increase in private consumption, retailing has become one of the hottest sectors of the emerging economy.

Retail Scenario in India

According to a CRISIL report, the $200-billion Indian retail market is one of the most fragmented markets of the world. The report states that only two percent of the entire retailing business is carried out by players in the organized sector, while the unorganized sector still accounts for the lion's share of the retail business.

According to Euromonitor, retailing accounts for global revenues over US$ 6.6 trillion and is the largest private sector industry in the world economy. In most of the developed nations, organised retail accounts for over 70-80 per cent of the total retail business. However, the organised retail segment in India has still a long way to go even when comparing to some of its Asian counterparts such as China, South Korea and Thailand. Much of the business of "traditional retailing" happening in India is handled by local kirana stores, according to analysts tracking the sector. In spite of its largely fragmented structure, retail business in India is one of the largest in the world and a by McKinsey estimates the size of the Indian retail market at US$ 200 billion, with the market growing at a rate of 11-12 per cent annually.

The retail sector in India is growing by leaps and bounds. India tops the list in the 2005 Global Retail Developed Index (GRDI) released by AT Kearney - an international management consulting firm. The GRDI ranks 30 emerging countries on the basis of various macroeconomic and retail specific variables. This index, which is published annually, is a tool to help retailers define their global developmental strategies. India has managed to ascend steadily on the GRDI and has now displaced Russia to occupy the numero uno position. A large portion of the growth in Indian retail business, according to A T Kearney, would be in the food and the apparel sectors. Indian consumers spend 45 per cent of their income on food and grocery and this category is a sure-fire way for retailers to attract consumers initially. Thus, it is apparent that food retail industry is indeed a booming sector in India and has the potential to generate large revenues.

The objectives of the study are:

- To explore the factors that influence shopping at a retail store
- To measure customer satisfaction towards retail dimensions
- To understand the purchase preference of customers from the stores
- To analyze the five dimensions of retail performance i.e
  - Price (the extent to which the store provides products at lower prices and whether the customer finds value for money paid to products)
  - Product (whether the store displays a wide range or not, to what extent the products are of good quality, availability of advertised merchandise in stock, product availability)
  - Layout (store layout is convenient for customers to move easily and pick up products, an aesthetic and appealing ambience, and convenient store parking)
  - Communication (the store effectively communicates the discounts and special offers, the signboards are easy to spot)
  - Customer Service (includes the salesmen's product

knowledge, helpfulness, courtesy and manners, and promptness in handling customers' complaints)

- To explore the association between the area and customer relations dimension of retailing
- To identify areas for improved customer retention and methods to attract new customers by offering a perfect environment to shop

Data was obtained by administering questionnaires to the customers at three retail outlets in the twin cities of Hyderabad and Secunderabad. The three supermarkets are located at Himayatnagar, Dilshuknagar and Chaitanyapuri. A structured questionnaire was administered to the customers who walked into these outlets covering four main dimensions, Price, Products, Store layout, Communication and Customer services offered. As most of the customers wouldn't wish to answer the questionnaires at the store, they were interviewed with questions based on the questionnaires.

The collected data was analysed in the following way for obtaining results

- The frequency and means of the considered retail dimensions are shown to measure the satisfaction levels of customers at the retail stores
- Chi-Square test was implemented to understand whether there was any association between area and customer service

In the factors influencing the choice of store for shopping, six factors were included, namely proximity, product variety, product range, discounts, customer service and brand name. Some of the customers have given preference to more than one factor while choosing the store for shopping. From the above table, it is evident that 28.3 per cent of the customers prefer a retail outlet for three reasons i.e., proximity, product variety and product range. It is also found 22.8 per cent of the customers preferred a retail store due to proximity. From this, we can draw a conclusion that almost 51.1 per cent (28.3 per cent + 22.8 per cent) preferred retail stores which are near to either their house or office. Proximity becomes a very important factor for deciding on the store for shopping, as customers find it very convenient to buy things from stores near to their homes or offices. Also, impulse purchases because of discounts or sales promotion schemes are more likely in stores which are conveniently located for the customers.

The customers were asked the different category of items they purchased from retail outlets. The category of items generally purchased were fruits and vegetables, processed food, ready to fry items, bakery items, grocery (staples) and toiletries. It was found that 31.5 per cent of the respondents preferred to purchase fruits and vegetables, grocery items and toiletries from the retail outlets. Around 16.3 per cent of the customers preferred to purchase fruits and vegetables, processed food, grocery items and toiletries. So, we can conclude that frequently purchased items from retail outlets are fruits and vegetables, grocery and toiletries.

Among the various parameters, proximity is an important parameter drawing majority of the customers to the retail store. So, the retail store should concentrate remaining parameters like product variety, discounts, services etc.

The most frequently purchased items by the customers in the retail store are fruits and vegetables, grocery items and toiletries. Therefore, the retail stores need to improve the visibility and merchandising of other items such as processed food items and bakery items in order to drive up the sales of these products.

With consumers looking at convenience and choice of products under one roof, consumer demand is truly the driving force for organized retailing in the country. As evident from the above, the three major issues pointed by the customers are pricing, customer service and communication.

All brands and items within a category are not perceived by consumers in the same way. Therefore, retail stores must identify "known-value" items - that is, items purchased frequently across outlets and are recognizably higher or lower in price relative to a consumer's previous shopping experiences.

A remarkable observation is that people with income below Rs. 5000 do not shop in these retail outlets. This can be due to various reasons like high price which is found in the present study, the difference in customer service which is also proved through the chi-square test where it was found that there is association between area and customer service, the communication should also be such that it attract every income group. All these factors can draw even the low income group also to the store.

The average time spent by the customer is 15-30 minutes, which is by far a very small amount of time. Efforts should be made to increase the time spent by the customer in the retail store, which could be achieved by improving the customer service and by managing the customer experience in the retail store.

Customers who throng to retail stores buy there because they perceive that they get better quality products. However, the battle would be lost if efforts were made only to draw customers who are price conscious and increase the traffic. Therefore, a greater need is being perceived for strategic articulation in prices across various categories.

Since most retailers have access to the same merchandize, it is very hard to differentiate one retail outlet from another in terms of quality. The same reasoning can be extended to prices of some of the merchandize. So the question is how pricing should be done to increase traffic and retain loyal customers.

Retail stores need to develop strategies that build on existing pricing techniques and focus more on meeting customers' needs and desires. Customer-focused approaches in which retailers identify and exploit the items most important to customers, i.e., items that will help build and sustain a positive price image would help the stores derive the maximum mileage. The brands and items that the largest segment of shoppers is likely to remember should be identified and aggressively priced. A pricing strategy which would enable the retail stores to derive maximum benefit is discussed below:

Five point pricing strategy: (Source: AT Kearney's)

- Offer attractive prices on image-enhancing brands and items
- Create opening price points in each category, sometimes through private-label brands

- Appeal to shoppers' "treasure hunting" mindset by establishing a highly visible discount price on a unique or limited item
- Offer large sizes and value packs
- Communicate an everyday low price to establish price credibility

Retail stores should begin advertising in newspapers about product availability, discounts and offers. This strategy is being followed by Trinetra, Big Bazaar, Spencers, and many other retail outlets. Retail stores also need to identify and reward their best shoppers, and encourage those who spend more through various loyalty programs.

The second important thing that surfaced from the study is importance of customer service.

"Successful retailers are those who view customer service as a means of gaining an advantage in comparison with the other retailers."

Customer expectations are changing. Earlier, the customer would casually walk into the store, look around, compare a range of items and their prices, zero in on a product and eventually buy. In case there was any indecision or hesitation on the part of the customer, retailer's recommendation was solicited while making the purchase decision. The retailer was considered an opinion leader. Today, the scenario is different. With the power of mass media advertising, the consumer now walks into the store armed with the necessary information about products and having already decided on the brands and items in his or her choice basket. As media has created awareness about the options available, the purchase decisions are already made. And tomorrow, there will be a different picture altogether. The modern consumer is perplexed about the plethora of options that are available. Decision-making on brand purchase would no be as simple as it was earlier. As this happens, a majority of all purchase decisions would be made at the point of purchase. This of course would vary from category to category. In this context, sales personnel would playa pivotal role in helping customers reach a purchase decision.

It has been observed that there is sale personnel employed at the store are very casual and not very committed to their jobs. This can be attributed to the reason that most of the assistants employed are under the opinion that their job is not to improve sales, but just to keep the store clean 'and assist whenever asked for. This could however be improved through proper training of the sales personnel. Alternatively, managers at these stores can be directed to inculcate the real responsibilities into the sales personnel.

Retail stores can improve customer service by providing value-added services such as home delivery, meeting the health and wellness needs of the aging consumer, and giving the educated consumer more knowledge about what they are buying. Through discussions it was found that the retail store at one of the area employs only one home delivery person and this is the reason given by the store for taking one day to deliver goods at the customer's place. Comparing the same service with other retail outlet which is located very close by is found that they have more than one person employed for the same job. The customer experience should be such that the goods home delivery so be so efficient that goods would be delivered at customers residence even before the customer reaches her/his residence

The Customers should experience the world class courtesy from the employees of the retail store. Why do we need sales personnel moving around the store to assist people? On one occasion, a customer was asked to describe his shopping experience. During the discussion, he made a point that the particular retail store where he was shopping needed to improve in terms of product availability. When asked in particular about the products he was unable to find, he said he was looking for plastic fridge bottles. When the manager was asked, he immediately took the customer to that particular section of the store where bottles were displayed. The customer then told me that he wanted to buy these and since he couldn't locate them himself, he looked for assistance which wasn't there. The store could have missed a sale here. And one can imagine how many more would the store loose if no such assistance is provided.

As most of the customers who visit the stores are women of all ages, focus should be placed on vanity products. For these, a small portion of the store could be used to display all these items. Also the same counter can be used to display perfumes and colognes. Many retail stores do, not offer any testers for perfumes so that customers can try these first. This would reduce sales for some untested and rare brands. The investment lost in these testers could be regained by selling some less know (imported) brands that fetch higher margins.

It's not just important to attract new customers, customers from the secondary trading areas and passer-bys, but 'also to attract the lost customers. Customer complaints and suggestions box was placed only at one store. However, the box was placed in a corner and was not really visible to the customer. If information a bout why a customer is not happy with the store and what improvements are to be made at the store is not managed properly, how can the store understand changing customer expectations?

Retail stores should also target price, conscious customers, which would be possible by providing goods at a lower price, communicating discounts and offers with better visibility and by providing value-added customer service. This can also be done by communicating about lower denominations or economy packs, customer friendly schemes, monthly draws etc.

Conclusion

Therefore, in a nutshell, we can conclude that the key to effectiveness of a retail store is the management of customer experience. Customer experience management would ensure that retail stores can strategically manage a customer's experience and by doing so, allow them to be truly customer centric. To accomplish this, the following five step framework can be utilized (Source - 'Customer Experience Management' by Schmitt)

Step 1: Analyzing the experiential world of the customer

Step 2: Building the experiential platform

Step 3: Designing the ,brand experience

Step 4: Structuring the customer interface
Step 5: Engaging in continuous experiential innovation

8

Emerging Trends in Indian Retail Market.

M.S.R. Seshagiri and P. Pinakapani

Retailing is gaining lot of importance day by day, from past three to four years there is a quick, consistent and continuous change occurred in marketing with special reference to retail marketing. In this context an insight into the retail markets helps us to understand the growth of retail markets which are crossing leaps and bounds .The evolution started with weekly Haats and Melas. The concept which is called as modern in western sides is in practice at India since early civilization days. However things started taking new shapes since early 1980's when India first began opening its economy. For a long time a few corporate houses like Bombay Dyeing, Raymond's, S.Kumars', Grasims and Titan Watches have run the organised retail show. By the year 2000 the size of the organised Indian retail Industry has increased to approximately Rs. 13,000 crore. The various segments that make up the organised retail industry along with their size are in table given below. However this industry is expected to grow by 30 percent in the next five years.

Thus the growth potential for the organised retailer is enormous. Development of India as a sourcing hub shall further make India as an attractive retail opportunity for the global retailers. Retailers like Wal-Mart, GAP, Tesco, JC Penney, H&M, Karstadt-Quelle, Sears (Kmart), etc stepping up their sourcing requirements from India and moving from third-party buying offices to establishing their own wholly owned/wholly managed sourcing & buying offices shall further make India an attractive retail opportunity for the global players

Retailing: Consists of those business activities involved in the sale of goods and services to consumers for their personal, family, or household use.

All transactions in which the buyer intends to consume the product through personal, family or household use

Store concepts are now being tested on a global base. Communication networks and mass media have made expansion across national borders more feasible. One event that has made this possible is the spread of communication networks and mass media. Accessible markets have enticed US retailers into Mexico, Canada, Europe, Japan and China through the North American Free Trade Agreement (NAFTA) and the General Agreement on Tariffs and Trade (GATT).

The top five retail companies in terms of investment are:

Company	**Investment**
Wal-Mart-Bharti	Yet to announce
Reliance	$ 5.5 billion
Aditya Birla Group	$ 3.3 billion
Pantaloon	$ 1 billion
Tatas	$ 89 million

In commerce, a retailer buys goods or products in large quantities from manufacturers or importers, either directly or through a wholesaler, and then sells individual items or small quantities to the general public or end user customers, usually in a shop, also called store. Retailers are at the end of the supply chain. Marketers see retailing as part of their overall distribution strategy.

Retailing is the media between the producer and the individual consumer buying for personal consumption. This excludes direct link between the manufacturer and institutional buyers such as the government and other bulk customers. A retailer is one who stocks the producer's goods and is involved in the act of selling it to the individual consumer, at a margin of profit.

As such, retailing is the last link that connects the individual consumer with the manufacturing and distribution chain.

Apart from the Cooperative Societies, Public Distribution System (PDS), Canteen Stores as well as Post Offices, in India are also part and parcel of retail chain across the country.

Table 8.1: Market Size in Various Segments

Segment	Market Size (Rs. crore)
Textile	4050
Jewellery	2,000-2,500
Consumer Durables	15,000
Footwear	1,300-7,500
Food and Personal Care	1000
Non-Store retail	900
Luggage, Watches and Tyre	500
Books and Music	390

Source: Knight Frank-Indian Retail Review – Quarter 2005

Table 8.2: Facts about Various Types of Retail Outlet

Type of Retail Outlet	Facts – Numerical
Haats	Average Sales per Day-Rs.2.25 lakh Number of sales outlets per Haat- 300+ Number of Visitors per Haat- 4500+ Average Sales per Outlet-Rs 900 Villages covered by a Haat – 20-50
Melas	Annually held (Approx) – 25,000+ Outlets held at every mela at an average – 800+Average Sales per Mela-Rs 143 Lakh
Mandis	At average exists – 6,800 Catering to a population of –1.36 Lakh

Source: BW Marketing Whitebook, pp. 99-101

Evolution of Retail Marketing in India

In the Post Liberalisation era one can observe the advent of malls with a considerable pace. The advent of malls have not confirmed to metros 'A' Grade cities but also leveraging into 'B' and 'C' grade cities too.

Table 8.3: Mall Development in India

City	Number of Malls		Area (Million Sq.Ft)	
	2005	2006	2005	2006
NCR	14	18	3.35	6.67
Mumbai	7	14	2.45	4.60
Bangalore	5	1	1.06	0.50
Hyderabad	3	4	0.74	0.65
Kolkata	2	1	0.45	0.70
Pune	2	6	0.41	2.20
Lucknow	2	1	0.34	0.40
Indore	1	0	0.30	0.00
Jaipur	1	1	0.20	0.25
Ludhiana	1	1	0.20	0.20
Cochin	0	2	0.00	0.85
Chandigarh	0	2	0.00	0.40
Chennai	1	2	0.40	0.65
Ahmedabad	0	1	0.00	0.65

Source: ICICI Property Services Research

A decade ago it is difficult to find a single mall. But few years ago, we can trace hardly half a dozen or so. However, today around 54 malls can be listed out apart from the emerging malls. From the above table it is understood that there is 138 per cent growth in the shopping malls and contrarily 189 per cent growth in floor space. But the industry forecast is that around 300 malls will spring up in coming two years offering, 41 million Sq.Ft Space. These 300 malls tentatively include 35 Hypermarkets, 325 large departmental stores, 1500 Super markets and over 10,000 new outlets. Here, arises a series of questions that what are those forces, which propel the growth of the retail malls. Some of the networking facts are

- Changing Income Profiles and Consumption Patterns
- Diminishing difference between Rural and Urban India
- Growing number of Young Earners

Changing Income Profiles: Though concept does not much vary, study and interpretation will vary. The NCAER classification is one of the studies in deciding about the changing profiles. The average middle class family's disposable income rose by more than 20 percent between 1999 and 2003.It has also projected that there could be enormous expansion in middle income and upper middle income categories. Hence, the echelons will provide a demand for the niche and branded products. 300 millions odd middle class are the real consumers who are catching up the attention of the world.

Diminishing Difference between Rural and Urban India: Nearly 72 per cent of the Indian population is spread in rural areas. Rest of the population spread from 'A' grade cities to 'C' grade cities. While food grain production has steadily increased, resulting in the increase of spending power of the average rural family. Market giants have rightly identified through various surveys the latent demand for retail markets. The Indian economy is showing positive indicators from past few years .For example 50 per cent policies of LIC were purchased by rural customers during the year 2002-03. BSNL is having around two billion mobile phone connections out of which 50 per cent are located in small towns and villages. Number of Internet or Communication Café's have sprung up almost in every town, though not in villages which helped companies to win 55 per cent to 60 per cent customers from other than cities and out of which 50 per cent customers did shopping and purchase transactions through Internet The fact that the 20 million Kisan Credit Card (KCC) issued so far exceed 25 million credit plus debt cards issued in urban India. A Whopping Rs. 65, 000 crore have sanctioned under the KCC Scheme.

Changes in Consumption Patterns: Growing literacy rate and increasing employment opportunities in private sector especially in IT and IT Enabled services Tourism, Hospitality, Insurance and Medical Services and also increase in the gender (both male & female) employment, leading to changes in income levels whereby resulting on consumption patterns.

Another Interesting factor, which has enhanced the consumption pattern, is introduction of credit cards. Almost every leading bank and identified financial institutions of both Public sector and Private sector, offering various types of currency related plastic cards. For example in September 2004, around 11.94 million cards are in the hands of customers against 0.3mn in 1990 as per industry sources. By the end of FY 2005 these cards accounted for a spending of Rs. 20 bn per month, with an average of Rs. 1659 per card. Most of the expenditures are because of availability of easy finance at lower interest rates with payment option in EMI's. This scenario leaving much less for discretionary spending. For example, in 1975 car sales averaged 30,000 a year. In April 2005, in one month 63,930 cars were sold.

Growing Number of Young Earners: The great asset at present for India is youth under the age of 34 years who constitutes to 70 per cent as per the census, 2001. This age group people are the deciders of the shape of the business forms in India by redefining service and consumption patterns. Approximately 3 Crore youth are employed in various service sectors earning and spending around one lakh crore in a year leaving indications of a prosperous and promising society. The consumers' horizon has broadened with advent of media and communication technology. In fact, this is one of the aspect for the growth of retail markets during 1996-2001.

Retail in India: Structure

The retail formats seems to be rosy in India. However, in reality the market is a blend of organised and unorganised sectors. But, overall size is estimated to be US$ 180 billion, which provides jobs to almost 15 per cent of employable Indian adults considerable contributor to India's GDP .As per industry estimates there are approximately twelve million retail outlets are existing in India of which two-thirds are located in rural India. In the retail structure only 2 per cent of the market is organised and the rest is in unorganised sector (98 per cent). Where as, growth potential for the organised retailer is enormous.

According to India Retail Report 2007, the total private consumption touched Rs. 20,000 billion (US$ 445 billion) at current prices in the calendar year 2006 with organised sector accounting for Rs. 55, 000 crore (US$ 12.4 billion) business increasing its share to 4.6 per cent of the total Indian Retail Value that stood at Rs. 12, 000 billion (US$ 270 billion). Moving forward, organized retailing is projected to grow at the rate of about 37 per cent in 2007 and 42 per cent in 2008. Organised retail in India has the potential to add over Rs. 2,000 billion (US$ 45 billion) business by the year 2010.

The consumer spending is ultimately pushing the economy into a growth-and-liberalisation mode. The Indian market is becoming bolder by the day, with the economy now expected to grow at over 8 per cent and average salaries being hiked by about 15 per cent, there will be lot more consumption.

Challenges Ahead

Lack of Industry Status: As 98 per cent of the business is in unorganized sector, could not get recognized as an industry, which is hindrance factor for availability of easy finance to the operators. Apart from the Lack of Industry status, complex tax structure too is a pulling down factor of the growth of industry.

Inadequate Facilities: Inadequate Facilities like lack of adequate godowns, cold storages, improperly maintained market yards; improper roads etc are hindrances for the growth retail Industry in India. These facilities demand capital investment.

Presence of Global Players: Many of the Multinational Corporations are yet to unfold the wings in Indian market. Few days ago Wal-Mart decided to make its presence in India strategically with the help of Bharati Enterprises Group. Vice-versa other players like Tesco, CARYFURE etc. binocularing for suitable, competent, strategic partners.

The MNC' s show their preference with sound investment and state of art technologies and quality at competent prices.

Bargaining Power of Suppliers: The price at which the product is available to the retailer for selling to the end consumer is very important in retail as it plays a large role in the actual profitability. Those companies also offer finished products, as output usually will be the supplier to the retailing industry. Hence, if the numbers of suppliers are fewer and dominate, it results on final price of the product. The emergence of private labels in apparel and food has in fact played a key role in controlling the bargaining power of suppliers.

Government with the help of chamber of commerce, CII and other such relevant organization and professional bodies, make changes in taxation procedure pertaining to retail sector where by it should act as simulative motivation factor for the growth of the industry as such. Government by adopting policies like Built, Operate and Transfer (BOT) can develop world-class relevant infrastructure facilities (Cold Storage, Market Yards etc). Government with the help of professional organizations should create more awareness about consumerism among consumers so to develop proper retail formats.

At a glance if one have look towards Indian Retail Industry, one can realize the changing face of the Industry. Formats, new to the Indian market place have emerged hastily over the past seven years. Apart from the change in retail formats there occurred changes in living styles, living spaces, family composition, aspirations, off course raise in income levels and awareness through media have changed the consumer profiles of the country, which were dreamt a decade ago. Though see through changes are occurring at a pace in retail industry, there is no immediate treat to the small retailers as against much spoken giant players in retail industry who are operating in organized retail sector which hardly constitute two percent against 98 per cent of the unorganized retail markets and hardly confined to metros and 'A' grade cities.

References

Baker, Julie; A. Parasuramam; Dhruv Grewal; and Glen voss. "The influence of multiple store Environment cues on perceived merchandise"

Barsh, Janna; Blair Crowdford; and Chris Grosso. "How E-Tailing can Rise from the Ashes"

Bond, Ronald L. Retail in Detail

Dhruv Grewal; Gopalkrishnan Iyer; and Michel Levy "Internet Retailing".

Goldbrick, Peter and Gray Davies . "International Retailing"

Henderson, Terilyn and Elizabeth Mihas, Building Retailing Plans

Karr, Albert. "A Hot New Job is Chief of Customer Service for Internet Retailers

Karr, Albert. "A Hot New Job is Chief of Customer Service for Internet Retailers.

NICOM-2006(national seminar book)

Niraj, Rakesh; Mehendra Gupta; and Chakravarthi Narasimham. "Customer Profitability in Supply Chain"

Retail Management, Text & Cases; Swapna Pradan,

White, John Robert and Kevin D.Gray. "Shopping Centres and other retail properties"

9

Recent Trends in the Retail Sector

Priya Deshpande and M. Nalini

India is on the threshold of a great era in retailing. Over the last five years or so, shopping has been revolutionized with the arrival of malls, departmental stores, specialist boutiques, in an otherwise fragmented Indian retail market. The Indian retail industry, which was traditionally dominated by small family-run kirana stores, seems to have finally come of age. The traditional grocery stores have embraced the modern retail formats. Consumers now value convenience and choice on a par with getting value for their hard-earned money. A range of modern retailers is attempting to serve the needs of the 'new' Indian consumer, and what's new is the speed at which shoppers are shifting allegiance to modern format of "experiential stores." To tap this growth opportunity, Indian retail organizations need to be prepared for a quick scale up across dimensions of people, processes and technology in addition to identifying the right formats and value propositions for the Indian consumer. This paper focuses on trends to gain a better insight into the retail sector.

Introduction

India is witnessing an unprecedented consumption boom. The economy is growing between 7 and 8 per cent and the resulting improvement in income dynamics along with factors like favorable demographics and growth in aspirational consumption are the drivers. Retailing in India is currently estimated to be US$ 200 billion, of which organized retailing (i.e. modern trade) makes up 3 per cent , organized retail is expected to grow at 25-30 percent p.a., and is projected to attain US$ 23 billion by 2010.

The positive demographics and the Indian consumer's increasing disposable income have been highlighted by several studies. Increasing double income families in cities is another positive factor. With the retail industry seen as the next sunrise industry after the InfoTech industry, several retail companies have collectively through business associations and chambers, asked the government to set a policy and framework for the industry so that it can reach its full potential and become a growth industry. According to Pricewaterhouse Coopers (PwC), the rapid urbanization and growing working population in India are fueling modern retail growth, contributing 13 per cent of the GDP.

Table 9.1: Share of Market: Urban vs. Rural

Category	Urban	Rural
Food	33	44
Clothing	50	57
Footwear	61	64
Miscellaneous Goods	67	56
Durables	50	43

Source: NSSO 5th round; KPMG in India Analysis 2005

AT Kearney's Global Retail Development Index 2006 ranked India as the world's most attractive market for retail investments. India has the youngest population in the world, with 50 per cent of its population under the age of 25. The World Bank ranks India as fourth in purchasing power, after the US, China and Japan. Factoring the size of the rural population and agricultural income growth in rural India, the rural market is definitely an opportunity for retailers with an innovative retail proposition. A clear indicator of this potential is the share of the rural market across most categories of consumption. Key challenges in tapping this potential are the fragmentation of the market, given the geographic spread, and infrastructure issues like lack of distribution and logistics. Across the country, retail sales in real terms are predicted to rise more rapidly than consumer expenditure during 2003-08. The forecast growth in real retail sales during 2003- 2008 is 8.3 per cent per year, compared with 7.1 per cent for consumer expenditure. Sales from these large-format stores are to expand at growth rates ranging from 24 per cent to 49 per cent per year during 2003-2008, according to a latest report by Euromonitor International, a leading provider of global consumer-market intelligence.

Table 9.2: Formats Adopted by Key Players

Retailer	Current Format	New Format
Shopper's Stop	Departmental Store	Quasi Mall
Ebony	Departmental Store	Quasi Mall, Smaller outlets, adding food retail
Crossword	Specialty store	Corner shops
Piramyd	Departmental Store	Quasi Mall, food retail
Pantaloon	Own brand store	Hyper market
Subhiksha	Super market	Considering moving to elf service
Food world	Food supermarket	Hyper market ,Food world express(Spencer)
Globus	Departmental Store	Small fashion stores
Metro	Cash n Carry	
Reliance Fresh	Super market	Hyper market
Piramyd	Discount store	Tru Mart
Big Bazaar	Hyper market	
Hyderabad Central	Mall	
Food Bazaar	Supermarket	
Tata/ Trent	Department store	Hypermarket (Star India Bazaar)
Lifestyle	Department store	Hypermarket (TBA)

Source: KPMG in India Analysis 2005, Format Choices by Indian Retailers

What is Fuelling Retail Boom?

Market liberalization and increasingly assertive consumers are sowing the seeds of a retail transformation that will bring bigger Indian and multinational players on to the scene. The market is huge at US$ 162 billion overall. The entry of multinational companies (MNC) has certainly transformed this sector. The supply chain, and consumer interest and awareness in branded products have been built from scratch. The Indian consumers are divided into three categories, viz., high-income urban consumers, and low-income urban and rural consumers. The high-income urban consumers are willing to pay a higher price for having the choice of quality products and the complete shopping experience in the large retail stores. But, the low-income urban and rural consumers will go for the price- sensitive products which are easily available in the smaller stores located nearby. The markets in both categories are very large and hence, there is little direct competition between the two retail sectors. As the awareness and disposable incomes increase in India, the two categories will merge slowly, before the competition actually begins. But in rural areas, competition will be present, and the minor players will prevail. In a developing country like India, a large chunk of consumer expenditure is on basic necessities, especially food-related items.

Different Forms of Retailing: Space Hyper Marts

- Large supermarkets, typically (3,500 - 5,000 sq. ft)
- Mini supermarkets, typically (1,000 - 2,000 sq. ft)
- Convenience store, typically (7,50 - 1,000 sq. ft)
- Discount/shopping list grocer

Traditional retailers trying to reinvent the wheel by introducing self-service formats as well as value-added services such as credit, free home delivery etc. there is high potential for food service players. Food sales account for 63 per cent per cent of the total retail sales. The organized retail food sector constitutes the largest opportunity for growth and account for 2 per cent of total sales at present. Urbanization, working spouses, increasing household disposable incomes and convenience of one-stop shop with good ambience have been the drivers of growth of retailing in India

The country is on the brink of becoming an economic powerhouse ready to unleash its largely untapped potential for those who are willing to take the right step forward. In the retail sector, in spite of a 1.07 billion strong population, the target consumer base for most retailers in India stands at about 405 million. Till the end of 2006, over 60 per cent of malls in India will be in the 6 big metros which account for about 80 per cent of the sector's revenues. Delhi and the National Capital Region (NCR) will account for about 50 per cent of these malls. Tier I cities such as Mumbai, Delhi and Bangalore clearly have the upper hand in terms of higher disposable incomes, better infrastructure, awareness levels, propensity to spend and an affluent urban youth population. Availability of space will usher in the next level of Competition as requirements of mall space for new players are bound to heighten the intensity of competition. Increased mall space will also attract new Indian entrants. A clear indication of this is the plans of domestic retailers like Piramyd Retail and Lifestyle to scale-up operations and raise capital through the IPO route. With the entry of property funds and investment trusts, this trend of space availability is likely to continue.

Opportunities in Retailing

Retail is a capital intensive business - large investments are required in real estate, leasehold improvements and working capital. Foreign investments in retail are necessary for the growth of the industry. Government has permitted 51 per cent FDI taking the right steps to balance the needs of the individual retailers as well as the needs of the consumers who are demanding better and improved retail formats, where shopping is a pleasure.

In the current scenario of technological advancement, the new innovations in the bar code sensors, scanners Smart label technology, RFID, EDI are of great help in the growth of this industry.

Retailing has evolved from bricks to clicks ie e-tailing. The hardware and software tools that have now become essential for retailing can be put into 3 broad categories.

Technology in Retailing

Computers have evolved as cash registers for billing. The bar-coded products using UPC and EDI are scanned for billing. The point of sale systems uses scanners and bar-coding to identify an item, use pre-stored data to calculate the cost and generate the bill for the client.

Tunnel Scanning: Tunnel Scanning is a new concept where the consumer pushes the full shopping cart through an electronic gate to the point of sale. In a matter of seconds items in the cart are hit with laser beams and scanned. All the consumer has to do is to pay for the goods.

Internet: Internet is also rapidly evolving as a Customer Interface removing the need of a Consumer physically visiting the store.

Operating Support Systems: Various ERP Packages in retail specific systems help in integrating all the functions from warehousing, distribution, front and back office store system.

CRM Systems: Customer Relationship Management Systems are a boom in relationship. The rise of loyalty Programmes, Mail Order and Internet have provided the retailers with real access to Consumer Data. Data Warehouse and Mining Technologies offer retailers the tools they need to make sense of their Consumer Data and apply it to business.

Advance Planning and Scheduling Systems: Advance Planning and Scheduling Systems can provide improved control across the supply chain. APS packages complement ERP. The future trends aided by technological innovations like Personal Preference Card will be reality by the end of the decade.

As retail gets into tailspin, the spotlight is slowly shifting from the product to the space where all the action happens in the store. The shopping ambience has never been as important as now, with retailers looking to Designers and Retail Consultants to give their stores a contemporary and Consumer friendly design. Retail design and visual merchandising play a crucial role in creating the difference. Retail today has become a point of direct interaction for the brand with the target audience ie Touch Points. The retail shop represents every business parameter, supply chain, procurement, replenishment, Consumer footfall, conversion, and retention and wallet share growth.

Point of Sale: Check outs with scanning is common enough, but, Tesco has gone one step ahead with a possibility of scanning the products themselves by customers at point of sale.

Category Management: It is a model in which a retailer chooses a number of variants to offer in each category and the consumers of multiple categories (Basket Shoppers) make their store choice between the retail store and an exogenous outside alternative based on their utilities from their shopping basket.

Four-Gear Path

First Gear: Focus is on price control. This phase was driven by entrepreneurs like Subhiksha and Vivek's (durables) in the South and real-estate players like the Raheja's who started Shopper's Stop.

Second Gear: focus is on meeting customer expectations. It is highly customer driven, where buyers are exposed to new retail formats. This leads to a scenario where first generation retailers expand to multiple locations (Pantaloons, Lifestyle, Stopper's stop) to woo consumers. Retailers also get into initiatives like dial-n-order, free parking, convenient timings, provisions for trial a taste, prices below MRP and an Indian retailing can be said to be currently in this phase.

Third Gear: It also involves backend management, cost savings in terms of initiating vendor partnerships and increasing stock turns take priority. Many retailers in China and South Asia are in this phase. The focus is on efficiency and profitability of investment.

Fourth Gear: It is the period of consolidation. The organized sector acquires a significant share of the retail pie. It is start of cross-border movement, with mergers and acquisitions gaining momentum. Retailers in North America and Europe, like Walmart, Tesco, M&S and Carrefour are examples. The third and fourth phase the retailers exert great influence than manufacturers and, therefore, have strong bargaining power.

Emerging Trends

- Indian retail network is getting organized and corporatised and spreading across the country. Indian retail corporates are using multi-formats e.g. Pantaloons etc
- The Indian retailers are also becoming media players in indoor retail e.g. Stop-Fash media, the creators of digital signage. Pantaloon-Future media.
- Retail companies are increasingly spending on both the environment and fixtures and fittings emphatic lightings and digital signage and are all in for an international appeal and inviting feel so that they are selling an experience and not just goods.
- The retail business is an early adopter of I.T and various levels of usage are emerging such as data warehousing/mining, supply chain management, scanner data bar-coding, UPC, EDI&RIFD.
- The latest fad for fragrance retailing is now enamoring the great Indian retail dream, so also the emergence of private labels.
- Loyalty schemes and reward points are being extensively used to retain and reward customers e.g. First Citizen (Shoppers-Stop)Green Card(Pantaloons), Club West(Westside),Inner Circle (Lifestyle).
- Pantaloons have tied up with ICICI bank to launch ICICI - Big Bazaar credit /debit card.
- Store design is becoming international e.g. HyperCity has partnered with JAP of London for its store design. Future Group (Pantaloons) has its own in house design company Idiom, which constantly is working on design ideas.

- The emergence of retail brands e.g. Stop, Fresh & Pure etc.

Key Drivers of Growth

Indians with an ability to spend over US$ 30,000 a year (PPP terms) on conspicuous consumption represent 2.8 per cent of the entire population. But with a population base of 1.07 billion people, this number amounts to 30 million people, a market next only to USA, Japan and China. While consumer demand is driving retail growth, it is in turn being driven by the following factors:

Economic Growth: This has meant greater disposable incomes for the booming Indian middle class, which currently comprises 22 per cent of the total population. This figure is expected to increase to 32 per cent by 2010. Disposable incomes are expected to rise at an average of 8.5 per cent p.a. till 2015.

Demographics: More than 50 per cent of the population is less than 25 years of age and strong growth is expected to continue in this age bracket.

Urbanisation: The Indian urban population is projected to increase from 28 per cent to 40 per cent of the total population by 2020 and incomes are simuitaneously expected to grow in these segment.

Credit Availability: Retail loans have doubled in the last three years to reach USD 38.7 bn by 2005.

Challenges Ahead

In most emerging retail markets, such as Eastern Europe, Latin America and China, hypermarkets have been the major high growth format. Supermarkets dominate most cities, but there has been a clear shift towards hypermarkets, driven by the combination of good prices, overall shopping convenience and experience, product range and quality.

In China, most hypermarkets are located within city limits as consumers do their shopping more than once a week. This is primarily because Chinese consumers prefer fresh produce, have low car penetration and limited refrigeration space at home. The same factors apply to Indian consumers and we believe that successful hypermarkets in India will have to be centrally located - in big as well as Tier II cities. Pantaloon's Big Bazaar hypermarket at Phoenix Mills, Mumbai, has sales of USD 20 million per year - the highest by any retail outlet in India. Yet, there are only about 25 hypermarkets in India, operated by 4 major retailers. India's 67 retail destinations can therefore absorb over 1000 hypermarkets by 2010. 3 out of India's top 5 retailers already have aggressive hypermarket strategies in place. This is going to be one of the most preferred formats for international retailers entering India. The clothing segment is positioned for further organized retail penetration due to the high level of branding activities by apparel retailers and merchandising spread across formats such as department stores, hypermarkets, own retail outlets and franchises.

Distribution, or the lack of it, is a major hindrance for retailers in India. The lack of quality infrastructure across the country and a non-existent distribution sector results in inefficient logistics systems. Infrastructure is the weakest link in India's path to progress and there is an urgent need to address issues plaguing this area. Urbanization is driving an increasing need to upgrade or create infrastructure facilities. Fraud is going to be one of the retail sector's primary challenges in the future. Fraud and theft, including employee pilferage, shoplifting, vendor frauds and inaccuracy in supervision and administration costs the Indian retail industry about Rs 550-600 crore (US$ 0.12-0.13 billion) every year. This is despite the fact that most large modern format retailers use standard security features such as CCTVs, POS systems and anti-shoplifting systems for greater control over fraud and theft. In financial terms, cost of this fraud constitutes about 2 per cent of the organized retail sector's revenues. We believe that the implications and size of this loss will be more significant as retailers continue to scale up and increase product lines.

Conclusions

The Indian retail network is getting organized, corporatised and the network is spreading across the country with new retail formats and combinations are emerging. The attitudinal shift of the Indian consumer in terms of "**Choice Preference**", "**Value for Money**" has changed the face of Retailing in India. As retail gets into tailspin, the spotlight is slowly shifting from the product to the space where all the action happens in the store. The shopping ambience has never been as important as now, with retailers looking to Designers and Retail Consultants to give their stores a contemporary and Consumer friendly design. Retail today has become a point of direct interaction for the brand with the target audience and is creating new Touch Points.

Organized retailing in India is surely poised for a takeoff and will provide many opportunities both to existing players as well as new entrants. Technology promises to make the Indian retail market a real happening place in the day's ahead while same time offering immense business opportunities to the domestic entrepreneurs. In fact, this is likely to transform the whole contours of the India's market making it a part of the overall global market.

References

Call of the Mall, Indian Management, vol. 44, issue 6, June 2005.

CII, Retail Scenario in India: Unlimited Opportunity.

Gibson Vedamani, Retail Management: Functional Principles and Practices, Jaico Books Ltd.

Great Future for Hyper Markets, Business Line dated 17th Aug 2006.

India's Growing Working Population Fueling Retail Growth, The Hindu Business Line; Wednesday, August 23, 2006.

KPMG Analysis "Consumer Markets in India - The Next Big Thing", September 2005.

Levy Weitz, "Retailing Management", Tata McGraw Hill Publishing, 5th edition.

Majumdar S, "FDI in Retailing: India as a Supermarket"' www.business world India.com, September 17, 2002.

Retail mantra: 'Better, Simpler and Cheaper", The Hindu, 14th August, 2006.

The Hindu, Business Line, "Brand Line" Feb 8th2007.

The Main Roads to Retail Nirvana, Indian Management, vol. 44, issue 6,

June 2005.

There's No Looking Back for Retail Giants, Economic Times, dated 11 and 12th Aug 2006.

10

Revolutionary Trends in the Indian Retail Sector

A. Suryanarayana and Smitha Sambrani

Introduction

Retailing is an important social institution because about 30 percent of what we spend goes on products and services that we buy from retailers. Today, it is the most potential and upcoming industry in India and worldwide, and is also known as 'Sunrise Sector'. Ample of employment opportunities are available in retail industry and immense changes are noticed in today's retailing. Increasing number of supermarkets, shopping malls and hypermarkets indicate the changing face of retailing. India has moved into 21st Century and is showing marked changes to push the organized retail development even further, India is making its presence felt in all sectors. India is rated as the fifth most striking emerging retail market. There are several factors that are fueling the growth of the retail sector. The young working populace, due to the rise of nuclear families in urban locale, is increasing with more women joining in. This has given rise to promising opportunities in the service sector. Moreover, the consumer is cash rich because of the finance boom. More consumers are using credit cards and their spending patterns have also changed.

Retailing has emerged as one of the most profitable sectors worldwide and it is dominating the economies of many countries. It is the single largest industry by revenues, employment, etc and is undergoing a metamorphosis in many exciting ways. Retailing has become an intrinsic part of everyday life. The nations that have enjoyed the greatest economic progress have a strong retail sector.

According to Philip Kotler, "Retailing includes all the

activities involved in selling goods or services to the final consumers for personal, non-business use." Retailing involves a direct interface with the customer and co-ordination of business activities from end to end. The retailer is the final and important link between a producer or other intermediaries and the buyers, who are the end users. Retailing is a dynamic activity that has major contribution in achieving customer service and customer satisfaction as well as it has a major influence on the economy.

Retailer includes large number of people and institutions. Any organization selling to final consumers whether it is a manufacture, wholesaler, or retailer- is doing retailing. There are retailers of goods like general stores, department stores, etc or retailers of services like banks, transport services etc.

Indian retail sector is highly unorganized. There are unaccounted number of low cost retailers such as small corner shops, tea stalls etc. Retail sector consists of small, independent and owner- managed shops. Today, with increase in the disposable income of middle class households, retail trade is rejuvenated in India. Rural market is waking up hence many manufacturers of consumer goods are developing new products and designing different strategies with the rural consumer in mind. Considering these changes and opportunities many multinational retailers are entering Indian market to grab the tremendous potential. Apart from the traditional 'kirana' or 'baniya' shops, new attractive retail formats like self-service supermarkets, shopping malls are slowly making their footprints in India.

Although retailing in India is still in front stage, certain global trends have already entered and quite established. Organized retailing is slowly making its place. Many amazing retail forms have been developed in the past two decades, and the basic retail forms are now be gradually replaced by large retailers and other new forms such as hypermarkets, convenience stores, fixed price shops, etc. Change is the true driving force behind retailing today.

India: An Emerging Retail Market

India's retail sector is globally recognized as the Sunrise

Industry. The country is rated as the 2nd most attractive retail destination among emerging markets. The Indian retail Industry is now on the threshold of quantum growth. Even though today organized retail is only US$ 6 billion i.e. 2 per cent of total Indian retail market, it is predicted to reach US$ 25 billion by 2010. Just a decade ago, India didn't have a single mall but today there are over 96 malls in India, thus the retail revolution has just about begun creating significant value to the Indian economy.

Retailing in India is gradually inching its way towards becoming the next boom industry. The whole concept of shopping has altered in terms of format and consumer buying behaviour, ushering in a revolution in shopping in India. Modern retail has entered India as seen in sprawling shopping centres, multi-storeyed malls and huge complexes offer shopping, entertainment and food all under one roof. Retail industry in India is at the crossroads, it has emerged as one of the most dynamic and fast paced industries with several players entering the market, since the future is promising the market is growing, government policies are becoming more favourable and emerging technologies are facilitating operations.

Retailing companies such as Shoppers' Stop and Crossroads have entered the fray to entice the middle class. A host of traditional companies as Tata and Reliance and many other have entered the retail business. International companies such as Metro AG of Germany are operating under the cash and carry format, while there has been talk of allowing up to 26 per cent FDI in certain retailing activities, a decision is yet to be taken by the government.

The retail business in India is one of the largest in the world and a joint CII-McKinsey report has pegged the size of the Indian retail market at US$ 180 billion. Currently the organized market size and growth is leaping in the following segments

- Food beverage and Consumer goods
- Apparel and footwear
- Consumer durables
- Health and beauty products

- Home furnishing and household goods
- Leisure and personal goods (Music and Books

Current Scenario

Modern retail formats in India – over and above discount stores, convenience stores and malls we will see the concept of hypermarkets, supermarkets and E-tailing emerging. With over 12 million retail outlets, India is one of the biggest retail markets world-wide.

Shopping malls are becoming increasingly common in large cities and announced development plans project at least 150 new shopping malls by 2008. The number of department stores is growing much faster than overall retail, at annual 24 per cent supermarkets have been taking an increasing share of general food and grocery trade over the last 2 decades.

The Indian population is witnessing a significant change in demographics, a large young working population with age of 24 years, nuclear families in urban areas, along with increasing working women population and emerging opportunities in the service sector are going to be the key drivers of the organized retail sector in India.

Rising disposable incomes, demographic changes, higher aspirations for branded products, better access to consumer finance/loans and increasing affluence in smaller towns have triggered a gigantic fillip to organized retail activity.

The retailing scenario has changed extensively over the years. Shopping malls and varied product choice are providing the customer with good shopping experience. Shopping in the present age has become a new experience, a celebration and an entertainment for the Indian middle-class customers. Lifestyle in India is undergoing a rapid change and the concept of 'value for money' is rising. The credit card has made shopping more convenient. These shopping malls have emerged with a large array of products at competitive prices.

The main drivers for the growth of the industry are increased consumer demand, improved sourcing options and increasing availability of real estate. Most of the business houses are making a foray into retailing. Example:- Reliance

Retailing is followed by the IT boom, attracting public attention. Change in lifestyle has put a premium on the consumers' time; the right shopping experience is encouraging Indian consumers to spend more, and the tendency is frequent. Retailers are paying more attention to consumers and encouraging them to buy more, which started yielding greater dividends.

Table 10.1: Important Retail Chains in Indian Cities

Department Stores	Super markets	Specialty Stores	Hyper markets	Food Services
Shoppers' Stop	Food World	Music World	Giant	Pizza Hut
Lifestyle	Nilgiri's	Tanishq	Big Bazaar	Barista
Pantaloons	Margin Free	Health & Glow	Star India Bazaar	McDonald's
Trinetra	Subhiksha	Reebok	---	Qwiky's

This has created an opportunity in organized retailing, which is evident from retail outlets like Shoppers's Stop, Food World, Music World and Pantaloons. With many supermarkets coming up in the urban market across the country, the retailing sector has begun to grow in the Indian market. Retailing industry, creates opportunities for meeting consumer expectations, increasing value proposition and right mix of prices, product differentiation, experience and service. The retailing business is highly fragmented and a few retail chains are in operation: data shows that only 2 per cent of the retailing comes under the organized sector, which shows that the supply chain management is not in proper shape. According to a survey around 8 per cent of India's population is engaged in retailing compared to 20 per cent in the US. The per capita retailing space is about 2 sq ft compared to 16 sq ft in the US, which is the lowest in the world, which indicates a huge potential for retailing. It has an overwhelming proportion of the Rs. 400,000 crore shows that the retail market in India is highly unorganized.

On the other side, the highly fragmented Indian retail system has poor traditional shops and operational inefficiencies, higher cost and overall poor price and service to the consumer. High income households are growing particularly in the urban areas, there by creating new business, employment opportunities and wealth.

Organized retailing has a huge potential for growth, leading to higher GDP contribution and also generate employment. It could also drive the transformation of agricultural supply chain, remove the inefficiencies in the distribution of consumer goods and improve overall labor productivity and employment. The consumers will be benefited with the quality of product and service with a competitive price and good ambience for shopping.

Marketers need to understand the existing scene in India before they invest in organized retailing here. Local kiranas are incorporating changes with time, and people still prefer to buy their daily commodities from them. As the spending capacity in rural areas is still low, organized retailing is concentrated only in the cities.

This gives rise to few queries:

- What's the impact of organized retailing on the major urban scene and what's its effect on the growing middle class?
- In turn what will be the effect on manufacturers, distributors and small retailers?
- What options will be followed by foreign investors-franchising or joint ventures?
- What precaution India as a country needs to take before going in for foreign investments?

Organized retailing with its creative and innovative nature has been attracting the average middle class consumers to large cities and has been providing them a new shopping experience. To encourage the development of retail trade, which is currently the largest contributor to our GDP, the current marketing environment needs to be improved. India's infrastructure needs to be improved in order to make the supply chain of products more efficient.

The retail scenario in India is unique. Present retailing activities and trends in India can be understood with the help of following observations:

- Retailing in India is largely unorganized. There is no supply chain management perspective. According to a survey by the global management consultancy AT Kearney, an overwhelming proportion of Rs.400,000 crore retail market is unorganized.
- Just over 8 per cent of India's population is engaged in retailing compared to 20 per cent in the United States.
- Given the size, and the geographical, cultural and socio-economic diversity of India, there is no role model for Indian suppliers and retailers to adopt or expand in the Indian context.
- The first challenge facing the organized retail industry in India is competition from the unorganized sector. Traditional retailing has established in India for some centuries. It is a low cost structure, mostly owner-operated, has negligible real estate and labour costs and little or no taxes to pay. Consumer familiarity that runs from generation to generation is one big advantage for the traditional retailing sector.
- In contrast, players in the organized sector have big expenses to meet, and yet have to keep prices low enough to be able to compete with the traditional sector. High costs for the organized sector arises from: higher labour costs, social security to employees, high quality real estate, much bigger premises, comfort facilities such as air-conditioning, back-up power supply, taxes etc. Organized retailing also has to cope with the middle class psychology that the bigger and brighter sales outlet is, the more expensive it will be.
- International retail majors such as Benetton, Dairy Farm and Levis have already entered the market. Lifestyles in India are changing and the concept of "value for money" is picking up.

Examples of Organised Retailers

Wal-Mart is the world's largest retailer with over 3000 stores in the US. **Carrefour** meaning crossroads in French is the single largest retailer in Europe and the second largest in the world.

Royal Ahold is the third largest with several chains throughout Europe, Asia and North/South America and has its headquarters in the Netherlands.

In India, apart from **Pantaloon**, some of the well-known retailers include the **RPG** group, **K Raheja (Shoppers' Stop), Tata (Trent, Westside and Star India Bazaar)**, and the Landmark group. Organized retailing is more visible in urban areas because of people's high aspirations, their high purchasing power and splurging habits due to rising incomes. Availability of everything under one roof has fueled the growth of organized retailing--- the one stop shop has revolutionized the retailing sector. Quality, building trust, genuine material, good consumer care, and prompt after sales service are some of the main reasons which differentiate traditional stores from modern retail stores.

India's first true shopping mall—complete with food courts, recreation facilities and large car parking space was inaugurated as lately as in 1999 in Mumbai known as "Crossroads".

Factors Responsible for Changes in Retailing

Retailing in India is undergoing several changes. It is becoming more important. New retail formats are emerging. Although earlier retail sector was highly unorganized, today organized retailing is growing rapidly. There has been significant evolution in Indian consumer and increasing awareness of consumer movement over the last decade.

The factors responsible for changes in retailing in India are discussed below:

- Rising incomes
- Consumer pull and change in consumer behaviour
- Explosion of media
- Awareness of consumer rights, consumer movement
- Demographic shifts and increasing urbanization
- Emergence of hubs of retail activity
- Entry of corporate sector

- Entry of foreign retailers
- Expansion of family-owned business
- Technological impact

Retailing Facts

- **Number of Retailers:** India has about 78 per cent of small businesses utilizing only household labour. There are only 14 companies that run department stores and two with hypermarkets, while the number of businesses operating supermarkets is higher most of these had only one outlet. The number of companies with supermarket chains was less than 10.
- **Retail Sales:** In a developing country like India, a large portion of consumer expenditure is on basic necessities; especially food, beverages and tobacco accounted for as much as 71 per cent of retail sales in 2002. The remaining 29 per cent of retail sales are non-food items. Sales through supermarkets and department stores are small compared with overall retail sales. This high acceleration in sales through modern retail formats is expected to continue during the next few years with the rapid growth in numbers of such outlets in response to consumer demand and business potential.
- **Government Policy:** There has been vigorous opposition to foreign direct investment (FDI) in retailing from small traders who fear that foreign retailing companies would take away their business, lead to the closure of many small trading businesses and result in considerable unemployment. In order to safeguard the small trading community, Government has laid down certain regulations on FDI.
- **Organizational Characteristics:** For Indian retail sector, the organizational characteristics of retail enterprises are very basic in nature. Most of them belong to independent enterprises in the form of small family businesses. Economic liberalization, competition and foreign investment since the 1990s led to a proliferation of brands with both foreign and Indian companies acquiring a strong brand equity for their

products. Hence franchising emerged as a popular mode of retailing. Sales of franchises grew at a rapid pace of 14 per cent per annum over the review period. In 2002, there were over 5,000 franchised outlets. The other major retailing organization format is multiples, known as "chain stores" in India. In 2002, there were about 1,800 chain stores.

Strategies at Different Phases

A strategy in would mean the plan or the method by which an organization wishes to achieve its objectives. At the beginning, the retailers opt for low-end strategy and serve to price sensitive customers. They may use market penetration strategy, targeting a mass audience with the lower prices. Price sensitive customers are not loyal and they can switch to other retailers with still lower prices. Hence, when the retailers move to next phase, they open doors to many new entrants offering lower prices.

At the second stage, when they reach to trading-up phase, they go for medium strategy i.e. prices are moderate, facilities are improved, and they too serve value-and-service conscious customers. They try to gain customers that are more loyal.

At the maturity stage, they use high-end strategy. They offer excellent services and facilities. The prices are high and hence there is no room for price conscious customers. Prestige conscious customers like shopping at the retailers with high-end strategies. The retailers use market skimming strategy by serving quality, prestige conscious and valued customers. Number of customers is relatively less compared to that which are served at the first two phases.

Thus, retailer passes through these three phases and move in clockwise direction. The best example would be of the change from corner shop to supermarket because of the price vulnerability.

Example: In the 1950s, **McDonald's** and **Burger King** had very limited menus of hamburgers and French fries. Most stores had no inside seating for customers. Over time, these chains changed by altering their stores expanding their menus. Today,

McDonald's has expanded its menu by offering varieties in pizza. The store aesthetics and atmosphere have changed tremendously and thus attracting more number of status conscious, hygiene conscious customers.

Emerging Retail Strategies

Since it is difficult to categorize retailers solely by one type of merchandise they carry, it is useful to view store types in terms of their basic strategy mix. However there are two strategies used that is low-end and high-end strategy, there are usually an assortment of firms that attempt to operate between the two extremes.

For example, in general merchandise retailing, department stores have moderately to extremely good quality, they also provide significant sales assistance, credit, delivery and other services in a store atmosphere that is spacious and visually appealing.

Supermarkets provide a further example of a differential retail strategy. The Bureau of the Census identifies six different supermarket store categories.

Superspeciality Strategy: These stores are generally small in size and very narrow in merchandise line offering. Their strategy revolves around meeting customers' need in one of the two ways:

- Offering a broad, deep selection within a very limited product category.
- Catering to very narrowly defined market segments.

Mass Merchandising: While some retailers will follow a "superspecialist" strategy, others select the opposite approach. As consumers continue to place high value on convenience and time saving in shopping, very large stores that combine apparel, household items, electronics, hard goods, and in some cases, food continue to grow.

Example: Wal-Mart and K mart.

Discounting Strategies: Discounting as a strategy continues to grow, often in combination with other retail strategies. Two distinct discounting strategies have emerged.

- One approach features frequent promotions and reduced-price "sales" in the store.
- Another approach, known as the "everyday low price" approach, features a consistent day in, day out low price but few promotions or "sales" events.

Example: K.K. Bazaar and Mega Mart are known as discount stores, whereas Mantra and Tru Mart offer consistently low prices.

Focused Service: The key to this strategy is defining service in terms that are meaningful to a particular group of customers. The specific services offered may differ by retailing format, but the service focus strategy has been successful for many firms that have determined characteristics leading to customer satisfaction.

Example: Mantra, Tru Mart offer free home delivery services to its customers, Tru Mart also offers membership cards to its regular customers by ensuring a 5 per cent discount on the total sales procured by them between 25th to 10th of every month and add on points on the other days.

Direct Retailing: Direct retailing includes the traditional mail-order business as well as telephone shopping, vending, and the more recent electronic formats such as television's Home Shopping Network. The consumer's increasing desire for conveniences at the root of the success of direct retailing.

The Threat of Retail

An eminent threat for the industry, is the emergence of organized retail, retailers give huge discounts to consumers specially on the consumer electronic goods in order to win over the consumers. Ireena Vittal, Principal, McKinsey points out another trend that is of launching their own store brands.

Example: Electronic Bazaar, the consumer electronics division of the retail chain Big Bazaar, has started importing air conditioners and microwave ovens from China and is selling them, under the brand name Koryo, at prices that are over 40 per cent cheaper than those of companies products. Initial response to these products have been good says Kishore Biyani of Big Bazaar and they intend to import more products like TV and washing machines soon.

The challenges faced by the retail industry are the large-scale availability and feasibility of retail real estate, availability of trained manpower, financing etc. Another big challenge faced by the organized sector is the competition from the unorganized sector. Although, facilities are given by the organized sector to the consumer, retailers have to concentrate o supply chain in proper way.

Future of Retail

The Retail sector opens up opportunities for the growth of other sectors too which are related and support retailing i.e. Logistics, It, FMCG, which will eventually find more shelf space and tremendous employment opportunities across all sectors of the economy. The retailing sector also opens up education opportunities with many teaching Institutes designing courses leading to standard qualification and thereby jobs in the emerging retail sector.

The local big names about to make a splash in the ertai sector include the Reliance group, Birla's, Tata's, the Mittal's and almost all the eminent industrialists and businessmen. And amongst the global players it is Walmat, J.C. Penny, Costa coffee and Dixy Chicken, Carrefour and Tesco, to name a few who are awaiting Government FDI approval and the regulatory feasibility to make a foray in the Indian retail revolution.

Ethics are cornerstone of business success in general and marketing in particular. We must be sure that ethical behavior should in itself be rewarding one day or the other. Business is an internal part of society and Major Avenue of employment and livelihood. For our youth, value based business can herald piece and prosperity for the future. Companies may also appoint ethical advisors to guide its employees about right conduct.

References

Bhattacharya S.K. (1989), Achieving Managerial Excellence- Insight from Organization, Macmillan.

Charaporty S.K (1995) Human Values for Management.

Chonki, Lawrence B, "Ethical Decision-making in Marketing", Sage Publication, California, 1995.

Indian Management, Business India Group publication, vol. 38, no. 10 and 11,October-November, 1999.

Kotler Philip-Marketing Management, Analysis, Planning, Implementation and Control.

Lakue Tone Homer (1995) - The Ethics of Management.

Murray, David, "Ethics in Organization"- Kogan Page Ltd., London, 1997.

Parekh. D. "The Business Ethics" in Indian Management.

Peters. T. J and RH Waterman Jr. 1982 in Search of Excellence.

Schiffman L G and Kanuk L- (1997) Consumer Behavior.

11

Role of FDI in Retail Sector of India

Mohd. Mujahed Ali and Shaik Masood

Retailing is a very important part of the distribution process; it is the last link in the chain and a direct interface of the process with the customer. In the words Philip Kotler retailing is all about the activities involved in selling goods or services to the final customer for personal use. In today's scenario retailer is not static like a brick and mortar form, as it is much more dynamic as we do the business by using the telephone, direct mails, using television in the form of teleshopping networks, e-mails, through Internet or absolutely impersonally by vending machines to secure the customer and skim the cream of the market.

In the light of changing business environment, the Indian retail segment has started contributing 20 percent to GDP, but it remains one of the most unorganized sectors in the country with less than 3 percent that offers huge opportunities for Indian economy. Moreover a joint report by McKinsey and the Confederation of Indian Industry (CII) has pegged the Indian retail market at US$ 180 billion, and it adds that the market is growing at a steady rate of 11 to 12 per cent and which accounts for around 10 per cent of the country's GDP.

Success in Retail Operations

Retailing includes all the activities involve in selling goods or services directly to final consumer for personal non-business use. The various type of retail organization were consumer can shop for goods and services are

- Store retailer
- Non store retailer
- Retail organization

Success in retail operation is governed largely by two parameters margins and turnover.

A retailing organization must be strong in at least of these parameters. But in real the retail enterprise will be a low margin one, or a high margin one, or a low turnover one, or a high turnover one depends in a basic sense on the nature of the products or items handles.

Ronald Gist has provided an easy to follow conceptual framework of retail structures by using the margin and turnover as parameter. According to him the retailing operation of the organization may fall in one or other four quadrants, which was prepared by him. L.L. signifies low position on both margin and turnover. H.L. signifies a high margin but low turnover position. And H.H. signifies high margin and turnover position and L.H. signifies low margin and high turnover position of the organization.

Low-margin, High-turnover Stores: The low margin high turnover operations assume that low price is the most important determinant the store in this category they price their products below the market. In all their marketing communication they emphasis the price, they provide very few services and wherever they do so, they are usually optional and are provided at extra charge here customer "Buy" products rather than the store selling them.

High-margin, Low-turnover stores: The high margin and low turnover operations assume that services distinctive merchandise and sales approvals are the most important patronage determinants. The stores in this category price their products above the markets. These stores provide many services and sell select categories of products. Here the store is located in a downtown area or a major shopping center in a good cluster, in proximity to other institutions.

High-margin, High-turnover Stores: These stores stock a narrow line of item, which turnover rapidly. Typically they are located in a non-commercial location but in proximity to a major thoroughfare. Because of locational convenience, they can charge above market prices. Overhead costs may be high because of the long hours the store is open. Moreover the lack of large volume requires that the store charge above market prices to ensure profitability.

Low-margin, Low-turnover Stores: Outlets ion this category are the once that have been forced by prices competition to maintain low margin at the same time they do not sell high volume, may because of poor location, or incompetent management, or under capitalization. The turnover also will be poor here. As a combined result of the low margin and the low turnover, this types of outlet is a candidate for bankruptcy

Corporate Retailing

Corporate retail organizations achieve economies of scale, greater purchasing power, wider grand recognition, and better-trained employees. The major types of corporate retailing are:

Corporate Chain Store: Two or more outlets owned and controlled, employing central buying and merchandising, and selling similar lines of merchandise.

Voluntary Chain: A wholesale sponsored group of independent retail or engaged in bulk buying and common merchandising.

Retail Co-operative: Independent retailers using a central buying organization and joint promotion efforts.

Consumer Co-operatives: A retail firm owned by its customer members contributes money to open their own store, vote on its policies, elect a group to manage it and receive dividends.

Franchise Organization: Contractual associations between a franchiser and franchises, popular in a number of products and service areas.

Merchandising Conglomerate: A corporation that combines several diversified retailing lines and form under central ownership, with same integration of distribution and management.

Indian Government's Policy towards Foreign Capital

At the time of independence, the attitude towards foreign

capital was one of fear and suspicion. This was natural on account of the previous exploitative role-played by it in 'draining away' resources from this country. But in the developing countries capital is very important to exploit the resources, which they have, so foreign capital plays an important role in developing the nation. Now we see what are various forms of components of foreign capital.

Components of Foreign Capital: Foreign capital takes two main forms

- Private foreign investment and
- Foreign aid.

Private Foreign Investment can either be direct foreign investment or indirect foreign investment. As far as the direct foreign investment is concerned, the private foreign investor either sets up a branch or a subsidiary in the recipient country. Of particular importance has been the increasing role being played by the multi national corporations (MNCs) in the under developed countries. These corporations have set up a large number of branches and subsidiaries in these countries and have brought with them new technological expertise, machinery and equipment, better management and organization, superior marketing techniques etc. In fact, this is the main advantage direct foreign investment.

Indirect foreign investment or portfolio investment takes place when the nationals of one-country purchase shares or debentures floated by industries in some other country. The government of India presents data on foreign investment in the following categories (1) direct investment comprising a) investment as approved by SIA (secretariat for industrial approvals) and FIPD (foreign investment promotion board), b) investment as approved by reserve bank of India, and c) investment by Non resident Indians (NRIs), and (2) Portfolio investment comprising a) GDRs (global depository receipts), b) investment by FIIs (foreign institutional investors), and c) off-shore funds and others

Foreign aid can be defined to include "all official grants and concessional loans, in currency or in kind, which are broadly aimed at transferring resources from developed to less developed nations on developmental and/ or income distributional ground". The chief characteristic of such aid is that it is made available on concessional terms so that the interest rate is lower and the grace and maturity periods are longer. A small part of such aid is made available in the form of grants, which do not carry any obligation of repayment. Foreign aid (in the form of grant and loans) is made available either by foreign governments or foundation or international agencies like the international development association, World Bank, international monetary fund, etc.

In addition to grants and concessional loans, underdeveloped countries can also receive direct supplies of agricultural commodities (food grains, etc.) or industrial raw materials to face temporary shortages in the economy. The principal element in this form of aid is the U.S. contribution of surplus farm products under the provisions of public law 480. The developed countries also make aid in the form of technical assistance available.

Need for Foreign Capital

The section on the "Need for foreign capital" and the "reasons for the growth of MNCs " mention some advantages of private foreign investment as well. In this section we proposed to highlight some specific advantages of private foreign investment. These are as under:

1. Private foreign investment goes directly into capital formation and thus it constitutes a net addition to investible resources in the recipient country. Thus it helps in pushing up the rate of growth of the economy.
2. Being subject to business calculation of private profit it is likely to be employed more productively as compare to public financial aid.
3. When made available in the form of direct business investment (as in the case of investment by MNCs) foreign private investment promotes the spread of modern technology and efficient management methods.

4. Foreign investment may also induce more domestic investment. For instance, and ancillary domestic units can be set up to "feed " the main industrial unit set up by the foreign investor
5. By setting and example, and through the training that they sponsor, foreign direct investments (as by MNCs) contribute to the transfer of technology to the under developed countries and in encouraging the growth of skills.
6. Since returns on foreign investment are linked to the profits earned by the firm it is more "flexible" as compared to foreign loans, which are guided by rigid interest and amortization requirements.
7. Foreign investment results in a pattern of growth that is desirable from the point of view of under developed countries since new products are introduced and marketed, new tastes are created, and specific needs of the recipient country are met.
8. Free flow of capital is conducive both to total world welfare and to the welfare of each individual country. The operations of foreign firms, especially of modern multinational firms, knit countries together and closer into the web of international commerce both by (internal and horizontal) economic integration and by the transmission of tastes, design, ideas and technology.

Foreign Investment Flows

To understand how the recent changes in foreign investment policy have influenced the economy, quantitative information is needed on broad dimensions of the investment across industries, regions and by size of projects, firms and industry level production accounts and audited financial statements. Table 11.1 provides us the information relating to the direct investments and portfolio investment, of the total foreign investment inflows into the country.

As it is clear from the Table 11.1, there has been massive increase in foreign investment inflows into the country since

1991-92 from US$ 133 million in 1991-92, and rose to US$ 4153 million in 1993-94, i.e. just a span of two years basically due to rapid increase in portfolio investment. Foreign investment inflows reached a peak of US$ 6133 million in 1996-97 because of impressive increase in both FDI and portfolio investment but declined thereafter. In 1998-99, there was an outflow of funds amounting to US$ 390 million by FIIs with their result that overall portfolio investment was negative. However portfolio investment recovered strongly in the very next year to US$ 3,026 million.

Table 11.1: Foreign Investment Flows into India

(US$ million)

Year	Direct Investment	Portfolio Investment	Total Foreign Investment
1991-92	129	4	133
1993-94	586	3,567	4,153
1998-99	2,462	-61	2,401
1999-00	2,155	326	5,181
2000-01	4,029	2,760	6,789
2001-02	6,131	2,021	8,152
2002-03	5,035	979	6,014
2003-04	4,673	11,377	16,050
2004-05	5,652	9,315	14,967
2005-06	7,751	12,492	20,243

Source: Government of India, *Economic Survey* (various years).

As stated above higher levels of FDI witnessed since 2000-01 are partly due to the revised definition of FDI. In terms of revised definition, FDI rose to US$ 4,029 million in 2000-01 and further to US$ 5,035 in 2002-03 and further it has increased to US$ 5,652 million in 2004-05 and further it has increased to US$ 7,751 million in the 2005-06. And the portfolio investment has also taken a massive increase when compare to 1999-2000 which was US$ 326 million and has increased to US$ 12492 million in 2005-06 which shows the foreign investor confidence in the Indian economy.

Retail Business Scenario at Global Level

Retail is such a part of everyday life that people often take it for granted, but it is one of the fastest changing, most dynamic industries in the world today.

Today, perhaps more than ever before, retailing is a mirror of society. The diversity, variety & change in society offer an opportunity for retailers to respond and succeed.

Retailing globally is far more organized than when we compare to Asia. In United States and Europe the majority of the retail sector is organized and in Asia only 20 percent is being organized retail sector in Malaysia, Thailand and China. And in India it is very low organized retailing. To have a clear understanding of the organized sector of retail industry, Table 11.2 is given below.

Table 11.2: Retail Business Scenario at Global level

Country	Organised Retail Sector (per cent)
United States	80
Western Europe	70
Brazil and Argentina	40
Korea and Taiwan	35
Malaysia, Thailand and China	20
India	4

Retail Industry in the Indian Economy

India is witnessing an unprecedented consumption boom. The economy is growing between 7 and 9 percent and the resulting improvements in income dynamics along with factors like favorable demographics and spending patterns are driving the consumption demand.

Indian Retail Industry is ranked among the ten largest retail markets in the world. The attitudinal shift of the Indian consumer in terms of "Choice Preference", "Value for Money" and the emergence of organized retail formats has transformed the face of

Retailing in India. The Indian retail industry is currently estimated to be a US$ 200 billion industry and organized Retailing comprises of 3 per cent (or) US$ 6.4 billion of the retail industry. With a growth over 20 percent per annum over the last 5 years, organized retailing is projected to reach US $ 23 billion by 2010.

The Indian retail industry though predominantly fragmented through the owner -run " Mom and Pop Outlets" has been witnessing the emergence of a few medium sized Indian retail chains, namely Pantaloon Retail, RPG Retail, Shoppers' Stop, Westside (Tata Group) and Lifestyle International.

Given the attractiveness of the Indian retail sector, foreign retailers like Wal-Mart, Carrefour SA, Europe's largest retailer and Tesco Plc, the UK's largest retailer, were keen to enter this growing market, despite the Indian retail sector being closed to foreign direct investment (FDI). In February 2006, the Indian Government had announced its decision to allow FDI of up to 51 per cent in single brand retailing. Wal-Mart had said that India was high on its priority and that it was closely monitoring the Government's policy on FDI in the retail sector.

In the last few years, Indians have gone through a dramatic transformation in lifestyle by moving from traditional spending on food, groceries and clothing to lifestyle categories that deliver better quality and taste. Modern retailing satisfies rising demand for such goods and services with many players entering the bandwagon in an attempt to tap greater opportunities.

Conclusion

India in present context to meet the Global standards may allow to bring in FDIs in retail sector to open their own showrooms and stores through franchising, but the Government of India should develop policies have to safeguards and ensure livelihood of a large section of small traders and shopkeepers in the domestic market through location restrictions, allowing foreign investors in retail to operate only in big cities. On the other hand, banks may soon be allowed to use business correspondents for disbursal of credit and collection of interest in the rural sector.

Organized retail industry is the indicator for the development of a particular Nation. When new see our country where only 4 per cent of the retail industry is organized and remaining 96 per cent of the retailing is dominated by small out lets. Where we can observe that there is a great potentiality in our country for the organized retail industry

India has a strong manufacturing base in consumer durables, so the FDIs in retail market are not a panic towards devastate of small businesses. Similarly, we need to accept FDI flows into retail market on account of evolving consumer demands and lifestyles, shortage of retail space and global competition has made FDI in retail inevitable perhaps. So we have to welcome big retailers like Wal-Mart and others like China to bring in opportunities of employment and give a boost to our exports too.

12

Indian Retail Industry: Trends and Challenges

G. Deepika and Sowmya Katyayini

Retailing in India is set for a big leap. Retailing is the industry of the future in India. The rise in double income families lending to higher disposable incomes and fuelled by economic growth has lead to a significant life style change and spending patterns of customers. Today, customers are increasingly becoming brand conscious and view shopping not as a routine chore but one, which is to be enjoyed and experienced. Retailing has seen such a transformation over the past decade that today retailing has changed from selling a product or a service to selling a hope, an aspiration and above all an experience that a consumer would like to repeat. Favorable demographic and psychographic changes relating to India's consumer class, international exposure, availability of increasing quality retail space, wider availability of products and brand communication are some of the factors that are driving the retail in India. Over the last few years, many international retailers have entered the Indian market on the strength of rising affluence levels of the young Indian population along with the heightened awareness of global brands and international shopping experiences and the increased availability of retail real estate space.

Introduction

During the late 1990s, Indian retailers underwent an experimentation phase when new formats (department stores like Shoppers' Stop & Pantaloon) and product categories (like consumer durables retailing, music retailing etc) were introduced. As the country marched into the new millennium, the organised retailing scenario began to stabilize, especially over the last 3-4 years when players like Big Bazaar, Barista, Pizza Hut, Shoppers' Stop etc became successful in establishing a national footprint. This was also the stage when international retailers like McDonald's, Subway etc adopted a mix of global and India-specific strategies in order to entice the local population. Most of the global powerhouses in the retailing sector such as Wal-Mart, Carrefour, Tesco etc have adopted multi-format and multi-product strategies in order to customize their product offering for distinct target segments. Similar trends are likely to be exhibited in India as all formats present prospects for growth.

Retail industry in India is greatly fragmented comparing to the developed and other developing countries. This presents enormous prospective for the structured retail industry to flourish throughout the country, as the market for the final product is huge. Organized retailing which now accounts for three percent out of the total retailing is predicted to extend to 10 per cent by the year 2010. In other means, organized Indian retail sector would triple its share of the total market within the coming four years, generating new 8mn jobs, in addition to the 21 mn jobs that are already created by retail sector.

Present Scenario

Indian consumers are rapidly evolving and accepting modern formats overwhelmingly. Retail Space is no more a constraint for growth. Retailers and suppliers/brands world-wide are willing to partner with retailers here. Further, large Indian corporate groups like Tata, Reliance, Raheja, ITC, Bombay Dyeing, Murugappa & Piramal Groups etc and also foreign investors and private equity players are firming up plans to identify investment opportunities in the Indian retail sector. The quantum of investments is likely to sky-rocket as the inherent attractiveness of the segment lures more and more investors to earn large profits. Investments into the sector are estimated at Rs. 20-25 billion in the next 2-3 years, and over Rs. 200 billion by end of 2010.

The following statistics reflect the Indian retailing scenario:

- New entrants: Reliance Retail and Bharti Enterprises
- Established retailers: Pantaloon Retail, Shoppers' Stop, Spencer's, HyperCITY, Lifestyle, Trent.
- An estimated US$ 412 billion is likely to be invested in the retail sector over the next five years.
- Food, beverages and tobacco make up 40 per cent of the retail sector.
- The organized food retail sector is estimated to be worth US$ 666 million and likely to reach US$ 33.3 billion by 2015.
- Branded apparel segment is estimated to be worth US$ 422 million and is growing strongly at 20 per cent annually.
- Major metro's such as Mumbai, Delhi, Chennai, Kolkata, Bangalore and Hyderabad is where 68 per cent of organized retail is located.
- There will be an estimated 220 malls by 2007, a significant rise from 30 in 2003. Current lease rates in major cites vary from Rs. 88-120 per sq ft per month.
- India's retail industry is the 2nd largest employer, after the agriculture sector, employing 21 mn people, roughly 6 per cent of the country's total workforce and contributes 13 per cent of the GDP.
- Foreign companies are permitted to hold only 51 per cent of equity in a single brand format only, whose products are sold under the same brand internationally.

Changing Prospects

The last few years have seen rapid transformation in many areas and setting scalable and profitable retail models across categories. Suddenly, retail is big business and big news. Reliance has recently opened its retail stores in Hyderabad, and conglomerates such as Godrej, Mahindra and ITC are all foraying into the retail sector. India has been rated as the second most attractive retail destination, coming, surprisingly, after Russia and ahead of China. The retail market has been sized at around INRI0 lakh crore, and surprisingly only about 3-5 percent is in the organised sector. The rest is in the form of local kirana shops and street vendors. This is the segment that will see a metamorphosis.

Traditionally, around 80 percent of our spending is on clothing, food, durables, footwear and catering. The main driver here is the agricultural sector, which is seeing a revolution of sorts. Agricultural production is valued at around Rs. 7 lakh crore and is purely in the unorganised sector. Big industrial houses are concentrating on leveraging this sector's potential and bringing it to the consumer. This is being done by cutting intermediary costs and finally delivering better quality produce at a lower price - a winning combination when dealing with the discerning consumer. The strategy is two-fold: forge strong backward linkages with the farm through contract/corporate farming, and produce better quality of produce while eliminating the middlemen (there could be up to between four and six such layers in traditional agriculture) and deliver superior products at a lower price. Combine that with the malls that provide the glamour quotient to an otherwise ordinary shopping experience.

Consumerism: The New Wave

Growing consumerism would be a key driver for organised retail in India. Several demographic indicators show favourable trends for the growth of organised trade as below:

- Rapid income growth: consumers have a greater ability to spend.
- Increasing urbanisation: larger urban populations that value convenience, coupled with the higher propensity of the urban consumer to spend.
- Growing young population: growth of the post-liberalisation maturing population, with the attitude and willingness to spend.
- Spend now vs. save earlier: consumers are willing to borrow for present consumption.

Size of the Opportunity

Research done by the Tata Strategic Management Group (TSMG) indicates that over the next 10 years, the total retail market in India is likely to grow at a compounded annual growth rate (CAGR) of 5.5 per cent (at constant prices) to US$ 374 billion (Rs. 16,77 ,000 crore) in 2015. The organised retail market is expected to grow much faster, at a CAGR of 21.8 per cent to US$ 55 billion (Rs. 2,46,000 crore) in the same time frame, garnering around 15 per cent of overall retail sales. Based on our projections, the top five organised retail categories by 2015 would be food, grocery and general merchandise, apparel, durables, food service, and home improvement.

Retailing Trends in India

Organised trade in India is very underdeveloped when compared with other emerging markets in Asia, Latin America and Eastern Europe. Figures show that developed markets like the US are far, far ahead. There are a few key trends that one observes in international markets that have a bearing on India.

- **Convenience stores and hypermarkets are gaining prominence:** These are driven by a consumer need for convenience and lower prices/higher value in mass categories. While supermarkets may emerge at the initial stages of retail market development, in the long term they are unable to match the consumer value proposition of convenience stores and hypermarkets.
- **Private label products become increasingly important:** Private labels today account for 17 per cent of global retail sales, with the highest share of 23 per cent in Europe and the lowest share of 4 per cent in Asia. Growing acceptance among consumers, increasing price competition, the need for differentiation among retailers and the ability to offer higher margins are the key factors contributing to the growth of private labels. Private labels provide the retailer an ability to offer a significant price advantage to consumers, their prices being 16 to 32 per cent lower than manufacturers' brands .
- **Smaller towns to face retail boom:** With consumption in metros already being exploited, manufacturers and retailers of products such as personal computers, mobile phones,

automobiles, consumer durables, financial services etc are increasingly targeting consumers in smaller cities and towns. In addition, petro-retailing efforts of petroleum giants scattered throughout the country's landscape have also ensured that smaller towns are also exposed to modern retailing formats.

On the supply side, mall development activity in the small towns is also picking up at a rapid pace, thereby, creating quality space for retailers to fulfill their aggressive expansion plans. Thus, the 'retail boom', 85 per cent of which has so far been concentrated in the metros is beginning to percolate down to smaller cities and towns. The contribution of these cities to total organized retailing sales is expected to grow to 20-25 per cent.

India: A Sourcing Hub

Development of India as a sourcing hub shall further make India as an attractive retail opportunity for the global retailers. Retailers like Wal-Mart, GAP, Tesco, J.C. Penney, H&M, Karstadt-Quelle etc. stepping up their sourcing requirements from India and moving from third-party buying offices to establishing their own wholly owned/wholly managed sourcing & buying offices shall further make India as an attractive retail opportunity for the global players. Buying volumes for many of these players are already in the range of Rs. 10-20 billion per year, with reported plans to step up to Rs. 100-150 billion within the next 3-4 years .

Retail Opportunities in Diverse Product Categories: Through lucrative opportunities exist across product categories, food and grocery, nevertheless, presents the significant potential in the Indian context as consumer spending is highest on food. Further, 'wet groceries' i.e. fresh fruits and vegetables is the most promising segment within food and grocery as very few organized retailers have tapped this opportunity in spite of wet groceries being the preferred choice of most Indian households.

The next level of opportunities in terms product retail expansion lies in categories such as apparel, jewellery and accessories, consumer durables, catering services and home improvement. These sectors have already witnessed the emergence of organized formats though more players are expected to join the bandwagon. Some of the niche categories like Books, Music and Gifts offer interesting opportunities for the retail players.

Changing Perception: Manufacturers in industries such as FMCG, consumer durables, paints etc are waking up to the growing clout of the retailers as a shift in bargaining power from the former to the latter becomes more discernible. Already, a number of manufacturers in India, in line with trends in developed markets, have set up dedicated units to service the retail channel. Also, instead of viewing retailers with suspicion, or as a 'necessary evil' as was the case earlier, manufacturers are beginning to acknowledge them as channel members to be partnered with for providing solutions to the end-consumer more effectively.

Challenges Ahead

However there are challenges on the way ahead. For one, retail still does not enjoy an industry status. There are still not many players in the organized retail sector, lack of skilled work force coupled with the fact that there are few takers for jobs in retailing makes it difficult to manage retail operations. Companies are tackling this by investing heavily in training programmes. There is also resistance from the unorganized sector, which feels that their very survival is threatened with the entry of organized retail chains. There is need to understand and react to the spending habits and cultural and regional diversity of the country while formulating retail strategies.

Although there is enormous scope for retailing in the urban and the rural market, manufacturers and service providers will also increasingly face a host of specialist retailers, who are characterized by use of modern management techniques, backed with seemingly unlimited financial resources. Organized retail too has opportunities but faces challenges in terms of product categories that it can profitably offer.

Indian retailing, though enjoys many unique features, is still done in a primitive way. Barring a few exceptions, Indian retailers, particularly FMCG retailers, are not in a position to implement world class practices of supply chain management. The concepts of Quick Response (QR) or Efficient Consumer Response (ECR) are unheard of in Indian retailing. The two bases of modern retailing management, the Electronic Data Interface (ED I) and better partnership among the channel members are essential for implementing these concepts. QR, in fact, helps in reducing lead-time between the order placement (by the retailer) and merchandise delivery. The very concept revolves around quick transmission of order and execution of the same in the minimum possible time. ECR is one step forward and links the consumers' demands and preferences with the QR network. In the whole process the retailer increases service outputs in terms of lower inventory coupled with negligible waiting time, and higher assortments and variety. To achieve this level of sophistication Indian Industry will have to fulfill the following musts -

- Retailer level computerisation including Electronic Point of Sales (EPOS)
- Supplier (manufacturer) level facilitation
- Computerisation of all Distribution Centers (DC), including other members of the channel.
- On-line link among all the institutions mentioned above.

Retailer level computerisation would ensure EDI between the Electronic Point of Sale (EPOS) and the server installed in the outlet. The front line Electronic Tracking Facility like scanners makes this easier. The outlet level server then is linked to the Distribution Centers (either owned by the retailer or by other agencies). DCs in turn are connected to the suppliers' Servers. This requires very complex software along with a very efficient hardware. There would be constant information flow in the network. Whenever there is any situation, which warrants action, this network takes necessary steps in this regard. Since every member is linked both ways to each other, the efficiency of the total system depends upon individual efficiency of the members.

Now that Indian business houses are ready to go on-line intermittently, apart from a few giant manufacturers like Hindustan Lever Limited, very few are exploiting the unlimited features of the technology beyond a certain level. However, the trend is getting in and many of the organisations at various levels are trying to use information technology in their day-to-day business. Nevertheless, the Indian retailing will take many years to go fully on-line which their counterpart W al- Mart of US had achieved even before 1992.

Infrastructure bottleneck is another area of concern in Supply Chain Management. Indian road and railways are nowhere comparable to the international standard. Therefore, the real time taken in execution of an order cycle is much more in India than its developed counterparts. Wal-Mart completes the order cycle in less than 36 hours, whereas any Indian company will definitely take days to complete a big order cycle.

Use of credit card is still scarce in the Indian economy. Apart from the metros and some big cities the infrastructure to handle magnetic card is not present at all. This would make customer tracking difficult and almost impossible, besides other difficulties associated with implementation of full EPOS systems. Even if the plastic money is available liberally, only the high end of the market is expected to use this in a day-to-day basis. Thus a large number of Indian retailer's customer would never use this.

To make Indian retailing world class many a challenges are to be overcome by the industry. Some suggestions to improve the situation are offered below.

- Use of technology to the greatest extent possible may help strengthening the retailer's position in the marketing channel. First step may be taken with setting up of a network of independent firms believing in use of technology for business excellence. Then a collection of strong retail organisations may pressurize the suppliers and other channel members to use compatible technology. This may open the door for implementation of QR or ECR or other relevant concepts for the retailers.

- An overall change is to bring about in the mindset of the retailers. They will have to think differently.
- They must find out and satisfy service outputs of the target customers. Unless there is a drastic change in the mindset of at least large and medium retailers and as well as that of the manufacturers, the required change is not going to come by easily. The retailers must learn and understand to lead the chain from the front.
- Setting up of franchisee organisation may also help in strengthening the position of the retailers. The franchiser can exert a tremendous control over the way retailing is done. Transnational service organisation like McDonald and KFC are being able to offer a centralised control over purchase and operation. Large and medium sized retailers may take up the concept of franchising to reach the market in a more meaningful way. Though the management of franchisee network is difficult than managing a retail chain in view of high level of investment and other obligations, Indian retailers should spread out its wings in profitable and efficient way.
- Merger and buy-out of weak retailers by a stronger one, especially in metros and big cities may be another step towards this direction. This would give the new retailer the desired leverage to be world class.

Future Prospects

The analysts foresee bright future of the retail sector. A huge number of shopping malls, nearly 100, have come up 'in the recent past, generating 20mn sq ft. retail space, extending more space of about I2mn sq ft to it. Nearly 60 malls are on the verge of completion and may be operational by the end of current financial year. A forecasted number of nearly 200 malls, in a move to make additional 50mn sq ft of retail space, will be completed within the next two years.

Indian industrial group Reliance has made its foray into retailing, formally opening 11 stores in Hyderabad. Branded

"Reliance Fresh", they are part of a US$ 5bn project planned for more than 780 cities and 6,000 rural towns in India over the next five years. The company aims to open stores in the top 70 cities within the next two years and have sales of US$ 25bn by 2011.

Companies like Shoppers' Stop, Trent, Reliance, Lifestyle, Tanishq, Crossroads, Akbarallys' and Tanishq already have planned to invest over Rs. 5,000cr. Trent is on the edge to take both its brands 'Star India Bazaar' and 'Westside' to new cities, meanwhile Shoppers' Stop has recently geared up for expansion of present ones and to add 11 new stores including two hypermarkets. Also, Pantaloon has planned to add eight Big Bazaar malls within the next 6 to 8 months.

The global retail giants like Wal-Mart, Gap, Tesco, Versace, K-Mart/SEARS, Carrefour, ZARA, FCUK, Fendi, NEXT, Mother Care, IKEA, Trussardi, DKNY and Debenhams have made plans to march in the Indian market. ESPRIT, GUESS, Chanel, Mango and many other global players have marked their presence in India by implementing licensing and franchisee agreements. However, the current scenario has encouraged Indian players to speed up retail expansion and fresh retail ventures.

Implications for Indian Retailers

Global trends have important implications for Indian retailers. The Indian consumer is very value conscious; willing to spend money in most cases, but constantly cost conscious, evaluating every rupee spent. It is therefore imperative for retailers to offer a price advantage through sourcing and operational efficiency, as well as a strong private label programme to attract customers. Existing and new entrants need to achieve scale quickly to drive efficiencies in procurement, supply chain and marketing. Else, they risk being marginalised by larger players.

Real estate and human resources will be the critical drivers to build scale. While there are a few hundred malls under various stages of development across the country at present, retailers will also need to think out of the box to ensure the availability of real estate. This may include acquiring and developing the real estate themselves, rather than wait for mall development. Given the rising demand for retail real estate, retailers will need to take a long-term view on rentals and look at alternative options like ownership or very long leases. Retailers that invest in training will be able to ensure the availability of quality manpower in a rapidly growing market.

In conclusion, the retail market in India offers an opportunity for a large player to build a Rs. 40,000-crore retail business spanning multiple categories by 2015 (at current prices). Compared to this, the revenue of the largest Indian retailer, Pantaloon, grossed only Rs 1,085 crore in 2005. Little wonder, that large domestic business houses and international retailers have expressed a keen interest to enter the retail sector in India. To capitalise on the opportunity, however, players need to be aggressive in outlook and build scale quickly.

References

A. J. Lamba, The Art of Retailing, 1[5t] edition, TMH, 2003.

Andrew. J. Newmann & Petes Cullen, 1[5t] edition, Thomas Learning, 2003.

Barry Berman Joel & R. Evans, Retailing Management - A Strategic Approach, 8th edition, Pearson Education, 2002.

Effective Retail Promotion Management: Use of Point of Sale Information Resources", Vikalpa, Vol. 25 (4), pp. 51 - 59.

Gilbert: Retail Marketing Management, Pearson Education.

Purchase Planning Horizon", Decision, Vol. 28 (2), pp. 43 - 80.

13

Foreign Direct Investment (FDI) in Retail Sector

P. Krishnama Chary, Satyanarayana and Srikanth Verma

Introduction

The Indian retail sector is highly fragmented in nature and has the highest retail density in the world. A broad consumer base and an ever-increasing population have given the necessary push to the Indian retail industry to grow prodigiously. But the unorganized structure of the retailing was unable to tap the real potential of the Indian retail market. However, the continued economic development and the growing middle-class have fortified the position of organized retailing in the country. Retailing is an important segment of any economy, both in relation to GDP contribution and share in total employment. The segment is labor exhaustive and contributes considerably to raise the employment level. The opportunities and scope for more employment in retailing sector can't be over accentuated. Currently, retailing is a new concept for the Indian market and is largely disorganized. Only 3 per cent of the total retailing sector comes under organized retailing. With the shopping mall culture catching up in the metros and plans of around 150 new malls are to be launched by 2008, the retailing sector is poised to boom in the country.

By 2010, the Indian retail sector is anticipated to become a Rs. 12.5 percent market. The share of organized retailing is supposed to jump to about 10 per cent from the existing 3 per cent. The anticipated staggering growth in the organized retailing provides opportunities to both established and new players to expand in the market. These opportunities are, Development of successful and profitable retail formats; expansion beyond geographical boundaries and vertical integration.

The United Nations Conference on Trade and Development (UNCTAD) has said that India is among the "dominant host countries" for FDI in Asia and the Pacific (APAC). India attracted more than three times foreign investment at US$ 7.96 billion during the first half of 2005-06 fiscal, as against US$ 2.38 billion during the corresponding period of 2004-05. In a bid to stimulate the sector further, the government is working on a series of ambitious economic reforms. The Center has divested some of its own powers of proving foreign investments that it exercised through the Foreign Investment Promotion Board (FIPB) and has handed them over to the general permission route under the RBI. In this research paper an attempt has been made to develop on insight as to what are the trends in Indian Retail industry and to present opportunities and challenges of FDI in retail sector. Finally, to examine the impact of retail FDI on Indian economy.

Government Policy on FDI

The Indian government has clarified on a number of occasions that foreign direct investment will not be permitted in India. Major international retailer organizations will be watching for signals of policy change especially because China has permitted foreign investment in retail. In opening up the retail sector, the government may consider various approaches such as insisting on joint ventures, limiting the foreign stake, or specifying the cities areas where investment is permitted. Thailand's example shows that in case of joint ventures, the local partner can play a significant role in the success of the joint venture. The Brazilian experience shows that local retailing groups can successfully compete against international chains if they adopt innovations and restructure operations in accordance with market needs. Some policy protection can be given to consumer cooperatives, which have been providing value to their members and customers. This protection can be in the form of allowing these organizations to access capital from the local market and operate in a more professional manner. The government can also play a positive role in simplifying or eliminating the plethora of regulations governing retailing. Specific laws relating to franchising will also be desirable for foreign and Indian brand owners to adopt the franchise route in a bigger way.

The then Finance Minister Dr. Manmohan Singh had changed the law to permit FDI in retail trade. Dairy Farm, a multinational corporation entered India on that opening. But, the next Finance Minister, P Chidambaram, to curry favour with the Communists in the then United Front Government, changed the law again in 1996 to ban FDI in retail trade, but as with every Indian law there is a loophole by which foreign retailers can (and some do) operate in India through local franchises. Now, in 2005, the new United Progressive Alliance government is grappling with same question whether or not to permit FDI in retail trade. Should FDI in retail trade continue to be banned? The answer is obviously 'no,' especially, after the World Trade Organization's Doha Round of talks. The WTO mandate now requires that India lift the ban or face WTO's 'cross-retaliation' measures, such as withdrawal of tariff and trade privileges that are available to India under the new General Agreement on Tariffs and Trade. The cost of continuing with the ban is therefore prohibitive and, in any case, much more than what the Leftist Swadeshites claim as the consequences of lifting the ban. A cost-benefit analysis clearly points to saying 'yes' to FDI in retail trade. The Leftists and Swadeshites in India have been continuously crying wolf about foreign goods and funds. They are however ready to accept that foreigners can guide their ideology (e g, Karl Marx) or that foreign doctors may do their heart by-pass or knee replacements.

Now it is being said that allowing FDI in retail trade would destroy this commerce! Will it? A study by the Associated Chambers of Commerce of Industry of India, New Delhi, concluded that at least for the next ten years that will not happen. Thereafter, the present fragmented system may get phased out or evolved into more integrated networked units. This is already happening without FDI. For example, ready-made garments have displaced the family tailor (but not tailoring), horse buggies or tongas have made way for the automobiles (but not reduced travel), and dharamshalas have been replaced by hotels (but not the cuisine). Labour has been retrenched, but re-tooled and made more productive. That is what happened with development in Thailand, South Korea and now in China. The Government approved sweeping reforms in FDI with a first step towards partially opening retail markets to foreign investors. It will now allow 51 per cent FDI in single brand products in the retail sector. Besides retail, other sectors are being opened:

- 100 per cent allowed in new sectors such as power trading, processing and warehousing of coffee and rubber.
- FDI limit raised to 100 percent under automatic route in mining of diamonds and precious stones, development of new airports, cash and carry wholesale trading and export trading, laying of natural gas pipelines, petroleum infrastructure, captive mining of coal and lignite.
- Subject to other regulations, 100 percent FDI is allowed in distillation and brewing of potable alcohol, industrial explosives and hazardous chemicals.
- Indian investor allowed transferring shares in an existing company to foreign investors.
- Limit for telecom services firms rose to 74 per cent from 49 per cent.

Allowing FDI has resulted in lower prices to the consumer, more consumption and higher profit for the producer. FDI in retail trade has forced the wholesalers and food processors to improve, raised exports, and triggered growth by outsourcing supplies domestically. The availability of standardized products has also boosted tourism in these countries. Hence, time is now for us to shake off the last vestiges of Soviet-style socialism and comply happily with the WTO mandate to permit FDI in retail trade. The Indian consumer and the poor farmer will be the two biggest gainers from it. Thus we cannot allow the way we do things to remain frozen just because of the paranoia of the Left and

Swadeshites. We need a rational approach toward FDI in India's retail trade; in particular, how after it is permitted free access, it is subject to regulatory supervision.

Trends in the Indian Retail Sector

Retailing in India is receiving global recognition and attention and this emerging market is witnessing a significant change in its growth and investment pattern. It is not just the global players like Wal-Mart, Tesco and Metro group are eying to capture a pie of this market but also the domestic corporate behemoths like Reliance, KK Modi. Aditya Birla group, and Bharti group too are at some stage of retail development. Reliance, announced that it would invest $3.4 billion to become the country's largest modern retailer by establishing a chain of 1,575 stores by March 2007. The last couple of years have been rosy for real estate developers and the retailers are finding suitable retail space in prominent locations. The industry is buoyant about growth and the early starters are in expansion mood. There is increased sophistication in the shopping pattern of consumers, which has resulted in big retail chains coming up in most metros; mini metros and towns being the next target. Consumer taste and preferences are changing leading to radical alteration in lifestyles and spending patterns, which in turn is giving rise to new business opportunities. Companies need to be dynamic and proactive while responding to the ever-changing trends in consumer lifestyle and behavior.

Retailing in India is currently estimated to be a US$ 200 billion industry, of which organized retailing makes up 3 per cent or US$ 6.4 billion. By 2010, organized retail is projected to reach US$ 23 billion and in terms of market share it is expected to rise by 20 to 25 per cent. The report also predicts a stronger retailer growth than that of GDP in the coming five years.

The generic growth is likely to be driven by changing lifestyles and by strong surge in income, which in turn will be supported by favorable demographic patterns. Rapid growth in international quality retail space brings joy to shoppers and shopping malls are becoming increasingly common in large cities, and announced development plans project at least 150 new shopping malls by 2008. The number of department stores is growing at a much faster pace than overall retail, at 24 per cent annually. Supermarkets have been taking an increasing share of general food and grocery trade over the last two decades. Development of mega malls in India is adding new dimensions to the booming retail sector. Shopping experience in the nation of shopkeepers is changing and changing very fast. There is significant development in retail landscape not only in the metros but also in the smaller cities. Even ITC went one step ahead to revolutionize rural retail by developing 'Choupal Sagar' a rural mall. On one hand there are groups of visionary corporate working constantly to improve upon urban shopping experience and on the other hand some companies are trying to infuse innovative retail experience into the rural set up.

Global retail giants such as Wal-Mart, Tesco and Carrefour are all clamoring to enter the Indian retail market, even though the government does not allow foreign direct investment as yet. Over half of India's population of 1.1 billion is under 25 years of age with rising disposable incomes, making it a goldmine of opportunity. Landmark Group announced that it would be investing US$ 96.5 million in the next three years to increase its retail presence in India. The company operates three brands, Lifestyle, a departmental store chain; Max, a hypermarket chain and Home Centre, a home focused chain. Lifestyle stores will be increased from the current 11 to 35 and Home Centers will increase from the current 2 to 10.

The total estimated commercial real estate stock is likely to grow by US$ 66 billion to reach US$ 366 billion by the year 2010. Most of this growth will be taking place due to the growth of organized retail, which is one the world's 10 largest retail markets and has a $250 million estimated turnover. According to a report by Deutsche Bank Research, by 2008 end, there will be an estimated 220 new shopping centers in tier I and tier II cities.

The sector has got its importance in the economy, and

particularly the diamond segment accounts for 80 per cent of total exports of the sector and is providing employment for close to 10 lakh artisans and workers, both directly and indirectly. The gold jewelry segment accounts for 15 per cent of total exports. Being one of the significant foreign exchange earners, the industry is contributing significantly to the economy. And being the largest consumer of gold in the world, the country is mated to hold nearly 14,000 tons of gold is accounting for around 9 per cent of the global cumulative mine production. According to a survey conducted by KPMG, the global gems and jewelry will grow up to US$ 185 bn by 2010 and US$ 230 bn by 2015. It says India, along with China, will play a dominant role and as a market equivalent to the US. In fact, the country is emerging as one of the biggest markets for premium products. The gems and jewelry sector is very popular among the people. We can judge its popularity from the fact that over one million are employed in this industry and it is still growing at the rate of approximately 15 per cent every year. Exports grew by 13 per cent to US$ 13.7 bn in 2005-06 against US$ 12.12 bn in the previous year. Majority of the growth was fueled by the branded segment, at an amazing growth rate of 40 per cent. According to a study by consulting firm McKinsey, the branded jewelry market in India would touch US$ 2.28 bn market by 2010.

Retail FDI: Opportunities and Challenges

India can become a giant in a short time span in food processing and textiles, for which we have the potential because Indian agricultural production is the lowest cost in the world, and textile labour is the cheapest internationally. Allowing FDI in retail trade, especially in groceries and garments marketing, is one sure way of doing it. Food processing and textiles will grow very substantially from the linkage effects of a modernized, globalized retail trade that only FDI can ensure. The employment generation for Indian youth would also be enormous. Indian retail trade is of enormous size (US$ 180 billion), nearly 10 per cent of GDP, employing 21 million persons, which is about 7 per cent of the labour force. It is six times bigger than Thailand and five times larger than South Korea and Taiwan. China's retail trade is 8 per cent of GDP and 6 per cent of employment. But the trade in India is fragmented, unorganized, un networked, and individually small. The 12 million kirana shops are mostly family or 'ma-pa' owned, with little capital for expansion or credit to receive or to extend to consumers. About 96 percent of these shops have 500 sq ft or less of space with limited stock or choice to offer. During all these years, instead of shedding tears for indigenous trade and resistlng FDI, had the government declared it an industry, it would done the trade a world of good.

The country is expecting a strong economic growth of about 8-10 per cent per year and this can be achieved by raising the rate of investments as well as by generating demand for the increased goods and services produced. Retail contributes about 10 per cent to the national GDP and is expected to increase over the next decade or so. PricewaterhouseCoopers estimates that Indian retail will get USD 412 million by 2011 and majority of the investment will be directed towards the two most popular retail formats: hyper markets and supermarkets. Growth of this sector holds paramount importance to the Indian economy, so any augmentation of this sector will have a resultant growth effect on the economy. Although at this point in time FDI in retailing is receiving mixed reaction, but our feeling is that FDI would bring a lot of positive changes both for the operators and the consumer. The infusion of much-needed foreign investment would result in: (1) retail consolidation and increase in the share of the organised retail sector, (2) increase in employment in retail (3) increase supply chain efficiency which would lead to lower prices, superior quality for consumers, (4) enhanced opportunity for domestic operators to join hand with global retail players to bring in technical know how and global practices, (5) making shoppers feel international shopping experience.

Modern retailing is designed not only to provide consumers with a wide variety of products under one roof, but also of assured home delivery and information feedback between consumers and producers. A modern retail outlet will also make it easy to buy on credit and provide for servicing and repair of products sold. With IT application, the modern retail store can cut transaction costs such as due to inventory, delivery and handling. That is precisely how the US based Wal-Mart grew to be a giant because it reduced its distribution costs to 3 per cent of sales compared to 4.5 per cent of others. With MIT Professor Sanjay Sarma's epochal innovation of RFID (radio frequency identification), which will do away with cash registers and clerks who are required to operate it, Wal-Mart will further reduce its costs. Wal-Mart had entered the Chinese market a few years ago.

These retail giant houses can bring their better managerial practices and IT-friendly techniques to cut wastage and set up integrated supply chains to gradually replace the presented disorganised and fragmented retail market. According to McKinsey, India wastes nearly Rs 50,000 crore in the food chain itself. These international retail outlets can help develop the food processing industry, which requires US$ 28 billion of modern technology and infrastructure. As India's urbanisation grows, these modern food delivery systems are required. Foreign companies want to come in, and we need their money and techniques to prepare our transition to the inevitable globalised market of the future. FDI in retail sector has been a key driver of productivity growth in Brazil, Poland and Thailand.

It is difficult to fit a successful international format directly and expect a similar performance in India. The lessons from multinationals expanding to new geographies too point to this. For example, Wal-Mart is highly successful in USA but the story is different in Asian countries like China. Therefore, it is important for retailer to look at local conditions and insights into the local buying behaviour before shaping the format choice. Considering the diversity in terms of taste and preferences existing in India the retailers may go for experimentation to identify the winning format suited to different geographies and segments. A Convenience store offers location advantage for the shoppers and provides ease of shopping and customized service to the shoppers.

It charges average to above average prices, depending on the product category and carries a moderate number of stock keeping units (SKUs). Normally it remains open for long hours and shoppers use it for buying fill-in merchandize and emergency purchases.

Table 13.1 reveals that in India, Convenience stores occupied 23 thousand sq. meter of retail space with sales of about Rs 1347 million in 2005 and are expected occupy 85 thousand square meter of selling space by 2010.

Table 13.1: Convenience Stores: Value Sales, Outlets and Selling Space, 2000-2005

	2000	2001	2002	2003	2004	2005
Value sales Rs million	15	68	225	431	998	1,347
Outlets	5	28	99	249	370	510
Selling Space '000 sq m	1	2	5	9	16	23

Source: Euromonitor Report on Indian Retail, 2006

Table 13.2 reveals that sales are expected to touch Rs. 5271 million and number of outlets is likely to grow from 510 to 2434. Twenty Four Seven a new format of convenience store is operational in Delhi from June 2005. Twenty Four Seven's portfolio comprises 3,500 stock keeping units (SKUs) of branded fast-moving consumer goods and another 3,500 SKUs of prescription and over-the-counter drugs besides 300 private labels products across food, focusing on staples such as pulses and rice. The promoter of this format, the Modi group, plans to set up 500 convenience stores in Delhi and Mumbai by 2007.

Discounters Wal-Mart, the largest retailer in the world is a discounter. Practically the discounters offer several advantages such as lower price, wider assortment and quality assurance. The discounters like Wal-Mart and Aldi were able to quickly build scale and pass on benefits to the consumer. However, in the long run success depends on the operational efficiency and consistent value delivery to the consumer. The same retailer Wal-Mart struggles in Asian countries like China but extremely successful in USA. It is believed that the average Indian consumer is highly price-sensitive and looks for savings in term of money in her grocery purchase. So price-value equation is a critical component in most of the grocery purchases. Despite this, there is hardly any national level discount chain operating in India. But retailers such as Aldi and Lidl are extremely successful in Europe. Due to regulatory issues no such retailers are allowed to sale their products directly to consumer.

Table 13.2: Convenience Stores Forecasts: Value Sales, Outlets and Selling Space 2005-2010

	2005	2006	2007	2008	2009	2010
Value sales Rs million	1,347	1,751	2,329	3,168	4,118	5,271
Outlets	510	710	974	1,347	1,813	2,434
Selling Space'000 sq m	23	32	43	56	71	88.4

Source: Euromonitor Report on Indian Retail, 2006

However, they can sell in a cash and carry format, which is exclusively B2B context. If these retailers are allowed to operate in India through their retailer stores they may find it extremely difficult in the early stages because of lack of experience in the grocery retailing in this market. Unlike the western markets where retailers largely depend on private labels to offer price advantage, here the concept of private label is very early stage. Some of the food retailers like Foodworld and Adani sell private labels but they are not discounters. Soft discounters are present in India, although their influence on grocery retailing in 2005 was very minimal with a value share at less than half a percentage point. The absence of strong discounters and the lack of local retailer's initiatives in discounters have several reasons. Unlike most Western countries, Indian retailers are mainly small stores and do not have much bargaining power with manufacturers in order to negotiate terms. Due to low economies of scale, retailers are unable to offer significant discounts on their own. Consequently, the presence of discounters is much smaller than that of supermarkets.

Table 13.3 reveals that according to Euromonitor Report on Indian Retail, 2006, in India there are 410 discount stores with 63 thousand sq, meter selling space and by 2010 that figure is going to be 555 discount retail outlets with 85 thousand selling space. Subhiksha, the Chennai based discount retail chain is going national. By July 2006 the retail chain had around 150 stores and planning to open 350 more by March 2007. The National Capital Region (NCR) is going to get a fair share of 145 stores. Apart from the NCR the retail chain is actively looking at markets in Maharashtra, Gujarat, Andhra Pradesh and Karnataka. The retail chain already started operation in Ahmedabad but the stores are largely selling fruits and vegetables at this point of time. They claim that they sell at a lower price compared to other places in the local market.

Table 13.3: Discounters Forecasts: Value Sales, Outlets and Selling Space, 2005-2010

	2005	2006	2007	2008	2009	2010
Value sales Rs. million	6,479	7,063	7,627	8,314	9,145	10,15
Outlets	380	410	440	470	510	555
Selling Space'000sqm	58	63	68	73	78	84.8

Source: Euromonitor Report on Indian Retail, 2006

Summary

The Government approved sweeping reforms in FDI with a

first step towards partially opening retail markets to foreign investors. It will now allow 51 per cent FDI in single brand products in the retail sector. The employment generation for Indian youth would also be enormous. Indian retail trade is of enormous size (US$ 180 billion), nearly 10 percent of GDP, employing 21 million persons, which is about 7 per cent of the labour force. It is six times bigger than Thailand and five times larger than South Korea and Taiwan. China's retail trade is 8 per cent of GDP and 6 per cent of employment. But the trade in India is fragmented, unorganized, UN networked, and individually small. The 12 million kirana shops are mostly family or 'ma-pa' owned, with little capital for expansion or credit to receive or to extend to consumers.

About 96 per cent of these shops have 500 sq ft or less of space with limited stock or choice to offer. During all these years, instead of shedding tears for indigenous trade and resisting FDI, had the government declared it an industry, it would done the trade a world of good. We need a rational approach toward FDI in India's retail trade; in particular, how after it is permitted free access, it is subject to regulatory supervision. Modern retailing is designed not only to provide consumers with a wide variety of products under one roof, but also of assured home delivery and information feedback between consumers and producers. A modern retail outlet will also make it easy to buy on credit and provide for servicing and repair of products sold. With IT application, the modern retail store can cut transaction costs such as due to inventory, delivery and handling.

References

Adawal Shankar, Economic Times. 6. Wednesday, August 2, 2006.

Agarwal, J.P. (1980), "Determinants of Foreign Direct Investment: A Survey", Weltwirtscaftliches Archiv, Vol. 116.

Aggarwal, A. (2000). Current issues in Indian retailing, European Retail Digest , Issue 25 70-71

Alexander, N. and Silva, M..D. (2002). Emerging markets and the internationalization of retailing: The Brazilian experience", International Journal of Retail Distribution and Management, 30, (6)

300-314

Anand, M. and Rajshekhar, M. (2001). The retail puzzle, Business World, 29 October, 38-42

Balasubramanyam, V.N., (1996), "Foreign Direct Investment and Growth in EP and IS Countries", Economic Journal, Vol. 106, January.Channels, (6th Ed). New Delhi: Prentice Hall of India Pvt. Ltd.

Bennett, R.C., Livstack, D.S., and Singh, D. (1998). Merging theories to explain Recent retail evolution", Vision, 2 (1) 27-32

Bennison, D. and Boutsouki, C. (1995). Greek retailing in transition", International Journal of Retail Distribution and Management, 23 (1) 24-31

Berman, B. and Evans, J.R. (2001). Retail Management, (8th ed) , Upper Saddle River, N.J., Prentice Hall

Bhattacharjee, P. (2001). Retail's new Godzilla" Business World, 28 May, 44-46 Bhardwaj. H.P. (1998), " Foreign Exchange Handbook", Bhardwaj Publications.

Fernandes, M., Gadi, C., khanna, A., Mitra, P. and Narayanaswamy, S. (2000) " India's retailing comes of age", McKinsey Quarterly,.4, 95-102

Foreign Direct Investment in India: htt://Indianground.com

Foreign Direct Investment Magazine http://www.fdimagizine.com

Jeevanandham (2002). "Foreign Exchange and Risk Management" Sultan Chand & Sons publications

Justin, (2004) "International Business" Himalaya Publications P.P. 141.

N.V. Sivakumar, India states that "India is the hot spot for large international retailers," and that "They cannot afford not to be here."

Radhakrishnan, K. (2003). Organised retail: Forging ahead, Praxis , 4 (1) 47-51 Ramaswamy, V.S. and Namakumari, S. (2002). Marketing Management. Delhi: Macmillan India Ltd.

Sarma, M.K. (2000). Some issues in retail management in India, Vision, 4 (1), 35-40

Shukla, S. (2001). Can India's largest retailer bounce back? Business Today, December 8 , 41-48

Sinha, P.K., Bannerjee, A. and Uniyal, D.P. (2002). Deciding where to buy: Store choice behaviour of Indian shoppers, Vikalpa, 27 (2) 13-28

Subramanian Swamy, "FDI in retail "February 24, 2005.

The ICFAI University Press "THE ANALYST" Chartered Financial Analyst, February 2007.

The New York Times. Wednesday, August 2, 2006 Piyush Kumar Sinha. Sanjay Kumar Kar " An Insight into the Growth of New Retail Formats in India " W.P. No.2007-03-04. Indian Institute of Management Ahmedabad-380 015.India

Wikipidia, the free encyclopedia http://en.Wikipedia.org/Wiki/fdrs

14

Organised vs. Unorganised Retailing

B. Srinivas Raj and K. Krishna Reddy

With a population of 1.1 billion, India is one of the world's most attractive future markets and the Indian subcontinent could potentially become the fastest-growing economy in the world over the next ten to fifteen years. The Indian economy has undergone considerable deregulation and privatization in the recent years. Since this process began, the country has grown rapidly and benefited handsomely from globalization. The service sector in particular offers plenty of opportunities for foreign investors to enter the Indian market: Call centers, software development, accounting and research and development represent only a small cross-section of India's huge service industry. The service sector now accounts for 53 per cent of the gross national product; agriculture contributes a mere 21 per cent. With the increase in the IT boom, buzzing activity of BPOs, KPOs, ITES companies, purchasing power has gone up and people now are able to afford everything ready made.

Recently, a family stepped into a hypermarket store, "Hyderabad Central" in central district of Hyderabad, and was surprised to find mall offering shopping, movies and food at one place which has World class standards in ambience, interiors and service, conceptualised with a theme and tagline that says ***shop, eat and celebrate***. Hyderabad Central has been established with an investment of some 700 million rupees, this is the second large-scale mall in the country, the first being in Bangalore. Hyderabad Central is popular because there are over 300 clothing brands to choose from, including the famous Marks and Spencer from the United Kingdom, besides a complete range of music, books, coffee shops, food courts, supermarket, restaurants, and movies it has everything under one roof.

Retailing play an important role in day to day life as it is a vital part of the business world as it is a link between consumers and manufacturers and they add value to products by making it easier for manufacturers to sell and consumers to buy. It would be very costly and time consuming to locate, contact and make a purchase from the manufacturer every time consumer wanted to buy chocolates, a sweater or toilet soap. Similarly, it would be very costly for the manufacturers of these products to locate and distribute them to consumers individually. By bringing multitudes of manufacturers and consumers together at a single point, retailers make it possible for products to be sold, and, consequently, business to be done. Retailers also provide services that make it less risky and more fun to buy products. They have salespeople on hand who can answer questions, may offer credit, and display products so that consumers know what is available and can see it before buying. In addition, retailers may provide many extra services, from personal shopping to gift wrapping to delivery, that increase the value of products and services to consumers. Thus, retailing not only benefits the consumers but also benefits the government and the economy as a whole.

The global retail industry employs more than 150 million people and accounts for about 9 per cent of Global GDP – and another 20 per cent indirectly. More importantly, global middle and upper-middle – income groups which are the target consumer segments will likely double in size over the next 10 years. As emerging markets attract modern retail, there are many possible benefits, including increased productivity, economic growth, capital investment, job creation and exports. Moreover, greater competition will lower prices for end consumers.

According to the National Retail Federation, 1 in 5 American workers are employed in the retail industry. The Department of Labor estimates that since 1990, 7,00,000 new jobs have been created in the retail sector. That's 13 per cent of all new jobs in the United States. At present, more jobs are provided in retailing than the entire U.S. manufacturing sector.

While retail stores means a one-stop shop, wherein pin to play station which include essential items to a common man, but there is a difference between various retail stores, the most common ones are Discount/Mass Merchandisers, Department Store, Specialty Stores, Warehouse/Wholesale Club, Factory Outlet and Online or E-Commerce stores.

Organised and Unorganised Retailing

The retail industry consists of organized retailing and unorganised retailing. Organised retailing refers to trading activities undertaken by licensed retailers, that is, those who are registered for sales tax, income tax, etc. These include the corporate-backed hypermarkets and retail chains, and also the privately owned large retail businesses. Unorganised retailing, on the other hand, refers to the traditional formats of low-cost retailing, for example, the local *kirana* shops, owner manned general stores, *paan/beedi* shops, convenience stores, hand cart and pavement vendors, etc.

Unorganised retailing include small local stores that have dominated Indian retailing over the decades and are present in every village and local community or street corner stores, addressing the needs of the population in the area and being the point of contact with the consumer. The distribution networks of brands extend right up to this point to stay in touch with customer needs and preferences. A good example of this is Coca-Cola, wherein it could penetrate to each and every village in the country.

India like most other countries has a very large network of local stores. You will find these in almost every village and locality. A lot of them function as paan and cigarette outlets with tea and coffee sometimes also offered. Besides this, these stores stock and offer eateries, soft drinks and other essentials. These small stores cater to the needs of their own local population and travelers who stop by for a smoke or a snack.

A little larger format is the neighbourhood grocery store that focuses on grains, foods, snacks and toiletries besides other home essentials.

Fruits and vegetables that are perishable are usually maintained and offered by exclusive vegetable stores and not by the normal groceries.

Every fair sized village is likely to have at least one grocery store, a fruit and vegetable shop and a paan and cigarette shop. The new addition of the past decade is to have a telephone booth that lets locals and travelers make local, national and international telephone calls.

This network is very large and spread all across India. It is not really a network since each store is individual or family owned and has no connection with the other. It does however represent a network since large consumer product companies like Unilever, Procter & Gamble, Colgate-Palmolive, Cadbury, Coca Cola, Pepsi and ITC uses them as their final point of retail to the consumer.

These small stores are very personal and have built strong relationships with the local population. They are points of news and connection. They offer credit to the local population and help out in times of crisis. They also have a very good understanding of requirements of the local population and have very low overheads enabling them to offer the best price for their products. Over the years, the local kirana merchants established personal touch/bonding with the local people, which make the customers to comeback to their place again and again. However, it is believed that the new retail chains will drive these small stores out of business.

Some of the examples of Organized Retailers are as follows. Wal-Mart is the world's largest retailer with over 3000 stores in the US. Carrefour meaning crossroads in French is the single largest retailer in Europe and the second largest in the world. Royal Ahold is the third largest retailer with several chains throughout Europe, Asia and North/South America and has its headquarters in The Netherlands. In India, apart from Pantaloon, some of the well-known retailers include the RPG group, K Raheja (Shoppers' Stop), Tata (Trent, Westside and Star India Bazaar), and the Landmark group. Recently, Reliance also joined the fray. Organized retailing is more visible in urban areas because of people's high aspirations, their high purchasing power and splurging habits due to rising incomes. Availability of everything under one roof has fueled the growth of organized retailing—the ***one stop shop*** concept has revolutionized the retailing sector. Quality, building trust, genuine material, good customer care, and prompt after-sales service are some of the main reasons, which differentiate traditional stores from modern retail stores.

In a relatively closed economy, where a few manufacturers can dominate some industries, the consumer and the retailer who is in direct contact with the consumer, drive the development and growth of the decline of a market.

The service, ambience and product of Shopper's stop and Lifestyle have influenced the expectations of customers to new levels. Similarly, Giant, Subhiksha and Big Bazar have recreated the value of low price, which are being expected by the customers in the recent past.

These retailers have become prominent in size as well as in the opinion leadership, their new and often more business processes influenced the suppliers to change and these developments also spread among the chain and networks of the suppliers as well.

The Indian retail market is estimated at US$ 350 billion. But organised retailing is estimated at only US$ 8 billion. However, organised retailing is expected to grow to US$ 22 billion by 2010. With the growth of organised retailing estimated at 40 per cent (CAGR) over the next few years, Indian retailing is clearly a promising industry. India is currently the ninth largest retail market in the world. Cities and Major towns like Dehradun, Nagpur, Salem, Lucknow, Nasik that will power India up the rankings soon because in these places the middle income groups purchasing power is growing, and this is the place where retailing is going to grow.

Employment in Retailing

Employment opportunities provided by these two forms

(Organised and unorganized) of trade in India makes us understand how effective retail sector is contributing in development of the economy – organized trade employs roughly 5 lakh people (Tables 14.1, 14.2 and 14.3), whereas the unorganized retail trade employs nearly 3.95 crore. According to a GoI study the number of workers in retail trade in 1998 was almost 175 lakh. Given the recent numbers indicated by other studies, this is only indicative of the magnitude of expansion the retail trade is experiencing, both due to economic expansion as well as the 'jobless growth' that we have seen in the past decade. It must be noted that even within the organised sector, the number of individually-owned retail outlets far outnumber the corporate backed institutions. Though these numbers translate to approximately 8 per cent of the workforce in the country (half the normal share in developed countries) there are far more retailers in India than other countries in absolute numbers, because of the demographic profile and the preponderance of youth, India's workforce is proportionately much larger. That about 4 per cent of India's population is in the retail trade says a lot about how vital this business is to the socio-economic equilibrium in India.

Table 14.1: Share of Retailing in Employment in Select Countries

Country	Employment (per cent)
India	8
USA	16
Poland	15
Brazil	12
China	7

Source: AT Kearney Analysis

Organised retail is still in the stages of finding its feet in India even now. Though organised trade makes up over 70-80 per cent of total trade in developed economies, India's figure is low even in comparison with other Asian developing economies like China,

Thailand, South Korea and Philippines, all of whom have figures hovering around the 20-25 per cent mark. These figures quite accurately reveal the relative underdevelopment of the retail industry in India.

Table 14.2: Retail Trade in India and South East Asia

Countries	Organized (per cent)	Unorganized (per cent)
India	2	98
China	20	80
South Korea	15	85
Indonesia	25	75
Philippines	35	65
Thailand	40	60
Malaysia	50	50

Source: AT Kearney Analysis

Recent Trends

Several Global Retail Players have entered India through different tie-ups and ventures. For example:

- Nuance Group, World's leading Airport Retailer has joint ventured with Shoppers' Stop. The venture aims to set up duty free shops in the new airports in India, as airports provide the last minute shopping destination for travelers.
- Pantaloon has also joint ventured with Talwalkars to provide health related products.
- Giordano has opened the first retail store in Chennai to provide seasoned collections. The space area of the store is 1000 sq ft. The company has planned to establish 20 stores by 2008, including in cities like Mumbai and Hyderabad.
- Mosa Shoes Private Ltd., has Joint ventured with Mauritius-based Tano India Private Ltd., to set up an exclusive retail outlet for Nike products. It is the first foreign private investment after allowing 51 per cent in single branded retail outlet.

Table 14.3: Global Retail Development Index 2006

Country	Region	Country risk	Market Attractiveness	Market saturation	Time Pressure	GRDI score
	Weight (per cent)	25	25	30	20	--
India	Asia	55	34	89	76	100
Russia	Eastern Europe	43	59	53	90	85
Vietnam	Asia	43	24	87	81	84
Ukraine	Eastern Europe	42	37	76	81	83
China	Asia	58	40	57	86	82
Chile	Americas	67	57	47	48	71
Latvia	Eastern Europe	58	50	31	88	69
Slovenia	Eastern Europe	78	52	25	70	68
Croatia	Eastern Europe	57	51	28	91	67
Turkey	Mediterranean	46	59	64	40	66

Source: Euromoney, The World Bank, Global Competitiveness Report 2005 and AT Kearney Analysis

Global retail development index 2006 finds that India is an attractive market for retail sector, and there is much scope for companies to grow, as the organized sector is hardly tapped. There is scope here for foreign players to invest and there is tremendous opportunity for domestic players till 100 per cent FDI is allowed in retail sector.

The developing economy of India is practically converting the country into a shopper's haven. India is on the threshold of a revolution in its retail industry, and if managed cleverly, it would pay handsome returns beyond retailers' expectations. The foreign investors would need to take care of which retail format they need to apply to India, as the business and economic models vary widely. So the main issue would be to identify an approach that has been successful in other markets that is suitable to India's needs. The challenge would be to find a pricing strategy and plan that caters to India's diversity, particularly in its food business. The high cost of real estate relative to the price and margin levels would have to be looked into. With the sound road infrastructure and better connectivity, rural India is bound to be influenced by the revolutionary retail sector.

Retailing is very diverse and at times the edges start to blur with other types of businesses. Generally, retailing is based more on whether the business deals directly with the public. Retail banking, service stations, local coffee shops are also retailers but not in the sense of a clothing store. Nowadays, with the emergence of online retailing, retailers are no longer concerned about location of stores. E-tailing, which is the selling of retail goods online through companies like Ebay, has changed the definition of the term retail.

There are several factors that are fueling the growth of the retail sector. The young working populace, due to the rise of nuclear families in urban locale, is increasing with more women joining in. This has given rise to promising opportunities in the service sector. Moreover, the consumer is cash rich because of the finance boom. More consumers are using credit cards and their spending patterns have also changed. Rural consumers have also changed their buying patterns, signifying the spread of consumer revolution to rural India.

The growth projections for retail business in India vary hugely. Investors who are willing to invest in India are concerned whether India is fertile enough to accept foreign retail investments.

Analysis of Indian Retail Sector

Indian retailing industry has seen phenomenal growth in the last five years (2001-2006). Organized retailing has finally emerged from the shadows of unorganized retailing and is contributing significantly to the growth of Indian retail sector.

Findings of the Indian Retail Sector Analysis Report are:

- Organized retail will form 10 per cent of total retailing by the end of this decade (2010).
- From 2006 to 2010, the organized sector will grow at the Compounded Annual Growth Rate (CAGR) of around 49.53 per cent per annum.
- Cultural and regional differences in India are the biggest challenges in front of retailers. This factor deters the retailers in India from adopting a single retail format. Hypermarket is emerging as the most favorable format for the time being in India.

The arrival of multinationals will further push the growth of hypermarket format, as it is the best way to compete with unorganized retailing in India.

Challenges Faced by the Retail Sector

The challenges for the organized retail industry in India are: Competition from the unorganized sector. Traditional retailing has been established in India for some centuries. It is a low cost structure, mostly owner-operated, has negligible real estate and labor costs and little or no taxes to pay. Consumer familiarity that runs from generation to generation is one big advantage for the traditional retailing sector. In contrast, players in the organized sector have big expenses to meet, and yet have to keep prices low enough to be able to compete with the traditional sector. High costs for the organized sector arises from: Higher labor costs, social security to employees, high quality real estate, much bigger premises, comfort facilities such as air-conditioning, back-up power supply, taxes etc. Organized retailing also has to cope with the middle class psychology that the bigger and brighter sales outlet is, the more expensive it will be. It is also understood that there isn't a single premier educational institute that offers training courses with a retail focus and an acute shortage of senior and middle-level retail professionals, high attrition rates and rising compensation costs will force other players to follow. India's organised retail industry needs 20,000 top-level management positions in the next one-year, eight lakh customer care executives in four years and a total of 2.5 million new jobs in five years.

The Road Ahead

Advances in technology, like the Internet, have helped make retailing an even more challenging and exciting field in recent years. The nature of the business and the way retailing is done are currently undergoing fundamental changes. However, retailing in some form will always be necessary. For example, even though the Internet is beginning to make it possible for manufacturers to sell directly to consumers, the very vastness of cyberspace will still make it very difficult for a consumer to purchase every product he uses directly. On-line retailers, like Amazon.com, Barnes & Noble, Fabmall, bring together assortments of products for consumers to buy in the same way that bricks-and-mortar retailers do. In addition, traditional retailers with physical stores will continue to be necessary. Of course, retailers who offer personal services, like hair styling, will need to have face-to-face interaction with the consumer. But even with products, consumers often want to see, touch and try them before they buy. Or, they may want products immediately and won't want to wait for them to be shipped. Also, and perhaps most importantly, in many cases the experience of visiting the retailer is an important part of the purchase. Everything that the retailer can do to make the shopping experience pleasurable and fun can help ensure that customers come back.

Conclusion

The retail scene is changing really fast. Retailers are rethinking their approaches towards the suppliers so that they can get the best pricing strategies from them. With the help of IT systems, retailers want to find out the exact percentage of shares in profits shared by others. Suppliers need to synchronize their understanding with the changes in the retail trade; otherwise soon they would be without consumers. Retailers want to work well with those suppliers who would help in generation of offers to strengthen the consumer faithfulness mainly to retain them from running away to competitors. Efforts have to be constantly made to introduce new products and services. The customer relationship management systems are important, as they help retailers in understanding the needs of customers. Retail is increasingly gaining global tone and those retailers wanting to enter new markets in other areas need the support of strong brand products, which would help them in presenting the same image for products universally. The advanced and emerging new technologies are progressively throwing up new opportunities for retailers to open their stores in India in the form of joint ventures.

References

Chengappa, P.G, Achoth, Lalith, Mukherjee, Arpita, Ramachandra Reddy B.M. & Ravi, P.C, Evolution of Food Retail Chains: The Indian Context, 5-6th Nov. 2003, www.ficci.com

Economic Times Intelligence Group, Changing Gears - Retailing in India, Times Multimedia, 2003.

Emerging Market Priorities for Global Retailers: The 2006 Global Retail Development Index at atkearney.com

Ganguly, Saby, Retailing Industry in India, www.indiaonestop.com

India Brand Equity Foundation, The Retail Industry, ibef.org

Indian Retail Sector Analysis (2006-07) – Market Research Report, researchandmarkets.com

Iyengar, Jayanthi, China, India Confront the Wal-Marts, Online Asia Times, www.atimes.com, January, 31,2004.

Monthly abstracts of Statistics, Central Statistical Organisation, GoI

S Shajahan, Emerging Influence of E-commerce in Retail Business in India - Indian Management, AIMA - Business India Group, New Delhi, October, 2000 pp 44-50.

Singhal, Arvind, " A Strong Pillar of Indian Economy," www.ksa-technopak.com

Singhal, Arvind, "Indian Retail: The Road Ahead" www.eretailbiz.com.

Singhal, Arvind, Changing Retail Landscape, www.ksa-technopak.com.

15

Emerging Retail Revolution: Issues and Implications

A. Sathish Babu and D. Guna Sankar

Introduction

The term Retailing refers to any activity that involves sales to an individual consumer, Retailing Business has been transforming from conventional Retail outlets to super stores, specialty stores, franchise stores, direct marketing and even telemarketing. Consequent to the introduction of Economic reforms there has been enormous transmutation in the Indian Economic Environment. Several sectors in our Economy are silently scaling significant peaks and India is emerging as the fourth largest Economy in the world in terms of purchasing power parity after the United States, China and Japan.

The Liberalization measures have yielded good results and there is a new sense of optimism about the Economy. Prominent among the promising sectors are Retail Business. This type of business has been vogue in the Indian society since ages and people are having a lot of affinity towards local stores. Service is the single most important factor in successful retail business. Local stores are coming forward to deliver the provisions at the doorstep of the consumer without additional cost. Another important factor for the success of local stores is that most of the customers are known to the shop owner and hence always get personal attention. Traditional shops owners are ready to extend credit to those who are familiar to them and they believe business depends on mutual trust.

Of late, the profile of local stores in the by lanes has been metamorphosing into aesthetically decorated, meticulously planned and properly arranged mega malls to allure customers.

The silent spectacular retail revolution has immense impact on the Indian society for the reasons that traditional stores have an inseparable affinity and at the same time most modern markets/malls are posing new challenges.

Changing Profile of Indian Consumer

Dynamic development and liberalization policies have brought a sea change in the attitude of Indian consumer. Indian market has been witnessing drastic changes in recent times. The life style of Indian consumer is undergoing a major diversification and consumers are preferring new brands that appear in the market. Due to the transformations of Demographic, Economic and cultural factors, Indian consumer is more active, mature and evincing keen interest to select best products irrespective of price range. As a result, Indian consumer is active participant rather than passive purchaser.

Information Technology has paved the path for more opportunities, young people are working hard and earning fat salaries and their preferences, choices are also fast changing, companies are also sensing the moods of consumers, reorienting their strategies with a focus on consumers. Innovative marketing strategies, product design, pricing, advertisements are the corner stones of success. In the olden days, the Indian companies did not have access to sophisticated technology. In those days, quality was a dream. Consumers are hesitated to purchase Indian made products. Today the situation has been reversed. Pragmatic policies of the Government especially after the prelude of Economic reforms are also another contributing steward for the growth of consumerism.

Today in the competing circumstances quality is mantra. Companies are spending huge amounts on quality improvements, corporate world is giving utmost importance to the selection of best raw material, virgin technology backed by good research and development, well trained employees, logistics management has helped in distribution of best products that surfeit the customers. Now the pertinent point for a marketer is how the consumer perceives the quality of the product. Buyers will take into consideration various factors such as advertisement, price, brand name and store name. Companies are realizing that their fortunes depend on quality. Quality is free. Quality can be seen in the eyes of the customer. For a company which supplies quality products opportunities are electrifying. Profits are plenty. Sky is the limit to expand in the Global arena. The dreams of companies are resulting into realities and Internet is being perceived as an innovative engine of resource. Netizens are playing a prominent position in the E-markets. These markets help in augmenting the exciting experiences to corporate world. Another factor behind this optimistic scenario is relationship marketing is satisfaction of the consumer's desires and aspirations. An elated consumer is a boon to the organization. This depends on quality, which is an important tool of the competition.

Indian Rural Scenario

"India lives in its villages" is the adage and rural markets have been an enigma and virgin land for un-tapped opportunities. Even though the rural consumer is not educated, but he is definitely astute with a lot of experience in handling the vagaries of life. In recent times, due to the widespread of Information Technology the rural consumer is able to understand what is happening around him and he is willing to shift his life style in accordance with the latest trends. These opportunities are giving an unlimited scope for the corporates to build insights and break boundaries. It is the passion and advertisements that takes the consumers towards new and novel products. Corporate world is also realising that progress is always propelled by professionalism and new ways are depicted to woo the consumer.

India is a biggest Geographical abstract with 28 states, seven union territories, hundreds of dialects, multiple cultures and with diversities. In such a diversified and enigmatic market belief is that the market system is a" matter of faith". It is understood that a house hold's spending and savings decision depend on its view of long term or permanent income.

Indian Retail Landscape: An Overview

The dawn of Retailing in India has a lot to do with the growing purchasing power of the buyer's unlimited choice of products, alluring advertisement attractions, Brand popularity etc. As a result, super markets and centrally air conditioned Shopping Malls are established. Mega malls offer the experience of shopping, dining, movies, leisure and entertainment games, exhibitions, all are available under one roof. Families are having the opportunity to visit these new fangled areas and spend their time that gives them a new experience.

India's new prosperity and opulence is attributable to the progressive policies of the Government. The saga of Economic reforms is a continuous process so that India is able to rebuild its Economy. Several measures have been initiated to contain and control inflation. Foreign reserves are mounting and in comfortable position. Indian companies are emerging as International companies and competing in the Global markets. India's hegemony in Information Technology and Bio-technology has opened new vistas and India is able to convert its population explosion into Human Assets. Several middle class families are educating their children and these young brains are bringing wealth to the Nation as well as their personal prospects are also ameliorating. All these endeavors have resulted in sharp rising of Incomes in the middle class. The neo-rich middle and upper middle class has disposable and discretionary income. Consequently, the life style of middle-income group is fast changing and present Indian cities are reflecting the situation.

Role of Women in Retail Business

The buying behaviour of Housewives in Indian context assumes splendid significance due to the reason that they are the cynosure of the family. Present middle class wife is educated, employed and also an expert in Home management. A successful housewife is competent to collect information about a product from various sources. She is capable of weighing pros and cons. Every housewife meticulously plans and executes the purchase requirements of the family. Now modern, educated middle class housewife gathers information from print media, electronic media, friends and from other available resources. Generally grocery items, fruits and vegetables are purchased by housewives, but cosmetics are her exclusive choice. In buying consumer durables the head of family takes final decision. Some times, even though the house wives are capable of taking decisions but the credit they wants to attribute to the husbands in the Indian society. Housewives can't take major decisions without consulting spouses, and they believe that family ties will be strong by mutual consultation and respecting each others opinions or views. If both husband and wife are employees they could not find time to cook and going out for dining twice or thrice per week is a prevalent practice. In good olden days or yesteryears joint families are the fulcrum of Indian society.

Over a period of time nucleus families are emerging in the present day society due to urbanization and income is not sufficient to meet and maintain joint families. Circumstances are such that unless both husband and wife are earning it is not possible to meet both ends. These types of working families are growing and they could not find time to cook and visiting restaurants very often to satiate their taste buds. In order to satisfy this segment companies are coming forward to produce ready to eat recipes and instant items are sold in the Retail outlets and they are exported to other countries to cater to the needs of Indian migrants.

Prominent Players in Indian Retail Landscape

In order to encash the present vicissitudes many Foreign and Domestic companies are establishing their retail outlets and they are believing that servicing is the most single important cause in successful retailing.

Following are the prominent retail players in India.

1. Pantaloon Retail (I) Ltd -Value and life style retailing
2. Bata India Ltd. - Foot Wear
3. RPG Retail - Value And Life Style Retailing

4. Shoppers Stop - Life style retailing
5. Life Style International - Life style retailing
6. Vivek Ltd. - Consumer Electronics
7. Trent Ltd. - Value and Life Style Retailing
8. Subhiksha Trading - Discount Retailing Food and Groceries
9. Margin Free - Discount Retailing Food and Groceries
10. Trinetra - Value Retailing –Food & Groceries
11. Nilgris - Value Retailing –Food & Groceries
12. Raymonds - Life style Retailing
13. Piramid Merchandising - Value Life Style
14. Vijay Sales - Consumer Electronics
15. Globus Stores - Life style Retailing
16. Nalli - Speciality Saree
17. E Bony - Life style Retailing
18. Madras Garments - Apparel
19. Arvind - Apparel
20. Levi Straus India - Apparel
21. Times Retail - Music Retailing
22. Barista - Coffee Beverage Retailing
23. Café Coffee Day - Coffee Beverage Retailing
24. Mc Donald's - Food Service
25. Pizza Hut - Food Service
26. Cross Roads - Mall Retailing
27. In Orbit - Mall Retailing
28. Forum Mall - Mall Retailing
29. Spencer Plaza - Mall Retailing
30. Nirmal - Mall Retailing
31. ITC E-Choupal - Choupal Fresh and Saagars
32. Metro India - Retail
33. Reliance - Retail
34. Bharathi-Walmart - Retail Outlets
35. Tata- Croma - Retail Outlets

The Retail format can be divided into three aspects.

- Convenience stores: That sells ready to eat Food. Beverages, Fruits, Vegetables etc.,
- Super Markets: A part from Food, Beverages, essential

commodities will be sold.

- Hyper Markets: Bigger in size Arranged in 4,000 or more square feet. Sells essential Commodities, House hold utilities and Apparel.

Organized vs. Unorganized Retailing

Traditionally small kirana shops are omini present in rural and urban India. Small shops are having inseparable affinity with the local people and depends on the integrity will sell the goods on credit also. Daily wage earners will purchase provisions out of their day's earning. Salaried people also purchase either on cash or credit. Hence, small shop owners are familiar with every face in that locality. "Repeated business is always a business". Since local customers will visit these small shops regularly, retail business is thriving. Nearly 4 crore people are directly depend on Retail sector and this sector is considered as an avenue for self employment. Retailers are purchasing produce from farmers in the season and sell through out the year. For some goods they will purchase from wholesaler or sole distributor and take their margin. In the present economic scenario Government is giving priority to privatize all possible works and to get a Government job is searching for water in the Desert. When avenues are narrowed day-by-day un-employed youth are desperately trying to stand on their own legs and small shops are one among the several options available to them. Thus, small shops in both rural and urban area are occupying significant status. Low capital, small space, reasonable prices, quality provisions, satisfactory service, personal attention are the inherent successful pillars for small shops. All these shops are in the un-organized sector and having impact on Indian society.

Many companies are grasping the situation and due to the introduction of Economic reforms, Indian Economic sector is in upbeat mood. At present, retail business is facing competition from both domestic companies and indirectly from foreign companies. Corporate world has understood that the level of economic activity can be calibrated by the level of money supply.

Since quality of work life is improved, standards of living are also refining. Money is flowing in our society due to pragmatic and progressive policies of the Government and people are willing to purchase modern articles. As a matter of fact, a household's spending and savings decision depend on its perception for future or permanent income.

In recent times, Reliance Industries has taken a decision to establish its Retail stores through out the country in a phased manner. Similarly ITC Ltd., has unveiled its plan to expand its fruit and vegetable retail and wholesale business by opening 54 new outlets called "CHOUPAL FRESH". Same company plans to increase the number of its rural malls "CHOUPAL SAAGARS". These are rural Hypermarkets, which provide multiple services under one roof. Main contributing conveniences for corporate presence in the retail sector are:

1. India's burgeoning population.
2. Middle class explosion.
3. Re-Structuring/ Re-engineering revolution.
4. Expansion of Information Technology.
5. Growing awareness among consumers.
6. Quality of work life.
7. Professionalism.
8. Opportunities in the private sector.
9. Incremental income levels.
10. Technology.
11. Sharp marketing strategies.
12. Large scale Economies.
13. Services under one roof.
14. Offering new exciting experience to consumers.
15. Remunerative price for farmers and reasonable rates to consumers.

At present, the farmers are not getting reasonable rate for their produce and as a result, Indian farmer is born in poverty, cultivates poverty, dies in poverty and inherits poverty. Agriculture has become un-economical due to various causes and many farmers are committing suicides in Andhra Pradesh and

Maharashtra. In these circumstances, corporate world is coming forward to help farmers by supplying seeds, suggesting solutions to the problems faced by formers, forward contracts to purchase the produce at reasonable prices etc. At the same time the corporate world is taking into consideration the consumer by offering quality products at reasonable prices. ITC's e-choupul is one of the novel methods and the company serves as a platform to purchase the farmers product directly and pay spot payment for procurement. It is hassle free transaction and the role of middlemen is avoided. Farmers can also buy quality products for their own farms and household's from "CHOUPUL SAAGARS" and access services of soil testing, Banking, Insurance, Medical facilities and Restaurants. At present, there are 6,500 E-choupals in over 38,000 villages in nine states. Similarly Tata's "crome stores" offer 6,000 products spread across eight categories including large appliances, small appliances, computers, communications, entertainment, music, movies and games. Reliance is also entering into the fray by investing Twenty five thousand crore and concentrating in two tier towns and commercial centers.

Leading among the foreign players & retail business are:

Wall mart is operating in 15 countries and having 6100 stores and servicing 138 crore customers. Second famous retail is "THE HOME DEPOT", its head quarters is in ATLANTA in America. This company has introduced automatic kiosks in which the consumers can enter the shop on seeing the price on the Barcode can purchase and pay. Third famous corporate giant is German based "METRO AG" It is operating from thirty countries. CARE forces-A is the largest in the world after Wall Mart. Its head quarters are in France. It is maintaining 11,000 shops in 30 countries.

Innovative Advertisement in Retail

Every Day new products are entering into the Market. Unless sufficient advertisement is given it is highly difficult to sell the products. Cyclonic changes are effecting in advertisement arena and companies are searching for new avenues to advertise their products. All these companies are relentlessly trying to convince the consumer directly. In the back drop of this scenario, media managers are conceiving "INSTORE ADVERTISEMENT". Due to the wide spread of organized retailing, companies are exciting to experiment with the concept of in store Advertisement. For example "PANTLOON" has erected large size TV screens to display their products. It is estimated that nearly 15-20 lakh consumers are visiting pantaloon shops and they are directly influenced by new products. Generally domestic consumers are impulsive purchasers and their shopping habits are un-planned. In such Circumstances In stores Advertisements gives information about various products, features prices and other services. Interactive TV is also playing a vital role in the Retail landscape.

Dilemma of Small Shop Owners

Un-Organized Retail Shops are catering to the needs of local people. In India lowest strata of the society depends on daily wages and they hesitate to peep into glittering Super and Hyper markets. Hence they wish to visit the shops in their locality and the small shop owner will have rapport with locals and this nearness makes the shop owner dearest to locals. The support extended by the locals is a fulcrum to the foundation of small kirana shops. Unless and until the fruits of liberalization, privatization and globalization reaches to the lowest strata of the society, it is conceived that there is no threat to unorganized retail shops in India.

Government Policy

As matter of policy Government has been discouraging Foreign Direct Investment in Retail sector. The government is of the opinion that if the organized Foreign Retailers are allowed, the un-organized Retail Sector will have to close their shops. But Retail Corporates are of the opinion that if organized foreign retailers are allowed Indian manufacturers, suppliers and farmers will be benefited. It appears until the domestic retail business is strengthened it is not possible to allow Foreign Direct Investment in this sector. Un-organized retail sector has to face severe competition both from the Domestic and Foreign outlets.

In China, during the year 2004-05, the retail business registered a 6.1 per cent growth rate. Thailand has registered 13.2 per cent, Singapore 10 per cent where as India had registered 10 per cent growth rate. Retail companies are trying to attract 30 crore middle class consumers. Another interesting factor is that sixty per cent of our population is below twenty years and they are purchasing latest varieties. At present Organized Retailing is concentrated in North and Western India.

Future Scenario and Conclusion

It is expected that in the years to come Organized Retailing will grow at the rate of 40 per cent. Many companies are interested to establish retail outlets. So far the Andhra Pradesh in concerned Retail Business is mainly concentrated in Hyderabad and it takes some time to spread the Retail boom to other areas and two tier towns.

In accordance with the changing times, the traditional stores have to understand the challenging changes. At present Indian farmer is not getting required remunerative price and at the same time, consumer is paying high prices. Consumer protection Act 1986 is not practically implemented in letter and spirit. Organized Retailing bridges the gap between the producers and consumers. Socio, cultural and Economic aspects will play a vital role in the development of Retail Business. Until and unless the fruits of liberalization and privatization reaches to common man both organized and un-organized retail business will thrive in India.

16

Growth of Retailing in India: A Diagnostic Analysis

K. Rama Mohana Rao

Retailing is one of the oldest forms of business in the country. It has passed through many mile stones over centuries. For quite a long period, the retailing is in the form of village level Kirana shops, Weekly Shandies, Village fairs and Melas which provided extensive reach in the country besides a source of entertainment. Convenient stores, Mom and Pop shops are the next generation retailing formats. The Government supported Public Distribution System outlets, Khadi Stores, Cooperatives, etc. provided alternative distribution system against the private sector. The modern era is represented by hyper/super markets, departmental stores, exclusive brand outlets, shopping malls, etc. India has the highest density of retail outlets in the world. There are more than 4.3 million outlets spread over throughout the length and breadth of the country. The retailing sector employs around 8 per cent of the workforce in India which is 6 times bigger than Thailand and 5 times larger than South Korea and Taiwan. This sector is the second largest employment provider in the country after agriculture. The total domestic retail market was estimated around Rs. 9,300 billion in 2003-04 and the annual growth rate is around 6 per cent. Thus, the retailing sector occupies a vital position in the Indian economy with excellent growth prospects.

Changing Scenario of Retailing

Organised retailing is the change driver of 21st century in the country in the retailing sector. For several obvious reasons organized retailing could not make a mark in the country until recent years. The data presented in Table 16.1 shows the comparative status of the Indian organized retailing against its neighbouring countries. It clearly shows that organized retailing in India is only 2 per cent leaving 98 per cent to traditional unorganized retailing. Kishore Biyani, the trend setter in organized retailing in India, started "Pantaloons" and expanded it throughout the country, signaling the business potential in organized retailing. The changing economic conditions during the last two decades provided the right kind of foundation for the development of organized retailing.

Table 16.1: Organised Retailing in India and Neighbouring Countries (%)

Country	Organized Retailing	Traditional Retailing
Malaysia	50	50
Thailand	40	60
Philippines	35	65
Indonesia	25	75
South Korea	15	85
China	20	80
India	02	98

The liberalization policies followed by the Government of India helped the country to become the second fastest growing economy in the world. The disposable income of middle class households increased significantly at a growth rate of more than 20 per cent and the middle income population is growing by 10 per cent per annum. According to an estimate, there are more than seven lakh people in the country who will have a liquid cash balance of Rs. 50 lakh by 2009. The number is expected to cross 10 lakh at a growth rate of about 12 per cent per annum. The changes including accessibility of information, the shift from saving to spending and consumption behaviour of consumers, the nuclear family system, etc. opened up exciting opportunities to the industry and business to offer a wide variety of products and services. In many product and service areas there is a conspicuous shift from sellers market to buyers market.

Organised Retailing

Organized retailing is the fastest emerging dimension of the retailing sector in India. The size of the organized retailing is estimated at Rs. 36,000 crore in India with an annual growth rate of 30 to 40 per cent. It is estimated that the size of the organized retailing will skew up in the years to come and by 2011, it might stand in between Rs. 2,76,000 crore and Rs. 3,22,000 crore. Even then the share of organised retailing is expected to be less than 20 per cent in total retailing. A sizable number of companies entered into organized retailing in a big way. Pantaloon, Shoppers Stop, RPG Group, Trend, Lifestyle, Subhiksha, Food World, Nilgiris, Ebony, Crosswords, Globas, Raymond, Titan, Bata, Trinetra, Chandana etc.. have already established retail networks in the country. Big business houses like Reliance, Godrej, Tata, Hero, Wadia, Malhotras and Mahendra have announced big business plans to establish large scale retail networks. Reliance already made its presence felt through Reliance Fresh. Vertical retailing, category retailing, E-retailing etc., became the reality in India and are emerging as profit generating business opportunities. In addition to the Indian corporate giants, many multi-national corporations have successfully established their retail networks in the country which include McDonald, Dominos, Levis, Lee, Nike, Adidas, Banetton, Sony, Sharp, Kodak, LG, Samsung, etc.

It may not be out of point to make a mention here that Price Water House Coopers (PWC) has estimated India among the six most attractive destinations in retailing along side China, Turkey, Thailand, Malaysia and Hungary. At present, there are more than 200 shopping malls established in the country. All these are located in cities. The current trends in terms of investments and the entry of Indian and international corporate giants increased the income and consumption in the Indian economy, the fast changing life styles, Government support and the changing cost and value perceptions of Indian consumers signaling the emergence of a strong, viable and promising organized retail sector in the country in the years to come.

Major Challenges of Organised Retailing in India

India is a typical society with diversity as its character. The global formulations of success largely proved to be misfits in the India scenario. The common values of entire India are very few and the diversity in values, culture, habits, lifestyles, traditions, languages, religions, incomes will not allow any company to take India as one. They may need to see around 50 India's with in India to develop and finalize business strategies. There are at least four major challenges for the corporate retailers in the country. They are:

- Changing dynamics of retailing
- Changing expectations of consumers
- Reaching semi-urban and rural markets
- Adaptation to technology and service quality management

Changing Dynamics of Retailing

One of the noticeable changes that can be observed in recent years is the conversion of traditional provision shops (kirana shops) into departmental stores or mini-departmental stores in large number throughout the country. Further, the growth of highly accessible, medium sized products specific or service specific retailing units are being established. The traditional self financing retailers are taking the support of financial institutions or banks for their expansion plans. In other words, the traditional retailing units are redefining the scope, size and growth prospects of their business and responding in a big way to the fast changing dynamics of the Indian markets. The corporate retailers can be successful only by generating and offering new values that are beyond the possibility of the ordinary retailers. The retail format is one dimension presently keeping the corporate retailers above the line. The Malls, Hypermarkets, Warehouse Clubs, Super Centers and the like could offer the experiences that are new to the Indian customers. But the sustainability of this value in future is a big question mark. Innovative value added services and customized offerings may go a long way for the organized retailers to provide an edge over the traditional and the huge network of retailing units.

Promotion of retailer brands and building brand image are the most critical challenges. The huge promotional expenditure can't be transferred easily to the consumers in the presence of severe competitive environment from small and medium retail outlets rather than from the corporate counterpart. The Indian consumers are typically price sensitive across the socio-economic and demographic profiles. Communicating and convincing consumers on the intangible additional value offering is not at all an easy problem to handle.

Changing Expectations of Consumers

Throughout the country the research studies confirmed that the consumer expectations are changing fast in this country. The emergence of nuclear family system promoted group shopping and the families are looking at holistic experiences in shopping. The expected experiences of the consumers from the retail formats can be classified into three. They are:

- Shopping experience
- Business experience
- Service experience

Shopping Experience: The consumers are not in a position to incur time cost and search cost in collecting information relating to the need satisfying objects. They are looking at the retailing units to provide high quality information relating to various products and services available. They are expecting comprehensive, accurate, credible objective and current information not only of the outlet in which they are shopping, but also about the competitors' offerings. The information provided to the consumers should be in such a way that it is easy to understand for different categories of consumers. Convenient access to information is another dimension that provides support to consumers. They are also expecting some assistance from the employees of the retailing outlets in evaluating alternatives and in arriving purchase decisions. The retailing outlets which provide shopping experience to the consumers should take care that the consumers are not pressurized, either hardly or softly to avoid counter productive results.

Buying Experience: Consumers expect not only fair price from the seller but also a fair negotiation process. They want the negotiation to be free of pressure, free of deception and dishonesty. The negotiation process designed by the seller should be easy to understand and should include a clear description of all the costs - either direct or indirect, purchase or post-purchase. The consumers look for buying convenience, the availability of required inventory and honest and courteous treatment. In short, after the exit from the shop, the buyer should feel that he/she got the products at a reasonable price, and was treated well with reliability and responsiveness. The consumer expects empathetic treatment and the totality of whatever they have expected.

Service Experience: The consumers expect qualitative interactions in spite of perceived deficiencies from their part. The retailing organization should be capable of not only performing its activities qualitatively but also should try to fill the gaps of the consumers to generate quality interactive experiences to them. For example, the consumer may be struggling to define exactly his/her needs and to find out the right objects that can satisfy his/him. The sales personnel should first focus on helping the consumer to define the problem and then recommend the needed products accurately and honestly. Therefore, diagnosing the consumer problem accurately and responding to them rightly is the major dimension of service quality. Each and every moment of the consumer interaction has to be designed in such a way that each moment can generate some quality experience. The retail organization needs trained and qualitative work force to provide qualitative service experience to the consumers. Today quality workforce is a very scarce. The retailing organisations in the country are facing a problem of acute shortage of qualitative workforce. The expansion of the business on one hand, scarcity of skilled human resource, and competitive threats on the other hand are making it a Herculean task to the corporate retailers to provide qualitative service experience to the consumers.

Reaching Semi-urban and Rural Markets

India is a developing country. A large part of this country consists of semi-urban and rural markets. There are six lakh villages in the country and 90 per cent of the Indian consumers are living in semi-urban and rural areas. The real challenge of the corporate retailing in the country is to reaching to these markets effectively. The market potential is very much attractive in this part of the country. To exploit the potential, the companies have to manage the following challenges:

- Heavy investment requirement
- Shortage of qualified man power
- Low profit margin
- Shaping consumer behaviour and consumption habits
- Poor transport and other infrastructure; and
- Localisation of services

Heavy Investment Requirement: Developing the network of retail outlets in semi urban and rural areas requires huge investment and also time. With the uncertain estimates of outcome, companies are not interested to venture into these areas. Hindustan Levers Limited made some efforts to reach these markets with their packaged product line. The ITC promoted an Agri-based retail network in a few states of North India. Though the response is very impressive it has a long way to reach the total Indian market. Reliance is planning to trap the rural market potential for retailing in agricultural products. Excepting a few companies of this kind, the vast majority of the companies are not entering into the area. The requirement of heavy investment is standing as the major hindrance for the growth of retailing in rural India.

Shortage of Qualified Manpower: While the companies are facing shortage of quality manpower in urban areas it is too much to think of finding qualified manpower in rural areas. The companies need to identify the potential human resource and train them properly for making use of for their business purposes. This is a difficult proposition and demands an altogether a different competency from the organization.

Low Profit Margin: The rural consumers are mostly lower middle and lower income people and they are obviously price sensitive. The companies can reach the markets with a very low profit margin which proves uneconomic against a huge investment requirement. The return on investment is expected to be very low and it takes a very long period to maximize profits.

Shaping Consumer Behaviour and Consumption Habits: The rural consumers are tradition bound and they are rigid in their buying and consumption habits. To find market for the packaged goods offered by the retail outlets, the consumers need to be influenced and persuaded to change their traditional habits. It is not an easy task in a country like India where traditions are deep rooted.

Poor Transport and other Infrastructure: Infrastructure is the most neglected area in India. During the first fifty years of Independence this area was not given the importance it deserved. As a result, India lost so much in the developing process. Only during the last two decades some focus has been given for infrastructure development. However, the urban areas have been under focus and the rural areas are still deprived of the infrastructure facilities. Transport, Storage, Electricity, Roads and Communication System are the most essential for building the retailing network and in all these areas the villages score negative marks. No retailing company can build infrastructure by itself in rural India. It is only the Government that should focus on development of infrastructure to promote retailing in rural areas.

Localisation of Services: The rural parts of the country are diverse in their traditions and habits. Therefore, the generalized products may not be suitable to the rural India. The localization of products and services is another major challenge to reach rural markets.

Adaptation to Technology and Service Quality Management: Organised retailing is an emerging business dimension in India while it is the most prominent business in the developed parts of the world. The retail companies of America and European Countries have achieved substantial progress by developing customer friendly technology and by managing service quality. The Supply Chain Management, Electronic Retailing, Visual Merchandising, Event Management, Internal Marketing, Interactive Marketing, etc. are yet to be adapted properly and efficiently by the Indian retailing companies. Development of technology to suit to the needs of Indian consumers is one of the major challenges for the retailing companies.

Societal Concerns: The growth of organized retailing in the country in recent years is raising societal concerns in many parts of the country. Some are questioning the need for promotion of huge shopping malls and networks in a country where high density of retail network already exists. They fear that the corporate giants will kill the large number of small retail outlets. This may cause a major disturbance in the lives of millions who are eking out their livelihood from this business. In a country like India, where unemployment is one of the poorly addressed problems, any attempt to multiply the problem is not appreciated. The reaction of the small retailers in some parts of the country against Reliance Fresh is an example to recognize the growing fears and concerns among the people. The big retail houses are encouraging use and consumption of many products and services by the people. This attempt also attracted criticism from some quarters. Their point of view is that, in a developing country like India, consumption habits need to be nurtured properly and carefully, avoiding all excesses. The excessive consumption is leading not only to the consumption of scarce natural resources but also is resulting in ill health and low productivity. The sales promotion campaigns of the companies making the consumers impulsive in buying. This unplanned purchases paying off are heavily and the family budgets are being seriously affected. The increased burden of expenditure, as is feared by some people, is leading to the search for secondary means of raising incomes and promoting corruption.

All these concerns can not be over emphasized. The Government should come out with a retail policy addressing all these concerns. Particularly the issue of allowing Foreign Multi National Retail Companies in the country in any form should be discussed thoroughly in different platforms before arriving at a decision. The Public Distribution System, which is a balancing and control mechanism of market forces need to be strengthened further as an alternate mechanism to protect the interest of the consumers in case of exploitative tendencies of organized retailers. Opening of the system will lead to progress and development in any sector. But design of an effective control mechanism is essential to transform such progress and development beneficial to the society.

17

E-tailing Practices in Bangalore Metropolitan Area

Jai Raj Nair

Concept of E-tailing

E-tailing consists of computer-interactive retailing activities over the Internet. It involves a website maintained by the E-tailer for buying and selling of products and services via computer networks.

E-tailing is the electronic version of non-store retailing. Consumers can shop from their homes or offices by using computers to interact with retailers using the Internet. The number of Internet websites, or "store-fronts", where products can be ordered has been growing very rapidly. A few years back, www.amazon.com (the most prolific E-tailer) was only an Internet bookstore, but today shoppers can find thousands of items ranging from toys to sporting goods to consumer electronics products at this web site.

The Internet, with its worldwide "audience", is dramatically changing the nature of retailing. Its impact is so great that it finds a place in the "focus areas of special importance" in the retailing business. Traditionally, the focus areas of special importance have been merchandise assortment, location, atmospherics, customer service, store image, and database management.

While everyone - expert analyst and eager entrepreneurs alike mourned the demise of the Web as a business proposition towards the end of the year 2000, E-business has been slowly and steadily growing. And, remarkably, the wildly astronomical predictions and estimates made by analysts during the peak of the dotcom boom have, in fact, turned out to be rather conservative. Forrester Research reported E-commerce worth $3.9 trillion worldwide in

2003; a figure that is almost double of predictions made back in 1999. More than 40 per cent of the 450 plus Internet companies that went public have turned around and become profitable.

Problem Statement

The E-tailing concept in India is still relatively new. Hence, there is a limitation to availability of information. There is a need to study and analyze the problems being faced by E-tailers, and the marketing dynamics involved in the E-tailing process. In order to do so, it is imperative to develop an understanding of the online consumer that can impact marketing and operational strategy for the E-tailer.

As the practice of E-tailing in India matures, a deeper and more complete understanding of the nature and relationships of the three critical components – BUYERS, SELLERS, & TECHNOLOGIES that bring them together has become very essential. While some firms have been led astray by technology and IT, the truly successful have used the net to apply the core concepts of traditional marketing in a new and powerful way. There is a paradox here – "Customer Focus" is traditional thinking, but its application on the net involves new and non-traditional approaches.

Understanding the important components of online consumer behavior is the key to success in E-tailing.

A clear and thorough understanding of the above components can help E-tailers improve the adoption of consumer online purchasing by implementing methods and technologies that help fill in the gaps between the physical world shopping experience and the experience online. However, in some instances, physical touch can never be substituted. Likewise, human interaction will continue to be desired for social reasons. Nonetheless, E-tailers should discover and capitalize on the unique advantages of the Internet over physical world shopping, if E-tailing in India has to achieve staggering growth.

Research Objectives

The failure of a large number of E-tail companies during the "dotcom bust" period epitomizes the challenges of operating through virtual channels and underscores the need to better understand key drivers of online consumer behavior

The specific objectives of this research are as follows:

1. To identify the antecedents of customer confidence in E-tailing, leading to actual online purchase
2. To identify the critical success factors, including technological factors, of making online sales
3. To identify the product / services profiles that hold promise in the electronic market
4. To examine, analyze, and evaluate the important marketing issues facing firms that want to compete in this revolutionary and dynamic new media environment
5. To assess wants, needs and unmet expectations/opportunities specific to E-tailing products and services

In summary, the study is an attempt to

- introspect the past,
- retrospect the present &
- prospect the future of E-tailing in India using Bangalore as a representative city

Research Background (Emanating from Literature Review)

The following sections will introduce some models and issues related to this study and will lay the foundation for the Research Model.

The **Theory of Reasoned Action (TRA)**, attempts to predict and understand an individual's intended behavior (Ajzen and Fishbein, 1980). An individual executes a unique behavior that is decided by his or her behavioral intention (BI), which in turn is determined by his or her attitude (A) and a subjective norm (SN). External variables were considered in TRA to be related to a person's behavior (Ajzen and Fishbein, 1980).

The **Technology Acceptance Model (TAM)**, is based on the TRA model (Davis et al, 1989). It was developed to understand and predict an individual's Information System (IS) acceptance behavior based on perceived usefulness, defined as "the degree to which a person believes that using a particular system would enhance his or her job performance", and perceived ease of use, defined as "the degree to which a person believes that using a particular system would be free of effort". Consistent with the TRA model, the TAM states that the two beliefs affect the attitude towards using "IS" and the attitude leads to behavioral intention to use "IS". Finally, behavioral intention to use leads to actual "IS" use.

While TAM focuses on beliefs about "perceived usefulness" and "perceived ease of use" to influence the "behavioral intention to use" becoming "actual behavior", some external variables like "computer self-efficacy" and "trust" may influence behavior. Examples of such external variables are - trust for Internet banking (Suh and Han, 2002), trust for online shopping (Gefen et al, 2003), habit for online shoppers (Gefen, 2003), and computer self-efficacy for Web-Based Learning (Gong et al, 2004). These variables have exhibited significant impact on behavioral intention to use).

A **Model of Consumer Trust** was developed to explain consumer trust in an online store (Jarvenpaa et al, 2000). The trust factors are "perceived size" (the store's size from customer's perception), and "perceived reputation" (the store's reputation from customer's perception). Their research indicated that there are no strong effects with antecedents of trust, but the perceived trust in the online store is correlated individually with attitude and risk perception in the consumers' willingness to buy from an E-tailer's online store.

Ramnath and Pavlou (2002) introduced customer trust in an E-commerce transaction to predict consumer intentions to use online shopping. The conceptual framework was the perceived security effect of encryption, protection and authentication, reputation and Trust in E-commerce transactions in the model. The key finding was the relative strength of perceived security on trust in customer adoption of online shopping.

Dahlberg, et al (2003) introduced a **Trust-Enhanced Technology Acceptance Model** to explain mobile payment solutions. The trust factors are perceived trust, (the degree to which a person perceives a particular technology solution as secure and trustworthy), and disposition to trust, (the extent to which a person is willing to trust others). The findings indicate that the proposed trust factors play an important role in customer adoption of mobile payment solutions.

An **Extended Technology Acceptance Model** has been used to understand consumer intentions to use online purchasing (Heijden et al, 2003). The conceptual framework includes trust in the online store, perceived risk, perceived usefulness, perceived ease of use, attitude towards online purchasing, and online purchase intention in the research model. The key finding was the relative strength of trust in customer adoption of online purchasing.

Vijayasarathy, (2004) introduced an Augmented **Technology Acceptance Model** to predict consumer intentions to use online shopping. New variables in the model are privacy (the degree to which personal information is protected), and security (the extent to which a consumer believes that making payments online is secure). The findings indicated that the proposed privacy and security play an important role in customer adoption of online shopping.

A review of scholarly research on IS acceptance and usage suggests that TAM has emerged as one of the most influential models in this stream of research. The TAM represents an important theoretical contribution toward understanding IS usage and IS acceptance behaviors.

TAM has been applied to a wide range of technologies and has been very predictive of individual acceptance and technology use. One of the criticisms of TAM has been that although it can effectively predict system acceptance, it is not particularly useful in providing explanations that can be used to design interventions that foster acceptance (e.g., Venkatesh and Davis 1996, 2000). While it is widely recognized that perceived usefulness and perceived ease of use affect acceptance, until we better understand what determinants affect perceived usefulness and perceived ease of use, it will be difficult to provide *actionable and practical guidance* from TAM. There has been some research on a set of general determinants that apply to a wide range of technologies and classes of technologies (e.g., Venkatesh 2000; Venkatesh and Davis 2000).

However, in using TAM for actionable guidance, it is essential to identify determinants that are tailored to specific classes of technologies that capture the nuances of the class of technologies and/or business processes (Benbasat and Zmud 2002). Thus, as a first step, it is important to extend TAM toward specific classes of technologies (Dennis and Reinicke 2003). A model focused on a specific class of technologies will produce a *narrower* but *stronger* model rather than a general model that attempts to address many classes of technologies simultaneously (Newell 1969). Given this background, there is a necessity to integrate constructs from E-tailing practices with TAM to present a model of acceptance of E-tailing to provide a rich understanding of the acceptance and technology use of this specific class of technology.

Technologies that facilitate interactions via electronic means have become an essential component of day-to-day life. Thus, it is not surprising that this class of technologies has received considerable research attention over the past five years (Vessey et al. 2003). However, several prior studies have been mainly in the field of collaboration technologies such as voice mail, E-mail, and group support systems (e.g., Adams, Nelson, and Todd 1992; Chin and Gopal 1995; Straub, Limayem, and Karahanna 1995). These studies are nevertheless important because they established TAM as one of the cornerstones of IS literature and a theoretical model applicable to a wide range of technologies.

A model that integrates technology acceptance with E-tailing practices is lacking, a void that this research seeks to address.

Research Model and Hypotheses

The conceptual research model, shown in Figure 8, is an extension of the above-mentioned models and their enhancements, customized to the specific and unique characteristics of E-tailing. As explained earlier, the generic model of technology acceptance has inherent limitations and there is a necessity to extend this model to address each class of technology usage individually.

The research model given below shows that the major factors that influence 'actual online buying' are 'confidence for buying' and 'technological comfort'. The antecedents of 'confidence for buying' are 'perceived trust', 'perceived value-for-money', 'perceived navigability' and 'perceived quality of E-services'. The antecedents to perceived trust are 'credibility', 'security', 'privacy', 'communication', and 'gullibility'.

There is a general agreement among researchers (e.g., Cheskin Research, 2000; Cheskin Research & Studio Archetype/Sapient, 1999; Fogg, Soohoo, Danielson, Marable, Stanford, & Tauber, 2002) on the significant importance of "perceived trust" in online activities.

There are several definitions and interpretations of trust, so much so, that it makes the concept confused across research areas. In this study, the definition of trust has been adapted from Mayer et al, 1995 & Jarvenpaa et al, 2000 - trust is "the willingness of a consumer to be vulnerable to the actions of an online store based on the expectation that the online store will perform a particular action important to the consumer, irrespective of the ability to monitor or control the online store". The following antecedents of perceived trust have been identified:

1. Credibility: This is defined as the extent to which the reliability, trustworthiness, existence of physical store and reputation of the E-tailer is ensured.

Derived Hypothesis: H_1: There exists a positive association between credibility and perceived trust.

2. Security: This is defined as the extent to which protection of customers' sensitive data from "hackers" and "crackers" is ensured

Derived Hypothesis: H_2: There exists a positive association between security and perceived trust.

3. Privacy: This is defined as the extent to which customer's belief that the E-tailer will not divulge his/her personal information to 3rd parties, willy-nilly, is maintained.

Derived Hypothesis: H_3: There exists a positive association between privacy and perceived trust.

4. Communication: This is defined as the extent to which customer's belief that the E-tailer will be in constant communication with him/her before, during, and after the E-tail sale transaction is maintained

Derived Hypothesis: H_4: There exists a positive association between communication and perceived trust.

5. Gullibility: This is defined as the extent to which customers get influenced and form opinions based on word-of-mouth communication from others.

Derived Hypothesis: H_5: There exists a positive association between the individual's gullibility and perceived trust.

The research model suggests that perceived trust, perceived value-for-money, perceived navigability and perceived quality of E-services are the antecedents to establishment of confidence for buying.

6. Perceived Trust: As explained earlier, perceived trust is defined as the extent to which the consumer is willing to be vulnerable to the actions of an E-tailer, based on the expectation that the E-tailer will perform a particular action important to the consumer, irrespective of the ability to monitor or control the E-tailer.

Derived Hypothesis: H_6: There exists a positive association between perceived trust and confidence for buying.

7. Perceived Value-for-Money (VFM): This is defined as the extent to which the consumer's belief that E-tail purchase would offer more convenience, faster processes, better bargains etc. as compared to any other form of purchase is maintained

Derived Hypothesis: H_7: There exists a positive association between perceived value-for-money and confidence for buying.

8. Perceived Navigability: This is defined as the extent to which the consumer's belief that the E-tail purchase process is "free of effort" is maintained

Derived Hypothesis: H_8: There exists a positive association between perceived navigability and confidence for buying.

9. Perceived Quality of E-Services: This is defined as the extent to which consumer's belief in service quality of the E-tailer in terms of fulfillment, efficiency, responsiveness, grievance-handling, interactive decision aids (presence technology, 3D presentation, online help, etc.) is maintained

Derived Hypothesis: H_9: There exists a positive association between perceived quality of E-services and confidence for buying.

The research model further suggests that confidence for buying is an antecedent for actual online purchase

10. Confidence for Buying: This is defined as the extent to which the consumer's confidence in making a purchase in an E-tailing environment is established

Derived Hypothesis: H_{10}: There exists a positive association between confidence for buying and actual online buying.

11. Technological Comfort: This is defined as the extent to which the consumer is comfortable using the computer and other electronic gadgets relevant to E- tailing

Derived Hypothesis: H_{11}: There exists a positive association between technological comfort and actual online buying

Research Methodology

The behavior of online customers is central to this study, as it is important to understand the dynamics of purchases made over the Internet. Hence, the major focus of the study was to understand whether credibility, security, privacy, communication, and gullibility affects a customer's perceived trust, and whether perceived trust, perceived value-for-money, perceived navigability, and perceived quality of E-services affects a customer's confidence for buying, and whether confidence for buying and technological comfort affects the actual online buying.

Data Collection Instrument

One of the greatest challenges in collecting data for research is the creation and formatting of a questionnaire. In order to minimize misinterpretations in this endeavor, a preliminary questionnaire was initially distributed to a pilot group of 25 subjects, selected on the basis of convenience sampling. This pilot group not only answered the questionnaire, but also suggested changes in nebulous, fuzzy areas of the questionnaire. The group also made suggestions in the order of the questions. This process had a significant impact on the original questionnaire, narrowing the scope of the questions and eliminating redundant and irrelevant questions.

The final questionnaire used for data collection contained close-ended questions to measure the various constructs depicted in the research model. This enabled respondents to answer questions quickly, yet objectively. The perceptions of the respondents were collected objectively using 5-point Likert scales thus reducing the complexity involved in collecting subjective data. Various items within the same construct group were randomized to prevent systemic response bias. An E-mail survey method was selected to float the questionnaire due to the following three considerations:

1. E-mail surveys (a derivative of the standard mail survey) are well suited for measuring respondents about self-reported or beliefs or behaviors (Neuman, 2003) .It provides a quick and efficient way of gathering large amounts of data from the population with a relatively low cost in comparison with other collection methods (Neuman, 2003). In this study, email survey was used to obtain information on the customer's demography and their perceptions on the factors that have influenced actual customer purchase.
2. The use of a mail survey increases reliability of responses by eliminating interviewer bias (Neuman, 2003). As this research attempted to identify factors that influence the actual buying behavior by testing the interrelationship of different variables, the E-mail survey was highly suitable.
3. An E-mail survey allows the researcher contact with inaccessible respondents. It allows respondents to complete

the questionnaire at their own convenience and at their own pace. With this flexibility, the respondents can take time to think and answer the questions. Therefore, the E-mail survey method was an appropriate way to collect the data.

Moreover, as this research dealt with Internet-based electronic retailing, it was assumed that using email mode for collecting data would not generate any kind of bias in the sample. Indeed, every online purchaser is also an Internet user and could therefore access emails.

Sample Frame

The population for this research comprised Bangalore-based Internet-savvy consumers, who are all working professionals.

Sample Size

Sample size has a direct bearing on how accurate the findings are relative to the true values in the population. Therefore, determining an appropriate sample size for this research was considered to be of paramount importance.

The required sample size was calculated using the following formula:

$$\textbf{Sample Size} = \frac{\{(Z^2) * (p) * (1-p)\}}{C^2}$$

where:

Z = no. of std. deviations a point on a distribution is away from the mean (e.g. 1.96 for 95 per cent Confidence Level)

p = percentage picking a choice, expressed as a decimal (p = 0.5 is used for calculating required sample size)

C = confidence interval expressed as decimal (e.g. 0.04 = $\pm$ 4 per cent)

Assuming, Confidence Level = 95 per cent & Confidence Interval = 7 per cent, the required sample size identified was:

$$\frac{1.96^2 * 0.5 * 0.5}{0.07^2} = \mathbf{196}$$

A response rate from an E-mail survey might be normally expected between 10 per cent and 50 per cent (Neuman 2000).

Therefore, to ensure that sufficient data was collected to allow in-depth analysis, and accurate inferences could be drawn from the data, it was decided to send emailed questionnaires to five times of the sample size (approximately to 1000 subjects).

Sampling Method

The concept of E-tailing is of recent origin in India. Hence, E-tail database of consumers is not publicly available (ala directories). Individual E-tailers do have their own customer databases but generally, they are not at liberty to disclose the list due to the security issues involved in the E-tail purchases.

As a result of the stringent privacy policies adopted by the E-tailers it was extremely difficult to locate samples by absolutely random means. The sampling method chosen was "snowball sampling" (sometimes referred to as "network sampling"). Snowball sampling is a non-probability method used when the desired sample characteristic is rare. It may be extremely difficult or cost prohibitive to locate respondents in these situations. Snowball sampling relies on referrals from initial subjects to generate additional subjects. In the absence of a publicly available database, this was the only technique that could be used. Snowball sampling came at the expense of introducing bias because the technique itself reduces the likelihood that the sample will represent a good cross section from the population.

It was practically impossible to track the number of respondents who finally received the questionnaire, as the questionnaire was sent as an email attachment with a request to forward it to as many Bangalore-based subjects as possible. Initially, it was sent to 137 respondents directly but there is no way that one can estimate how many subjects ended up with a copy of the questionnaire in their mailbox.

219 responses were received till January 23, 2007. Out of these, 17 responses were rejected, as they were incomplete. The balance 202 responses were retained for data analysis. Kaiser-Meyer-Olkin (KMO) Test was used to measure the sampling adequacy. The KMO measure obtained was 0.785 and as this is

more than the cut-off value of 0.5, sampling adequacy was established.

Data Analysis: The Preliminary Steps

This section discusses the initial screening of the data, the examination of the data for missing values and outliers, and the selection of analysis methods (Table 17.1).

Table 17.1: Descriptive Statistics of Various Constructs

Variable	Notation	N	Min	Max	Mean	Std. Deviation
Credibility	CRE	202	2.00	4.91	3.8245	.47247
Security	SEC	202	2.40	5.00	4.0020	.53233
Privacy	PRI	202	2.33	5.00	4.1238	.53052
Communication	COM	202	2.00	5.00	4.1574	.47991
Gullibility	GUL	202	1.80	4.60	3.2901	.60938
Perceived Trust	PT	202	1.25	5.00	4.1460	.58831
Perceived Value-for-Money	PVFM	202	1.17	5.00	3.4257	.76925
Perceived Navigability	PN	202	1.54	5.00	3.6413	.58571
Perceived Quality of E-services	PQ	202	1.55	5.00	3.9595	.54793
Confidence for Buying	CB	202	1.80	5.00	3.5851	.71095
Technological Comfort	TC	202	1.50	4.83	3.2129	.67945
Actual Online Buying	AOB	202	2.00	5.00	3.3000	.60000

Data Screening: After collection and compilation of the data, the analysis process commenced with data screening. Prior to analyzing the data, a critical first step was to examine the basic characteristics of the data in order to assist with the application of a multivariate analysis model as well as interpretation of the results (Hair et al, 1998). The data from the survey were first screened to identify out-of-range values by examining the minimum and maximum values for each question. Descriptive statistics ensured that the means and standard deviations were credible.

The next step was to examine the data for missing values, outliers, and reliability. The investigations of these three areas are discussed in the following sections.

Missing values: Using the missing value analysis function in SPSS, the number of cases or variables having missing data was identified. None of the cases and/or variables in the final 202 responses exhibited a high level of missing data and hence, all of them were retained for further analysis.

Outliers: An *outlier* is an observation that lies an abnormal distance from other values in a chosen sample. Outliers may occur for a number of reasons: a procedural error (e.g. data entry error), etc. No outliers were detected during the examination and hence, there was no need to eliminate any of the 202 responses.

Reliability: To assess reliability, the Cronbach's alpha score for each construct was examined. The alpha score was greater than 0.7 (Numally 1978) in all constructs and hence, the constructs were reckoned as reliable (Table 17.2).

Table 17.2: Cronbach's Alpha Scores for Reliability Measurement

Scale	No. of Items	Cronbach's Alpha
Credibility	11	0.7242
Security	5	0.7165
Privacy	6	0.7021
Communication	10	0.8201
Gullibility	5	0.7104
Perceived Trust	4	0.8075
Perceived VFM	6	0.8408
Perceived Navigability	13	0.8820
Perceived Quality of E-Services	11	0.8489
Confidence For Buying	5	0.7042
Technological Comfort	6	0.7319
Actual Online Buying	3	0.7020

Data Analysis: The data was then subjected to rigorous quantitative analysis using SPSS 11.0. The hypothesized relationships depicted in Figure-9 were tested using multiple linear regressions. Three models were initially tested.

Model 1: The dependent variable (perceived trust) and independent variables (credibility, security, privacy, communication, and gullibility) were entered into a hierarchy for testing hypotheses (H_1, H_2, H_3, H_4, and H_5). The hypothesized relationships can be represented in terms of the following regression equation:

$$PT = \alpha + \beta_1 CRE + \beta_2 SEC + \beta_3 PRI + \beta_4 COM + \beta_5 GUL$$

where: PT = Perceived Trust, CRE = Credibility, SEC = Security, PRI = Privacy, GUL = Gullibility.

Model 2: The dependent variable (confidence for buying) and independent variables (perceived trust, perceived value-for-money, perceived navigability, and perceived quality of e-services) were entered into a hierarchy for testing hypotheses (H_6, H_7, H_8, and H_9). The hypothesized relationships can be represented in terms of the following regression equation:

$$CB = \alpha + \gamma_1 PT + \gamma_2 PVFM + \gamma_3 PN + \gamma_4 PQ$$

where: CB = Confidence for Buying, PT = Perceived Trust, PVFM = Perceived Value-for-Money, PN = Perceived Navigability, PQ = Perceived Quality of E-services.

Model 3: The dependent variable (actual online buying) and independent variables confidence for buying, and technological comfort) were entered into a hierarchy for testing hypotheses (H_{10}, and H_{11}). The hypothesized relationships can be represented in terms of the following regression equation:

$$AOB = \alpha + \zeta_1 CB + \zeta_2 TC$$

where: AOB = Actual Online Buying, CB = Confidence for Buying, TC = Technological Comfort.

Results of Regression Analysis

Model 1 : PT versus CRE, SEC, PRI, COM, GUL

The regression equation is

$$PT = 0.108 - 0.0487CRE + 0.206SEC + 0.0374PRI + 0.482COM + 0.378GUL$$

Table 17.3a: Coefficients for Model 1

Coefficients

		Unstandardized Coefficients		Standardized Coefficients	T	Sig.	Collinearity Statistics	
		B	Std. Error	Beta			Tolerance	VIF
Model 1	(Constant)	.108	.311		.347	.729		
	CRE	-4.872E-02	.076	-.039	-.638	.524	.626	1.598
	SEC	.206	.058	.187	3.558	.000	.857	1.167
	PRI	3.745E-02	.067	.034	.556	.579	.638	1.568
	COM	.482	.086	.393	5.571	.000	.474	2.111
	GUL	.378	.051	.391	7.379	.000	.838	1.193

* Dependent Variable: PT

Table 17.3b: Summary of Model 1

Model Summary

Model 1	R	R Square	Adjusted R Square	Std. Error of the Estimate
	.734	.538	.526	.40487

* Predictors: (Constant), GUL, SEC, CRE, PRI, COM

Table 17.3c: Analysis of Variance (ANOVA) for Model 1

Anova

Model 1		Sum of Squares	df	Mean Square	F	Sig.
	Regression	37.438	5	7.488	45.677	.000
	Residual	32.129	196	.164		
	Total	69.567	201			

* Predictors: (Constant), GUL, SEC, CRE, PRI, COM

* Dependent Variable: PT

Tables 17.3a, 17.3b, and 17.3c indicate the following:

- PT (perceived trust) showed positive association with SEC (security), COM (communication), and GUL (gullibility) @ 1 per cent, 5 per cent, and 10 per cent significance levels. Thus, hypotheses H_2, H_4, and H_5 are supported. Hypotheses H_1, and H_3 are rejected.
- The model is powerful because the 'P' value of 'F' is significant @ 1 per cent, 5 per cent, and 10 per cent levels.

Model 2: CB versus PT, PVFM, PN, PQ

The regression equation is

$$CB = 2.3 + 0.136PT + 0.237\ PVFM - 0.142\ PN + 0.519PQ$$

Tables 17.4a, 17.4b, and 17.4c indicate the following:

- CB (confidence for buying) showed positive association with PT (perceived trust) @ 5 per cent, and 10 per cent significance levels. It showed positive association with PVFM (perceived value-for-money), and PQ (perceived quality of E-services), @ 1 per cent, 5 per cent, and 10 per cent significance levels. Thus, hypotheses H_6, H_7, and H_9 are supported. Hypotheses H_8 is rejected.

- The model is powerful because the 'P' value of 'F' is significant @ 1 per cent, 5 per cent, and 10 per cent levels.

Table 17.4a: Coefficients for Model-2

Coefficients

		Unstandardized Coefficients		Standardized Coefficients	t	Sig.
Model 2		B	Std. Error	Beta		
	(Constant)	2.298	.389		5.906	.000
	PT	.136	.098	.112	1.380	.017
	PVFM	.237	.073	.257	3.267	.001
	PN	-.142	.115	-.117	-1.236	.218
	PQ	.519	.134	.400	3.885	.000

*Dependent Variable: CB

Table 17.4b: Summary of Model 2

Model Summary

Model 2	R	R Square	Adjusted R Square	Std. Error of the Estimate
	.368	.135	.118	.66787

* Predictors: (Constant), PQ, PVFM, PT, PN

Table 17.4c: Analysis of Variance (ANOVA) for Model 2

Anova

Model 1		Sum of Squares	df	Mean Square	F	Sig.
	Regression	13.723	4	3.431	7.691	.000
	Residual	87.872	197	.446		
	Total	101.595	201			

* Predictors: (Constant), PQ, PVFM, PT, PN
* Dependent Variable: CB

Model 3: AOB versus CB, TC

The regression equation is

AOB = 2.67 + 0.216TCT + 0.637 CB

Table 17.5a: Coefficients for Model 3

Coefficients

Model 3	Unstandardized Coefficients		Standardized Coefficients	t	Sig.
	B	Std. Error	Beta		
(Constant)	2.674	.211		12.648	.000
CB	.637	.063	.688	10.052	.000
TC	.216	.066	.223	3.258	.001

* Dependent Variable: AOB

Table 17.5b: Summary of Model 3

Model Summary

Model 3	R	R Square	Adjusted R Square	Std. Error of the Estimate
	.594	.353	.347	.53129

*Predictors: (Constant), TC, CB

Table 17.5c: Summary of Model 3

Anova

Model 3		Sum of Squares	df	Mean Square	F	Sig.
	Regression	30.701	2	15.351	54.384	.000
	Residual	56.171	199	.282		
	Total	86.872	201			

* Predictors: (Constant), TC, CB
*Dependent Variable: AOB

Tables 17.5a, 17.5b, and 17.5c indicate the following:

- AOB (actual online buying) showed positive association with CB (confidence for buying), and TC (technology comfort) @ 1 per cent, 5 per cent, and 10 per cent significance levels. Thus, hypotheses H_{10}, and H_{11} are supported.
- The model is powerful because the 'P' value of 'F' is significant @ 1 per cent, 5 per cent, and 10 per cent levels.
- After conducting regression analysis on the three models, test for multi co-linearity was undertaken with the intention of conducting a stepwise regression analysis, if multi co-linearity existed.

Correlation coefficients exceeding 0.75 were considered significant. Table 17.6 shows that all the coefficients are less than the threshold value of 0.75, and hence, there was no need to conduct step-wise regression analysis.

Table 17.6: Correlation Coefficients of all the Constructs

Correlation Matrix

	Pearson's Correlation Coefficient	CRE	SEC	PRI	COM	GUL	PT	PVFM	PN	PQ	CB	TC	AOB
CRE	Z	1											
SEC	Z	.252	1										
PRI	Z	.425	.316	1									
COM	Z	.602	.326	.581	1								
GUL	Z	.277	.226	.254	.384	1							
PT	Z	.367	.404	.403	.600	.582	1						
PVFM	Z	.298	.307	.381	.415	.430	.370	1					
PN	Z	.436	.403	.543	.517	.383	.426	.486	1				
PQ	Z	..631	.452	.560	.705	.390	.569	.487	.695	1			
CB	Z	.204	.186	-.030	.204	-.045	.195	-.078	.084	.258	1		
TC	Z	.290	.215	-.019	.301	.105	.178	.066	.221	.354	.554	1	
AOB	Z	.259	.213	.002	.162	.187	.462	-.007	-.067	.185	.565	.158	1

A summary of the hypotheses test results is presented in Table 17.7.

Findings and Suggestions

- A positive association has been established between security and perceived trust. Thus, E-tailers need to beef up their website security measures to instill confidence in the buyers. The following measures are suggested:
- The E-tailers need to procure "security certifications" from trusted third parties like "for their website transactions and display them prominently on their website.
- Warnings of new fraudulent means adopted by hackers need to be displayed prominently on the website on a regular basis.
- Dynamic electronic keyboards should be provided on the website to prevent "keyboard stroke capturing". An example of such a key board is given below:

Such security features are being provided by the E-banks for online banking transactions only. E-tailers need to adopt this feature on their websites.

- All information required to complete an online transaction, including payment are available on the card itself, i.e. Card Number, Expiry Date, and CVV Number. This is a major concern as card theft has become very rampant. Furthermore, in merchant establishments, very often the cards are taken out of view of the customer for swiping. Any unscrupulous person can note down the above three details and make fraudulent purchases. It is suggested that appropriate biometric technologies be brought in to authenticate the person making the online purchase. This would give a major boost to trust in online sale transactions. Till then, the E-tail website should automatically generate a password and send it to the email ID / mobile number of the concerned person. No transaction should be completed without the password being entered on the E-tail website. Very recently, Citibank introduced this feature to authenticate online transfer of money from banking accounts.

Table 17.7: Summary of Hypotheses Test Results

Hypotheses Path	Hyp.	Coeff.	t-Test	Decision
Credibility -> Perceived Trust	H_1	-.039	-.638	Not Supported
Security -> Perceived Trust	H_2	.187	3.558	Supported
Privacy -> Perceived Trust	H_3	.034	.556	Not Supported
Communication -> Perceived Trust	H_4	.393	5.571	Supported
Gullibility -> Perceived Trust	H_5	.391	7.379	Supported
Perceived Trust -> Confidence for Buying	H_6	.112	1.380	Supported
Perceived Value-for-Money -> Confidence for Buying	H_7	.257	3.267	Supported
Perceived Navigability -> Confidence for Buying	H_8	-.117	-1.236	Not Supported
Perceived Quality of E-services -> Confidence for Buying	H_9	.400	3.885	Supported
Confidence for Buying -> Actual Online Buying	H_{10}	.688	10.052	Supported
Technological Comfort -> Actual Online Buying	H_{11}	.223	3.258	Supported

- Mobile phones can be integrated into the E-tailing paradigm, as mobile phones are much more personal than computers. The huge penetration of mobile phones could be tapped and channnelized into an efficient E-tailing service.
- A positive association has been established between communication and perceived trust. This indicates that the E-tailers must be in constant communication with customers before, during, and after the sale transaction. The following measures are suggested:
- The E-tailers need to inform customers about the payment status as soon as it is over through automated email.
- Courier details should be emailed automatically to the customer as soon as the goods are shipped.
- E-tailers should respond to complaints related to late / non-arrival of goods promptly.
- A feedback should be taken after the goods are received and the customer has had time to use the product.
- A positive association has been established between gullibility and perceived trust. This indicates that the E-tailers must cultivate opinion leaders and consider mass advertising.
- A positive association has been established between perceived value-for-money and confidence for buying. This indicates that the E-tailers must offer better bargains; better bulk discounts vis-à-vis retailers. In other words, there should always be a price differential in favor of online purchases. The price advantage should be prominently displayed on the website. Other cost savings like transportation, parking, time costs, etc. should also be highlighted. Institutional membership maybe considered, wherein a member-institute's employees could be offered good deals if they shop online.
- A positive association has been established between perceived quality of E-services and confidence for buying. This indicates that the E-tailers must provide efficient E-services that are superior to offline mode. The following measures are suggested:
- E-tailers need to ensure that order fulfillment takes place on

or before the promised date. This is a serious concern as the results of one delayed receipt could adversely affect future online purchases.

- The E-tailers need to continuously invest in innovative technologies to provide better and better quality E-services. Presence technology, 3D presentations of products, interactive decision aids, etc. should be considered as starters.
- A positive association has been established between technological comfort and actual online buying. This indicates that the E-tailers must invest in innovative user-interface technologies that would put the user at ease and not intimidate him/her. Voice-based E-tailing services could also be considered.

Concluding Thoughts

E-tailing is one of the critical business models for E-commerce in the competitive business environment. Without a theoretical model for analyzing E-tailing success, it is very difficult for E-tailers to achieve their business goals. An "E-tail Acceptance Model" was developed to enhance and advance the traditional model. This new model has identified the critical factors leading to customer confidence and eventual purchase in an E-tailing environment, thereby contributing to the rising body of knowledge concerning the determinants of customer confidence in an electronic environment. Many companies today are trying to increase their website sales. The theoretical framework that has been developed in this study will help to convert 'online visitors' to 'online customers'.

The results of this study provide at least two theoretical contributions to E-tail adoption research. First, the study presents four empirically tested, reliable, and valid constructs that were found significant in predicting E-tail use, namely gullibility, perceived value-for-money, perceived quality of E-services, and technological comfort. Second, the results corroborate the fact that specific technology acceptance models have to be developed for specific classes of technology use. The general model may not be adequate enough to explain the adoption and use of different types of technologies wherein the specific features of the technology play an important role.

Although this study makes contributions to the body of knowledge in the E-tailing domain, there are a number of limitations associated with the research, as follows:

- E-tailers have not been segmented while conducting the study and have been treated as generic. Specific categories of E-tailers need to be considered to check whether the empirically tested model is valid across all categories.
- The sample selection using snowball sampling has limited the ability to generalize the finding to the overall population, due to its non-random nature.

References

A Degeratu, Arvind Rangaswamy, et al, "Consumer Choice Behavior in Online and Traditional Supermarkets: The Effect of Brand Name, Price, and Other Search Attributes", Int'l Journal of Research in Marketing, Vol. 17, 2000

Alex Birch, et al, "The Age of E-Tail: Conquering the New World of Electronic Shopping", Capstone Publishing, 2000

Charles Steinfield, "Situated Electronic Commerce: Toward a View as Complement Rather than Substitute for Offline Commerce", Urban Geography, Vol. 25, No. 4, May-June 2004

Christian Homburg, et al, "Service Orientation of a Retailer's Business Strategy: Dimensions, Antecedents, and Performance Outcomes", Journal of Marketing Vol. 66 (Oct 2002)

E Constantinides, et al, "The Impact of Web Experience on Virtual Buying Behavior: An Empirical Study", Univ. of Twente, NL

Erik Brynjolfsson & Mike Smith, "Frictionless Commerce? - A Comparison of Internet & Conventional Retailers", http://ecommerce.mit.edu

Geke Van Dijk, "Consumer Behavioral Styles in Online E-Commerce Environments", http://mcs.open.ac.uk

Jacques Bughin, "Finding the Path(s) Towards Profitable E-Commerce", Research Notes, Working Paper Series, Jan 16, 2003, No. 7

Jacques Bughin, "There is Light at the End of the Tunnel: Profitable Strategies in Online Retailing", http://e-commerce.mit.edu

Kavita Kshatriya, "E-Retailing: A Critical Review", Aura Journal of

IISM, Vol. 1, No. 2, Feb 2004

Klaus Lenk, "Competition in B2C E-Commerce: Analytical Issues and Empirical Evidence", Electronic Markets - Vol. 12, No. 3, 08/2002

Lei-Da Chen & Justin Tan, "Technology Adaptation in E-Commerce: Key Determinants of Virtual Stores Acceptance", European Management Journal Vol. 22, No. 1, Feb 2004

M Krishna Chaitanya, "Competitive Advantage in E-Tailing: Use of Marketing & Technology", ICFAI Journal of Marketing Management, Nov 2004

Mike Milloy, et al, "Modelling Online Security & Privacy to Increase Consumer Purchasing Intent", Informing Science, June 2002

Pingjun Jiang, "Managing Customer Price perceptions: An Empirical Investigation on the Impacts of E-Tailing Services Services Marketing", Qtly, Vol. 24, Issue 4 dtd. 03/01/2003

Retailing in India, McKinsey & Confederation of Indian Industry Joint Study Report, 2004

Ruby Roy Dholakia, "Switching to Electronic Stores: Consumer Characteristics and the Perception of Shopping Benefits", http://ritim.cba.uri.edu

Sandip Krishnamurthy, "An Empirical Study of the Causal Antecedents of Customer Confidence in E-Tailers", http://firstmonday.org

Sang Yong Kim, et al "Consumers' Perceived Importance of and Satisfaction with Internet Shopping", Routledge, Vol. 11, No.3/July 01, 2001

Taylor Randall, et al, "Choice of Inventory Structure By Internet Retailers: An Empirical Examination of the Role of Inventory Ownership", http://e-commerce.mit.edu

Xing Pan, et a, "Why aren't the Prices of the Same Item the same at me.com and you.com?: Drivers of Price Dispersion Among E-tailers", http://www.smeal.psu.edu/ebrc/publications

Yuping Liu, "Generating Value through Online Interactions: Individual & Situational Differences", www.yupingliu.com

Zulima Fernandez, et al, "The Internet: Strategy and Boundaries of the Firm", http://docubib.uc3m.es/WORKING PAPERS

18

Growth Drivers in Indian Retailing

C. Ram Mohan and Satyanarayana

Retailing is a business activity that involves selling products services to customers for their non-commercial individual or family use. Normally, retailing is the last stage of the distribution process. Retailing has been one of the fundamental building blocks of the Indian economy. It is estimated that by 2010, retailing in India will comprise a US$ 300 billion industry if the economy continued to register a growth of six per cent of the G.D.P. (Gross Domestic Product) annually. The retail industry is ever more attractive now, with scores of players leaping into action and many more testing the water.

The Indian retail market has undergone an immense transformation in the post liberation era. Due to wide range of products available the increasing purchasing power of customers, superior supply chain management leading to economic of scale and a world class Customer Service, the Indian Retail Market is witnessing tremendous growth. Few years back, industrial Giants like Tata's (Westside), Eureka Forbes, RPG, (Food World, Giant Music World, Health and Glow) Pantaloons, Big Bazaar Shopper's Stop, and Life Style have make a foray into Indian Retail Market the association of these big names with the retail sector has helped in attracting a large number of customers.

Moreover, the resource available with these companies' in terms of capital, personal, and Technology allow them to invest in the retail sector thus insuring the sustenance of the retail industry. Indian consumers now spread a significant portion of their income on buying goods and services.

The following are the objectives of the study.

- To analyze the trends in retail sector in India.

- To present about the various segments of retail industry such as department stores, discounts stores etc,
- To examine that the retail market is building blocks of Indian Economy.

Description of Department Stores

Department stores are the general merchandise retailers with considerably large retail space with separate sections allowed for foodstuff, body care products and so on. They offer a wide selection of products to customers and generally the quality of goods sold in the store varies from average to very good quality, e.g. Westside, Pantloons, Shoppers' Stop, LifeStyle etc.

Discount Stores: Discount stores are similar to department stores, except that these stores offer products at less than the retail price. The purpose of doing so is to generate profits on volume sales. Discount stores are normally targeted at middle and lower middle class customers who are price conscious like Big Bazaar.

Super Markets: Super Markets are retail outlets that are based on the concept of self-service. The customer can pick up products on their own from a wide variety of brands displayed on the shelves, e.g. Food World.

Hyper Market: Hypermarkets are a recent phenomenon in Indian. These are very large supermarkets with the shop floor area ranging between two lakh to three lakh square feet. These stores also offer a wide variety of products ranging from needles to household equipments e.g., RPG Group in Hyderabad.

Direct Selling: In a process of selling the products directly to the customers by meeting them personally in their homes, offices or other non-store location products sold using this method include vacuum cleaners, water purifiers.

Direct Marketing: Is a process of exposing the customer to the product or service, though mailers, telephone calls, cable, satellite television, and subsequently so soliciting a response from the customer by asking him/her to contact the company through telephone, e-mail, or Post for Tele shopping Network?

Franchising: Is a contractual and legally binding agreement between a franchiser and a franchiser. A franchiser may be the owner of a trademark or a trade name, a producer of goods or a service provider.

Cases of Some Companies

The retail revolution sweeping across India estimated to US$ 300 billion is seeing corporate invading newer and niche spaces. The latest action is taking place in the Pharma retail vertical, which is seeing the entry of many new players.

Fortis Health Care is set to be the latest entrant into sector. It is expected to make the entry through a chain of pharma retail stores.

In India Pharma retail has traditionally has been a commodity business – with a presence of 8-10 lakh chemists – but the entry of large player is changing the face of the sector the estimated sector of the sector is around the estimated size of the sector is around Rs. 40,000 crore according to Harminder Sahni, chief operating officer, KSA.

The players currently operating in the space include Apollo Hospitals, which runs a chain of over 300 stores under the Apollo Pharmacy brand, Medicine Shoppe, Pills and Powder CRS Health, Health & Glow, Global Healthline and Himalaya Drugs.

Pantaloon was the company which launched 51 malls in 14 million sq ft. area across India. Ved Prakash Arya, chief operating officer (Coo) and Director (Operations) Pantaloon Retail (I) Ltd. says, "spending US$ 1 billion for the birth of Indian retail business, under the flagship store Westside, took place after the sale of Lakme to Hindustan Lever in 1996 for Rs. 200 crore.

The war chest allowed the renamed company to acquire the Indian operations of the UK retailer Littlewoods and kick off of a journey to becoming a key player in the organized apparel retail segment today. Trent boasts of about 23 stores with about 6 lakh square feet area in Ahmedabad under the Star India Bazaar name and is looking to add more such stores across metros starting with Bangalore.

More recently in August 2005, the company acquired a 79 per

cent stake in landmark, the leading book store chain, for 109 crore, the books and music retailer with five stores in Chennai and Bangalore and income of just under Rs. 100 crore in 2005-2006, is looking to double its store count to 10 this year and expects to notch up to turnover of Rs.500 crore in next three years.

The Westside base is also being widened with another six stores planned to be added this year this will increase the retail area for trend to 9,00,000 square feet in the next year 2008.

In 1999, Eureka Forbes Ltd., the leading vacuum cleaner and water/air purifier equipment company announced a major policy change that came as a surprise to the Indian Corporate World. The company regarded as the pioneer of direct marketing in India was planning to focus more on the retailing business in the future.

In January 2001, BPCL further upgraded the Bazaar stores, and launched the 'In & Out' stores at a round 40 outlets in Bangalore Mumbai, Delhi, Kolkata, and Chennai, to offer enhanced service to its customers BPCL tied up with various companies from a number of different industries fast food, photography, music, financial service ticketing cards, ATM and courier services.

Conclusion

The retailing industry in India has been attracting major manufacturing firms and is poised to 5 per cent to grow to 28 per cent per annum over five years, period starting from 2007. There are several factors contributing to this growth in the retail sector. There has been significant economic growth over the past few years with the gross domestic product figuring above 7 per cent. The government is trying to improve this further to 10 per cent in the next few years. Besides the economic growth, India is the second highest populated country in the world. Retailing provides the highest employment after agriculture. This trend is poised to growth further, with customers ready to spend higher prices for the products. If the retailers can provide high quality service quality with increased efficiency and a wide product range. With around 12 lakh retail outlets, India is now one of the countries with the highest number of outlets per capita in world. These retail outlets contribute over Rs. 14,000 crore to the GDP of the country. Since 2000, retailing of home appliances and consumer electronics has increased along with the fast food outlets. The major segmentation of retailing is customer durables followed by furniture, healthcare, garments, foods and services, retailing of personal care products and books is on the rise too.

References

BPCL – Petrol Pump Retail Revolution, ICFAI Center for Management Research.PP-302, 304.

Direct Marketing Pioneer, ICFAI and Center for Management Research. ICMR, May 2004.CH: 18 Retailing, PP-293, 294,295.

Eureka Forbes- The Direct Marketing Pionner, ICFAI Center for Management, PP-296, 297.

Pharma Drug Retailing: New Kid on the Block, Outlook Business Journal. November 05, 2006. PP-9.

Retail Par Excellence: The man who scripted the success stories that is Pantaloon- Outlook Business Journal. November 05, 2006. PP-12.

19

Retail Markets in India: Opportunities and Challenges

V. Krishna Mohan and V.V. Vara Prasad

Retailing which is a habit of living, as it is rightly said, is a part of life in the developed world like USA, Canada, UK, Germany and any EU countries with 80 per cent of the retailing in the organized sector. While organized retailing accounts for 60 per cent in countries like Malaysia and Japan, it is 20 per cent in China. The recent spurt in retailing activity in India has doubled the share of organized retailing to around 4.5 per cent from around 2 per cent a couple of years back. The available statistical data is also not valid due to this very reason of 95 per cent of the retailing activity being done in an unorganized way. However, with the efforts of FICCI and CII and the Ministry of Trade & Industry some information is available which puts the total revenue of the sector anywhere above Rs. 7,00,000 crore per year. This potential is luring all the major industrial groups in the country and worldwide to make a foray into Indian organized retailing.

The existing names start with Pantaloons, Food World, Big Bazaar, Shoppers Stop and Goenkas Spencers. The list of new entrants looks very attractive including Tatas, Ambanis, Birlas, Mittals and the like. The Subhiksha group from Chennai, Trinetra Super Markets in Andhra Pradesh are some notable regional players in south (Trinetra has been taken over by the Birlas in the month of May 2007).

The sector is no doubt in a nascent stage but already plagued with many problems, which are sectorial and situational exclusive to Indian Retailing. All the issues are important for the new as well as existing players to make their mark in the sector. Presently the sector is termed as 'sunshine sector' with a projected growth of around 45 per cent in the organized sector per annum.

The process of LPG has helped all the big guns in Indian business to look for new emerging sectors and Retailing is no exception to this, considering the vast scope of growth and development. However, the political dimensions in Delhi have played their role in restricting the FDI into this sector, which was the need of the hour, not only for the required finance but also for the expertise. The aim of this paper is to examine the emerging opportunities in retailing sector vis-à-vis the challenges

Overview of Retailing

According to Philip Kotler: "Retailing includes all the business activities involved in selling goods or services to the final consumers for personal, non-business use. A retailer or retail store is any business enterprise whose sale volume comes primarily from retailing. Any organization selling to final consumers whether it is a manufacturer, wholesaler or retailer is doing retailing. It does not matter how the goods or services are sold (by person, mail, telephone, vending machine or internet or where they are sold- in a store, on the street or in the consumer's home)"

The importance of retail as an industry can be gauged from the fact that Fortune 500 has about 50 retail organizations featured on its list. The number one company on its list is also the largest retailer in the world, Wal-Mart. Any study on retailing has to invariably start with the mention of Wal-Mart, the largest retailing group in the world with its presence all over the world. The issue is more relevant to Indian retailing due to the desperate efforts of Wal-Mart to make an entry into Indian Retailing. However with the strong opposition from the left lobby in Delhi, so far the efforts are not fruitful; even though, the group did enter into a JV with Bharti Group to give a shape to its dream, the modalities are still being worked out. Wal-Mart is also known as the Beast of Bentonville. Wal-Mart has built a reputation for low prices by cutting out layers of middleman and squeezing out suppliers and sharing the savings with consumers.

Presently 51 per cent of FDI is allowed in retail under single brand retailing and under the format of 'cash and carry' it is 100 per cent and no FDI is allowed in any other format of retailing. This is exactly what Bharti and Wal-Mart have decided to cleverly use the FDI by forming joint ventures in wholesale, cash and carry, supply chain and logistics, where there is no restriction on FDI.

Statistics reveal that there are about 15 million retail units (year 2007) in the country, this from about 12 million in 2004, which includes the pan stalls and neighbourhood kirana stores. About 50 million people were dependent for their livelihood on these. Retail and Wholesale thus absorbs 8.7 per cent of the country's total workforce. Most of the small retail units are neighbourhood *kirana* stores, pavement shops and pushcarts in urban, semi-urban and rural markets.

Despite the retail store density in India with regard to population being the largest, it is estimated that over 90 per cent of the stores are less than 500 sq. ft in size. This is clearly indicative of small-shop ownership crowding the unorganised segment of retailing. While this fragmented market structure does pose significant challenges for organized retailing, potential does exist if modern information and supply chain management systems are deployed to support the development of convenience shops that match customer expectations.

The retail industry is going to emerge as a major hirer in the coming years and approximately about eight per cent of the country's workforce may be working in this sector. Employment opportunities in retail are not just confined to malls and factory outlets alone. It is a field intersecting several other industries at various points and thus has multifaceted opportunities to offer employment right from designing to sales, supply chain to e-tailing, B2B to B2C marketing, location for an outlet to running a mall etc.

Organized retailing rests on the logic of taking control of the supply chain. Those lobbying for a liberal retailing regime usually bank their argument on better realization by farmers but also lower prices for consumers through effective supply chain management. However, the concern is to predict the adverse impact on the present kirana stores, most of which operate on a small budget, satisfying specific needs of communities in their own localities. Their main service is offering value to consumers by satisfying a felt need. For instance, they offer goods on credit to working-class or middle class Indian consumer, who is mostly a salaried employee with hand to mouth budget and any differed payment will have a welcome impact on his budget and life-style and subsequent buying influence.

All these arguments for and against the entry of big names into retailing is a continuum, while already action is on with Reliance planning to invest US$ 5.6 billion (Rs. 25,200 crore) in opening 4,000 stores in 1,500 towns across India. ITC, for instance, plans to expand its fruit and vegetable distribution network by opening 54 new outlets in select metros in the next three years. This appears to be a logical extension of its existing procurement business, and the rural support system, the *e-choupal*, a concept of close netted agriculture-industry interaction through which the company buys fruits, vegetables and grains directly from farmers thereby avoiding exploitation by middlemen.

Retailing today is not only about selling at the shop, but also about surveying the market, offering choice and experience to consumers, competitive prices to increase footfalls and customer retention.

Present Formats of Retailing

- Cash & Carry, The whole sale type
- Hypermarkets/Superstores
- Supermarkets
- Discount stores
- Convenience stores
- Kirana Stores or popularly known as the mom & pop stores

Opportunities for Increasing the Scope of Retailing

- Income and consumption growth of the Indians is on the steady rise for during the past decade under LPG scenario.
- Increasing literacy levels and impact of western materialistic life-style.
- Changes in family structure and women's role in the family
- Growing role of children as influencers in buying process.
- Growing influence of TV and impact of urbanisation.
- Organized retail from about 4.5 per cent at present, will form 10 per cent of total retailing by the end of this decade (2010)
- From 2006 to 2010, the organized sector will grow at the CAGR of around 49.53 per cent per annum.
- Cultural and regional differences in India create opportunities for various retail formats.
- Hypermarket is emerging as the most favorable format to reap the benefits of large scale economies.

Contributors to Indian Retail Growth

- Conducive atmosphere due to LPG.
- Growing Consumer Classes (Urban and Rural).
- Increasing Disposable Personal Income.
- Growing Economy.
- Increasing Wage and Salary Levels.
- Introduction of Private Labels.
- Mergers & Acquisitions.
- Growing Urbanization and Industrialization.

Challenges and Opportunities: An Indian Perspective

FDI in Retailing: The fear of FDI in retail has a challenging dimension as it is expected to affect the usual mom-and-pop stores, farmers, and small-scale manufacturers with the kind of monopoly buying power of the MNCs. The left parties in the coalition at the center are vehemently opposing any alteration whether minor or major on this issue. The Reliance Fresh has to taste the anger of the farmers in Hyderabad for it was delivering the vegetables etc., less than the *Rytu Bazaar* prices which affected the interests of farmers. However, the industry demands allowing up to 49 per cent foreign direct investment in the retail sector over a three to five year timeframe — to give the domestic industry enough time to adjust to the changes. The present policy restricts FDI in retail to single-brand ventures, with a foreign shareholding cap of 51 per cent. However, 100 per cent FDI is permitted in wholesale cash-and-carry, where one can only sell to retailers and distributors and not to consumers. Besides, 100 per cent FDI is also allowed under the automatic route in warehousing services and refrigeration of agricultural products.

The Policy on foreign direct investment (FDI) is reviewed on a continuing basis. An inter-Ministerial consultation on policy issues is an ongoing process. The policy was comprehensively reviewed in 2006 and the revised policy for FDI was notified. In the trading sector, FDI was permitted in single brand product retailing and the cash and carry format.

Government Policies and Laws: The differing tax, licensing systems and high stamp duties across states could raise some issues when organized retailers expand nationally, this could well protect the interests of regional retailers. But the key to success is to build a fairly extensive network of stores across the country to enable e-commerce transactions. Introduction of VAT has resulted in more confusion than easing the system. The need for amending the weights and measures act and a few labour legislations are all to be done by government in due course.

Real Estate Problem: Research estimates that the total space for shopping malls is likely to go up from 50 lakh sq. ft. to 75 lakh sq ft during the year 2007. India's per capita retail space is the lowest in the world at just about 2 sq. ft. when compared to the US figure of 16 sq. ft. Therefore, the industry's need for real estate, which is on the rise, could be well justified. However, this along with the overall development of the economy has pushed the costs of real estate in major metros and tier-II cities to exorbitant heights adversely affecting the finances and subsequent expansion plans of retailers.

Manpower Planning and HRM: For gaining employment in the retail sector one should have a graduate degree preferably in marketing coupled with specific domain knowledge like apparel manufacturing, shoe and leather goods, designing, product packaging which will be an added advantage. The knowledge of operating a computer, accounting and inventory management will also be considered as plus points. People with academic background of fashion technology, marketing, financial management, supply chain management, HR, customer service and advertising also have promising prospects in this industry at the middle management level. However the crux of the problem is the lack of qualified manpower, which is a concern for the sector. To offset this problem Shoppers' Stop has started its own Retailing College and it is mandatory for all the employees to complete the certified course while working. This problem may ease in the very near future as many universities and private management colleges have added specialized courses covering the entire gamut of retailing and its various dimensions of management.

Technology Advantage: Technology in the retailing industry has provided a new challenge. The introduction of point of sale equipment, bar codes and huge storage capacity for billing and payment database has facilitated the management of large set-ups with ease. Operations can be recorded in a structured and systematic manner, providing detailed analysis of the sales and volume of transactions. Electronic transactions have increased the volume of sales in the country. Flexibility in the mode of payment and cashless transactions has helped in driving sales. The technological dimension of communication creates a competitive advantage in attracting and retaining customers. The concepts of B2B and B2C are possible with effective computer applications.

The introduction of new technology may be intricate for retailers, but the convenience and cost effectiveness create the need for new advancements. Large stores need to monitor inventories and expenses of establishments. With automated machines and high-end computers making the task simpler, the focus of retailers can stay on retaining customers with new strategies. Using ERP packages and solutions like Retail Pro, higher-end solutions like JDA, SAP IS Retail or Retek, facilitate back-end operations. Along with business optimisation software, mobile computing and B2C concept assist retailers to cut costs and increase efficiency, but these solutions are mainly targeted at big retail stores with chains all over India. Though these solutions have been implemented, returns on these investments take a longer period. Management needs to learn how to make a web page in delivering a satisfying shopping experience.

Promoting Private Label: The concept of developing own label is an unknown feature in Indian retailing. However it is an effective measure to enhance the profitability index. Reliance in Andhra Pradesh, has successfully implemented this concept, with its own labeling. The consumer prices for the products have already shown a downward trend between 8 to 9 per cent and the money saved is for the middle class Indian consumer. During the next two years, the positive impact of modern retailing in India, irrespective of who owns it, will be far more positive for the economy. Companies such as Trent have their own labels, which is 60 per cent of their total merchandise.

Differentiation: The basic way to create differentiation is to concentrate on a particular category, such as a pharmaceutical chain or even books. In fact, books as a category have done extremely well. Brands such as Landmark and Crossword have gone through the pains of perfecting their formats and are now making a lot of money. For example, a format such as Subhiksha sells everything that any other grocery store would sell, but its key differentiator is the 10 per cent discount it offers on its entire merchandise and the promise that it would enable you to save money for your family. This was possible due to the strategy to take real estate in a residential area to avoid high rentals in a commercial area, and thereafter, simulate the neighborhood concept of retail. Shopping festivals is another differentiation strategy that has become the order of the day whether it is Singapore or Thailand people flock to these events to do bulk purchases. Promoting own label is a way of creating differentiation, as the merchandise that you get in the respective outlets will not be found anywhere else.

Integrated Supply Chain Management: Strength in physical distribution will remain the backbone of any retail arrangement. However, ongoing investment in bandwidth, development of internet facilities, and increasing adoption of IT among B2B partners is the key to success in this business category due to vapour-thin margins. Wal-Mart operates on margin of 3 per cent by passing all the advantages to the consumers for their retention; this is only possible with effective SCM and continuous vendor development process. Reacting to the pressure of retailers, suppliers are assessing technology-based solutions to drive down costs and become more efficient producers of goods. Mercantile models create consistency and increase consumer convenience by eliminating the need to figure out a new business process for every single vendor. Managing Channel Conflicts is the strength of any business and retailing is no exception.

Prevention of Loss: Prevention of loss is highly essential for retailing. Risk management issues pertaining to preventing thefts from the stores, managing the finance audit etc. are very vital concerns. Loss of any form is also referred to as 'shrinkage' in retailing. The shrinkage can be of any form; customer theft, wrong pricing, wrong packaging, not-in-stock items, employee theft, etc. Wal-Mart has a personnel policy to fire the employee for any resultant loss, which can be pinned as his/her responsibility. It is estimated that a mammoth 5 per cent is lost on an average in Indian retailing, which is 3 per cent in developed countries. This particular challenge has to be faced by the retailer by adopting such modern techniques like RFID (Radio Frequency Identification Device), bar coding, strict security surveillance with CCTV etc. Security systems also do help for a safer shopping, for retailers as well as customers, providing immense mental relief. Such technological advancements are only now entering into Indian retail market and the need for it has been acknowledged.

The point of sale (POS) applications will provide for quicker consumer checkout and multiple payment options like credit cards.

Customer Relationship Marketing: Retailers will need to concentrate on value by offering new product mixes that include not only merchandise but also bundles of entertainment and "recreational" shopping with movie theaters, restaurants, bookstores, libraries, and community meeting facilities, which results in ***tangibalization*** of retailing services. Retailing is expected to change with rapid development of new online sales and distribution channels that literally can be used from anywhere, anytime-- from home, work, a hotel, car, or airplane. Each consumer has a distinct way of doing shopping but still some generalization can be made about the way consumers do shopping. Mercantile model can be developed from two perspectives; consumer and retailer. From the consumer side, it specifies the sequence of activities a shopper takes in purchasing a product or service. From the retailer side, it defines the order of management cycle, which specifies the activities within an organization that must take place in fulfilling the customer's order.

The buying process which consists of three stages as indicated below should be well understood and strategies formulated.

- The pre-purchase preparation phase includes search and discovery for a set of products in the larger information space capable of meeting customer requirements and product selection from the smaller set of products based on attribute comparison.
- The purchase consummation phase specifies the flow of information and documents associated with purchasing and negotiation with merchants for suitable terms and electronic payment mechanisms that integrate payment into the purchasing process.
- The post-purchase interaction phase includes the customer service and support to address customer complaints, product returns, and product defects.

Strategy for Effective CRM

- Prospecting for potential customers, qualifying a customer, learning the customer's needs, understanding the customer's purchasing process, selecting the presentation to be made, making the presentation, adapting the presentation based on customer reaction, handling objections, negotiating with the customer, closing the sale, and building an ongoing relationship through service.
- Retailers know that consumers adopt a brand, and make it part of their lifestyle; they remain loyal and purchase the brand again and again. The adoption decision is preceded by a number of other steps: unaware, aware, interested, knowledgeable, positive attitude, experience, trial, repeat, and adoption for managing brands and private labels.
- A retailer should be concerned with simply inducing the purchase through the use of marketing mix variables with the concept of purchase-now, rather than later.

Conclusion

Retailing by its very nature, is a dynamic industry. Change is always to be regarded as an opportunity for better prospects. The business of retail in India has witnessed significant changes in the last few years. Indian retail market has seen the emergence of new formats and the application of global concepts and constructs albeit with modifications to suit the Indian environment. Retail markets not only provide the Indian buyer a wider choice at fair price, but also represent a very large employment opportunity for people with diverse skill set. When viewed from the investor, there is abundance of opportunities luring the potential investor but at the same time the threats and challenges have to be well managed for the synergy of all advantages to support the thin margins, survive and grow.

Managing retailing in an effective manner requires managing channel conflict through best practices of SCM, delivering a satisfying shopping experience, proper design of store lay-out, introduction of e-tailing with online shopping experience to customers, managing brands including private labels are some of the positive dimensions of modern retailing.

FICCI, Federation of Indian Chamber of Commerce and Industry, has in 2007 formed a committee on retailing. The objectives of this committee are to negotiate with the Government for a better and smoother environment for the functioning of the Distributive Trade Sector and help grow organized retail sector in this country. The FICCI has represented to the government in the past on issues relating to Sales Tax, Essential Commodities (Amendment) Bill and Weights & Measures.

Amidst the ongoing organized retailing boom, it is important to understand issues that will successfully have a far-reaching impact on effective handling of Human Resource Development (HRD). In the current scenario, organized retailing has finally emerged from the shadows of unorganized retailing and is contributing significantly to the growth of the Indian retail sector with multi dimensional and positive reflections on the entire economy.

References

Emerging Trends for the Retailing Industry, Jagdish and Seth, Journal of Retailing, Volume 59, Fall 1983

Main Raods to Retail Nirvana, Biyani Kishore, Indian Management/June 2005

Marketing Management, Philip Kotler, 12th edition, Prentice Hall of India, New Delhi, 2006

Modernization in Indian Retailing: Managerial and Policy Perspectives, Mulky Avinash/Nargundkar Rajendra, Udyog Pragati/April 2003

Old Pillars of New Retailing, Berry LL, Harvard Business Review, April 2001, pp 131-137

Retail Marketing Management, David Gilbert, 2nd edition, Pearson Education, New Delhi, 2006

Retailing Management: Text and Cases, Swapna Pradhan, 2nd edition, Tata McGraw Hill Ltd, New Delhi2007

Retailing: The Next Ten Years, Leonard Berry and I H Wilson, Journal of Retailing, Volume 53, Fall 1977

20

Problems and Prospects of Indian Retailing

R. Sudarshan and Syeda Parveen

Introduction

Retailing is the last interface between the producer and the individual consumer buying for personal consumption. 'Candiff and still' has defined retaining as "retailing consists of those activities involved in selling directly to ultimate consumers". This excludes direct interface between the manufacturer and institutional buyers such as government and other bulk customers.

A retailer is one who stocks the producer's goods and involves in the act of selling them to the individual consumers, at a margin of profit, retailer is an intermediary because he is both marketer and customer though producer may sell directly to consumers, method of distributing goods to ultimate users is inconvenient, expensive and time consuming. There fore manufacturer depend on retailer to sell the products to consumer. Retail store is any business enterprise whose sales volume generated through retailing through his own stores or by house-to-house canvassing or by mail order business. Retailers serve the whole sellers, producers and consumers in advertisement of new products, arrangement to sell the goods, information about consumer taste and needs, credit facility, sale on approval.

Traditionally, retailing has been considered as business function but now many of the non-business unit's activities under take deal with attempts to satisfy ultimate consumer or public. Hospitals, lawyers, schools, restaurants, automotive repair shops and equipment rental agencies, vegetable market all these institutions deal with ultimate consumers.

In India, the organized retailing has emerged from the

shadows of unorganized sector and is contributing significantly to the growth of the retail sector in India. Retailing is value-adding process as Indian economy has been heavily geared towards the service sector. If there aren't any goods being manufactured, then there will not be any goods to be retailed. This underlines the importance of manufacturing and retailing in a developing economy.

The Indian Scenario

Retailing is the single largest component of the services sector in terms of contribution to GDP. The Indian Retail Sector is booming and mall growth is being seen as a clear indicator of the economic prosperity in India, there were 96 operational malls in August 2005. Its massive share of 14 per cent is double the figure of the next largest broad economic activity in the sector. Indian retail industry is generating more than 10 per cent of the Gross Domestic Production and is the largest source of employment, providing employment to 7 per cent of total workforce and stands next to agriculture in the country. There are enormous opportunities existing in this sector. Growth in this sector will be supported by the favorable demographic patterns, life style, shopping patterns, etc. The Retail Space Growth is expected to be 100 mn sq ft for quality shopping center space by 2007-08 .To generate retail sales of over Rs. 50,000 crore (US$ 11 billion), Rs. 20,000+ crore (US$ 4 billion+) investment in pipeline for retail infrastructure, systems and shop-fit Space for 15,000+ new outlets, 100 hypermarkets.

The retail industry is divided into organised and unorganised sectors.

Organised Sector

Organised retailing refers to trading activities undertaken by licensed retailers, that is, those who are registered for sales tax, income tax, etc. These include the corporate-backed hypermarkets and retail chains, and also the privately owned large retail businesses. Organized retail will form 10 per cent of total retailing by the end of this decade (2010) from 2006 to 2010, the organized sector will grow at the CAGR of around 49.53 per cent per annum, organised retail in India has the potential to add over Rs. 2,00,000 crore (US$ 45 billion) business by the year 2010.

According to the India Retail Report 2005 the size of the organized retailing market (Rs. 35,000 crore in 2005) is expected to reach the figure of Rs. 1,00,000 crore by 2010 at an average growth rate of about 30 per cent.

However, going by the current growth trend and considering the fact that existing prominent players in organised retail have stepped up their expansion drive with Reliance announcing big plans and other Indian corporate houses too evincing keenness on investing heavily in this sector as also the inking of the joint-venture between the world's largest retailer Wal-Mart and Bharti - the expectation from organised retail will be double now of what was estimated two years ago.

Unorganised Sector

India's retail sector at present is largely unorganized, with about 15 million tiny outlets catering to the needs of consumers across the country – it employs the second-largest number of people after agriculture. Unorganised retailing refers to the traditional forms of low-cost retailing, for example, the local kirana shops, owner managed general stores, convenience stores, paan shops, handcart and pavement vendors, etc. Unorganized retailing is by far the prevalent form of trade in India constituting 98 per cent of total trade.

In India unorganized retail sector there is no supply chain management perspective. According to a survey by AT Kearney, an overwhelming proportion of the Rs. 400,000 crore retail markets are unorganised. In fact, only a Rs. 20,000 crore segment of the market is organised. Over 8 per cent of India's population is engaged in retailing (compared to 20 per cent in the United States).

An attempt is made to present the current scenario of retail sector in India.

Table 20.1 reveals that in 2006 , in organized sector , the share of the Indian retail segment in clothing, textiles and fashion accessories is Rs. 1,13,500 crore accounting for 18.9 per cent Jewellery accounted for Rs. 60,200 crore (2.8 per cent), watches Rs. 3,950 crore (45.6 per cent), foot wear Rs. 13,750 crore (37.8 per cent), health and beauty care services Rs. 3,800 crore (10.6 per cent), pharmaceuticals Rs. 42,200 crore (2.6 per cent), consumer durables, home appliances/equipments Rs 48,100 crore (10.4 per cent). Further, mobile handset accessories and services accounted for Rs. 21,650 crore (8 per cent), furnishings, utensils, furniture Rs. 40,650 crore (9.1 per cent), food and grocery Rs. 7,43,900 crore (0.8 per cent), catering services Rs. 57,000 crore (6.9 per cent) and entertainment accounted for Rs. 38,000 crore (4.1 per cent).

In un organized sector , the share of the Indian retail segment in clothing , textiles and fashion accessories is Rs. 1,13,500 crore accounting for 81.1 per cent Jewellery accounted for Rs. 60,200 crore (97.2 per cent), watches Rs. 3,950 crore (54.4 per cent), foot wear Rs. 13,750 crore (62.2 per cent), health and beauty care services Rs. 3,800 crore (89.4 per cent), pharmaceuticals Rs 42,200 crore (97.4 per cent), consumer durables, home appliances/equipments Rs. 48,100 crore (89.6 per cent). Further, mobile handset accessories and services accounted for Rs. 21,650 crore (92 per cent), furnishings, utensils, furniture Rs. 40,650 crore (90.9 per cent) , food and grocery Rs. 7,43,900 crore (99.2 per cent), catering services Rs. 57,000 crore (93.1 per cent) and entertainment accounted for Rs. 38,000 crore (95.9 per cent).

Employment in Retailing

A glance at the employment numbers reveals that organized trade employs roughly 5 lakh people, whereas the unorganized retail trade employs nearly 3.95 crore. According to a GOI study, the number of workers in retail trade in 1998 was 175 lakh. Given the recent numbers indicated by other studies, this is only indicative of the magnitude of expansion the retail trade is experiencing, both due to economic expansion as well as the

20.1: Components of Indian Retailing

Particulars	India Retail Value (Rs. crore)	Organised Retail (Rs. crore)	Organised in 2006 (%)	Unorganised Retail (Rs. crore)	Unorganised in 2006 (%)
Clothing, Textiles & Fashion Accessories	113,500	21,400	18.9	92,100	81.1
Jewellery	60,200	1,680	2.8	58,520	97.2
Watches	3,950	1,800	45.6	2,150	54.4
Footwear	13,750	5,200	37.8	8,550	62.2
Health & Beauty Care Services	3,800	400	10.6	3,400	89.4
Pharmaceuticals	42,200	1,100	2.6	41,100	97.4
Consumer Durables, Home Appliances/equipments	48,100	5,000	10.4	43,100	89.6
Mobile handsets. Accessories & Services	21,650	1,740	8.0	19,910	92
Furnishings, Utensils, Furniture-Home & Office	40,650	3,700	9.1	36,950	90.9
Food & Grocery	7,43,900	5,800	0.8	7,38,100	99.2
Catering Services (F & B)	57,000	3,940	6.9	53,060	93.1
Books, Music & Gifts	13,300	1,680	12.6	11,620	87.4
Entertainment	38,000	1,560	4.1	36,440	95.9
	12,00,000	54,999		11,45,000	

Source: Compiled from the Indian Retail Report 2007.

'jobless growth' that we have seen in the past decade.

It must be noted that even within the organised sector, the number of individually owned retail outlets far out number the corporate backed institutions. Though these numbers translate to approximately 8 per cent of the workforce in the country (half the normal share in developed countries), there are far more retailers in India than other countries in absolute numbers, because of the demographic profile and the preponderance of youth. About 4 per cent of India's population is in the retail trade is an indication of how vital this business is to the socio-economic equilibrium in India. Generating employment for some 2.5 million people in various retail operations and over 10 million additional workforce in retail support activities including contract production and processing, supply chain and logistics, retail real estate development and management etc.,

Retail as a 'Forced Employment Sector'

As retailing plays a vital role in generating various sources of employment, it is important to understand how retailing works in our economy, and what role it plays in the lives of its citizens, from a social as well as economic perspective. India still predominantly houses the traditional formats of retailing, that is, the local kirana shop, paan/beedi shop, hardware stores, weekly halts, convenience stores, and bazaars, which together form the bulk. Most importantly, Indian retail is highly fragmented, with about 11 million outlets operating in the country and only 4 per cent of them being larger than 500 square feet in size. In U.S 0.9 million square feet caters to more than 13 times of the Indian retail market size.

The Indian retail industry continued to be, highly fragmented over-crowded agriculture sector, the stagnating manufacturing sector, and the hard nature and relatively low wages of jobs forced millions of Indians to get rehabilitation in service sector. Thus due to lack of opportunities, it is almost a natural decision for an individual to set up a small shop or store, depending on his or her means and capital. Thus, a retailer is born, seemingly out of circumstance rather than choice.

As shopping malls are becoming increasingly common in metropolitan cities, and the announced development plans project at least 150 new shopping malls by 2008. Number of departmental stores is growing at 24 per cent per annum. Supermarkets have been taking a growing share of general food and grocery trade during the past two decades.

Organised retailing, which aims at providing an ideal shopping experience for the consumer based on the advantages of large-scale purchases, consumer preference analysis, excellent ambience and choice of merchandise, has been adopted in a large number of cities in India with many business houses investing in this segment.

Increasingly, the organised retail industry is realizing the importance of information technology in bringing about process improvements, which would result in greater operating efficiencies and hence increased profits. But the awareness of IT systems that are available is low, resulting in poor decision-making. A number of organised retailers in India have installed solutions ranging from simple Point of Sale systems to complex Retail ERPs.

The Indian retail industry is at a transition phase- a period that will be characterized by punctuated change. Suppliers need to address mechanisms to deal with the growing power of the organized trade. As for the organized trade itself, mindset to collaborate with competition has important implications to pro-actively increase their competitive advantages rather than reactively co-operate only when faced with the prospect of global competition. Even in the short term, joint initiatives such as procurement groups or loyalty programme alliances provide cost efficiencies or consumer value increments that are too significant to be ignored.

Indian Retailing: Problems and Prospects

A brief discussion regarding the problems and prospects of Indian Retailing is as follows:

1. The retail sector in India is growing and developing it is because of impact of rising incomes, low interest rates, competition, culture, structural changes in India, rising number of stores, brands, availability of credit. Retail sales grew by 10.5 per cent in rupee terms in 2005, equivalent to a volume rise of 6 per cent. Retailing is undergoing a structural change in India, as supply slowly moves from small, family-run shops to larger, organised retail outlets. The rising number of attractive stores and foreign brands, coupled with readily available credit, will support steady real growth in retail sales of 7.2 per cent a year between 2007 and 2010.
2. In the case of more expensive consumer goods, such as refrigerators, washing machines, colour televisions and personal computers, retailers are joining forces with banks and financial companies to market their goods more aggressively. Among departmental stores, factors that support rising sales include a strong emphasis on retail technology, loyalty schemes, private labels and the subletting of floor space in larger stores to smaller retailers selling a variety of products and services.
3. Organised retailing is relatively new to India, although it is expanding rapidly. This sector should benefit from rising wealth, industry deregulation and a greater openness to international influences. Only 3 per cent of retail sales in India are accounted by organised retailers. By 2010, however, the organised Sector is expected to account for as much as 20 per cent of the total retail sector based on current trends.
4. Opportunities for retailers in food and groceries sector are bright. Modern retailing involves large shops and super markets constitute less than 1 per cent of total food retailing sector. Indian food retailing however, is moving inexorably towards the supermarket format, and consumers in the affluent, upper-income segment are attracted to brand names, variety and convenience. Other sectors that are likely to see growth include consumer durables, information technology (IT), home improvement, and health and beauty. A more

sophisticated front-end retail infrastructure will also create more demand.

5. India's biggest retailer, Pantaloon, plans to increase its 300,000 sq meters of retail space to 1m sq meters by end-2007, enabling it to expand its Pantaloon department stores as well as its Big Bazaar hypermarkets and Food Bazaar supermarkets. India's biggest private-sector company, Reliance Industries, has plans to enter the retail sector. The company is thought to be considering investment of Rs. 100 bn (US$ 2.2 billion) over the next two years to establish more than 1,500 outlets across the country employing 4,00,000-5,00,000 people.

Measures to Strengthen Indian Retailing

The following measures are suggested to strengthen the Indian Retailing sector.

1. The retail sector in India is constrained by limited availability of bank finance. The Government and RBI need to evolve suitable policies to lenders that will enable retailers in the organised and unorganised sectors to expand and improve efficiencies. Policies that encourage unorganised sector retailers to migrate to the organised sector by investing in space and equipment should be encouraged.
2. Cultural and regional differences in India are the biggest challenges in front of retailers. This factor defers the retailers in India from adopting a single retail format, Hypermarket is emerging as the most favorable format for the time being in India. The arrival of multinationals will further push the growth of hypermarket format, as it is the best way to compete with unorganized retailing in India.
3. A National Commission must be established to study the problems of the retail industry and to evolve policies that will enable it to cope with FDI.
4. The proposed National Commission should evolve a clear set of conditionalities on giant foreign retailers on the procurement of farm produce, domestically manufactured

merchandise and imported goods. These conditionalities must be aimed at encouraging the purchase of goods in domestic market state the minimum space, size and specify details like, construction and storage standards, the ratio of floor space to parking space etc.

5. Entry of foreign players must be gradual and with social safeguards so that the effects of the labour dislocation can be analysed and policy fine-tuned. Initially allowing them to set up supermarkets only in metros make the costs of entry high and according to specific norms and regulations so that the retailer cannot immediately indulge in 'predatory' pricing.
6. In order to address the dislocation issue, it becomes imperative to develop and improve the manufacturing sector in India. There has been a substantial fall in employment by the manufacturing sector, to the extent of 4.06 lakh over the period 1998 to 2001, the contribution to the GDP has grown at an average rate of only 3.7 per cent. If this sector is given due attention it could be a source of great compensation to the displaced workforce from the retail industry.
7. The government must actively encourage setting up of co-operative stores to procure and stock their consumer goods and commodities from small producers. This will address the problem of limited promotion and marketing ability, as well as market penetration for the retailer. The government can facilitate setting up of warehousing units thereby lowering the cost of capital for the small retailers.
8. Prices for perishable goods like vegetables, fruits, etc. are not fixed and therefore, this is where economies of scale are likely to kick in and benefit the consumer in the form of lower prices. But due attention must be given to the producer also. Often the producer loses out, for example, when the goods are procured at Rs. 2 and ultimately sold to the consumer at about Rs.15 as in the case of potatoes. The Government themselves can tap into the opportunities of this segment, rather than letting it be lost to foreign players. And by doing so, they can more directly ensure the welfare of producers and consumers.

Conclusion

Indian retail industry is generating more than 10 per cent of the Gross Domestic Production and it is the largest source of employment, providing employment to 7 per cent of total workforce and stands next to agriculture in the country. There are enormous opportunities existing in this sector. Growth in this sector will be supported by the favorable demographic patterns.

Retailers operate in a fast changing environment, which offers opportunities and threats. The industries may suffer from chronic over capacity resulting in fierce competition, consumers demographics, life style, shopping patterns are changing rapidly as are retailing technologies retailers have to focus on segmentation, targeting and positioning carefully for executing competitive strategies. The trends in retailing are new retail forms and combinations, Growth of inter type competition, Growth of Giant retailers, growing investment in Technology, Global presence of major Retailers, Competition between store based and non store based retailing.

References

Concepts in Comparative Retailing – Journal of marketing by Cundiff Edward

Government of India, "India and W.T.O", the monthly News letter of Ministry of commerce (Various issues)

Performance of international retailers- A suggested theoretical framework- International Marketing Review.

Third world network India: flood of food imports could destroy Indian Agriculture by Binus Thomas.

Index

Index